The
Environmental
Crusaders

Penina Migdal Glazer and Myron Peretz Glazer

THE ENVIRONMENTAL CRUSADERS

Confronting Disaster and Mobilizing Community

The Pennsylvania State University Press
University Park, Pennsylvania

Library of Congress Cataloging-in-Publication Data

Glazer, Penina Migdal.
    The environmental crusaders : confronting disaster and mobilizing
community / Penina Migdal Glazer and Myron Peretz Glazer.
        p.   cm.
    Includes bibliographical references and index.
    ISBN 0-271-01775-9 (alk. paper)
    ISBN 0-271-01776-7 (pbk. : alk. paper)
        1. Environmentalists—United States.   2. Environmentalists—
Israel.   3. Environmentalists—Czechoslovakia.   4. Environmental
sciences—Societies, etc.   5. Environmentalism—Social aspects.
    I. Glazer, Myron.   II. Title.
    GE55.G54   1998
    363.7'0092'2—dc21   97-49828
                                                                                      CIP

Copyright © 1998 The Pennsylvania State University

It is the policy of The Pennsylvania State University Press to use acid-free
paper for the first printing of all clothbound books. Publications on uncoated
stock satisfy the minimum requirements of American National Standard for
Information Sciences—Permanence of Paper for Printed Library Materials,
ANSI Z39.48–1992.

We dedicate this book with
love and admiration

to our parents
Rebecca and Benjamin Migdal

to our children
Joshua, Jessica, and Tamar

to our new family
Esther and Haim Noam

Contents

	Preface	ix
	Introduction	xiii
1	Maintaining a Democratic Society	1
2	Breaking the Bands of National Security Secrecy	25
3	Marching Along with Mothers and Children	61
4	Preserving the Farmland from Contamination	99
5	Protecting the Precious Natural Resources	135
6	The Courage of Ordinary People	165
	Methodological Appendix: Tracking the Environmental Crusaders	183
	Notes	195
	Index	213

Preface

In 1982, as part of our ongoing interest in individual and collective responsibility for maintaining a democratic society, we began a six-year study of whistleblowers in government and industry. These men and women refused to countenance illegal and unethical behavior in the automobile or pharmaceutical industries as well as in the Environmental Protection Agency or the Veterans Administration. Their supervisors often responded by blaming the whistleblowers for their problems, hoping never to reveal "secret" data that would give credibility to the whistleblowers' allegations and require investigation and remediation. Despite the attacks mounted against them and the costly consequences for their careers and families, whistleblowers continued their ethical struggles. After paying a heavy personal price, many were ultimately vindicated, and most remained convinced that their battles and sacrifices had been necessary and worthwhile. They believed that they were right in not shrinking from personal responsibility. They were on the forefront of the nationwide movement demanding organizational accountability.

Whistleblowers did not act alone. None of these employees could have continued their battle to a successful conclusion without the assistance of numerous allies. Rather, they operated most successfully when they formed strategic alliances. Public-interest groups like the Government Accountability Project in Washington, D.C., served as major legal resources for those who became involved in long-term litigation. Investigative reporters gave credibility and ongoing media coverage to the whistleblowers' allegations. Congressional and state legislative committees mounted investigations and public hearings in which whistleblowers provided key testimony. Finally, and most significantly for our current study, community activists provided a vital political arm when insiders revealed policies that threatened the health and safety of local residents.

When whistleblowers exposed environmental hazards, such as the improper disposal of toxic waste or the unauthorized release of low-level radiation into the atmosphere, local citizen activists attended hearings and enlisted public backing wherever they could. For the whistleblowers, such crusaders were indispensable, for they supplied information and emotional support. The citizen activists were often the liaisons to public-interest groups that offered legal assistance and strategic advice. Where possible, activists also raised small amounts of money to tide over the ethical employees when they felt they had nowhere to turn after being fired, blacklisted, or threatened.

At the conclusion of our whistleblower study, we decided to continue our research on citizens who had the courage to identify environmental dangers and demand remediation. We wanted to study how this decision affected their lives, as we had studied how similar decisions had affected the lives of their whistleblower counterparts. We sought to understand their backgrounds and motivations, the manner in which they organized, the retaliation they faced, the impact on their families, and the ultimate consequences of their efforts. Most specifically, we determined to test our theoretical assumption that these grassroots environmental activists, like whistleblowers, played a crucial societal role. They were the bellwethers alerting their communities and nations that serious problems had arisen and had to be confronted. They were "civic innovators" who were willing to put themselves at risk for the well-being of their families and neighbors. They rejected apathy and, despite the personal costs, were able to engage in the long-term struggle so often necessary for the resolution of major social problems.

In the course of the last five years, we have interviewed more than 140 activists, public-interest-group members, journalists, union leaders, and corporate and government employees. We thank them all for their willingness to spend hours speaking to us and supplying us with documents and other materials. In many instances, we interviewed them more than once and continually requested information to update our understanding. We appreciate their patience.

We also are pleased to acknowledge the John D. and Catherine T. MacArthur Foundation for their grant supporting the project. Their generosity, supplemented (in the last stages of the book) by the Smith College Project on Women and Social Change, made possible our travel throughout the United States as well as two research trips each to Israel and the former Czechoslovakia.

We must also single out the essential contributions of two key associates. Dr. Ruth Glasser transcribed all of the interviews. She also provided probing questions and commentary for our consideration, taking time away from her own important research. Kathleen Gauger, administrative assistant of the Smith College Project on Women and Social Change, typed and retyped the many versions of the entire manuscript. No one could have provided more competent, efficient, and good-spirited support. We remain indebted to her.

Several students, assistants, colleagues, friends, and family members gathered research materials, read the early drafts, and gave critical commentary. We thank Arian White, Hayley Hovious, Sandra Lory, Louis Clark, Michael Lewis, Faye and Terry Lichtash, Miriam and Paul Slater, Randy Huntsberry, Jules Chametsky, Robert Kleidman, and Rex Warland. Lynn Schler served as our translator in Israel whenever necessary. She and Joshua Glazer also helped us contact prospective interviewees. Hannah Evans served as translator for a major interview in Prague. Ann Kraybill provided important editorial comments. The Citizens Clearinghouse for hazardous waste provided helpful assistance in locating activist groups.

We also thank the *Massachusetts Review* for permission to reprint Chapter 2, "Breaking the Bands of National Security Secrecy," which appeared in a slightly different version in the summer 1996 edition.

We acknowledge with appreciation and affection the contribution of Joel S. Migdal, who read the entire manuscript and urged us to submit it to Penn State Press. It was an excellent suggestion, for we have found the press and Peter Potter, in particular, to have acted in an exemplary manner throughout the process of publication. We could not have hoped for a more insightful, exacting, and considerate editor. We are also indebted to Keith Monley for his painstaking editing of the final manuscript.

This book would not have been possible without the generous cooperation of all the environmental crusaders and other interested participants who shared valuable time and information with us.

We will always remember with gratitude Harry C. Bredemeier, our beloved professor, who strengthened our commitment to sociological research and humane values.

Introduction

It is a truism that democracy requires an open society. For citizens to participate intelligently in the political process, they must have access to information, an opportunity to hear controversial issues debated, willingness to evaluate the evidence, and the desire to organize with others to promote their points of view. It is also true that all societies have counterforces. In modern nations, government and corporate bureaucracies are reluctant to disclose vital information, and technocrats are often the interpreters of voluminous reports characterized by highly technical data and inaccessible language. The requirements of national security and law enforcement further intensify the pull toward withholding important information. As a result, there is always a tension between the ideal of openness and the reality of relentless pressures toward secrecy. All democratic societies struggle to establish structural and normative arrangements to keep that tension in balance.

In the United States, there are both public and private institutions that defend open access to information. The Freedom of Information Act requires the disclosure of materials from government agencies that might otherwise refuse them to petitioning individuals. Right-to-know laws make available critical data on air and water pollution, waste discharges, and other vital environmental statistics. Within the federal government, agencies such as the Office of Management and Budget, or the inspectors general in various settings, are mandated to investigate abuse of office and to provide fair access to information. Outside the government, watchdog organizations ranging from the

American Civil Liberties Union to the Government Accountability Project are consistently on guard against government and corporate efforts that may undermine individual and collective rights.

Despite these safeguards, there are still situations in which citizens cannot gain access to vital information. Efforts to understand what a factory down the street is producing or what is being dumped into a local river are often stymied by corporate and government officials who fear that the public will "misunderstand" or "misuse" data. Managers worry that they will be held responsible for improprieties or for damages that resulted from earlier policies.

Grassroots Activism and Democratic Participation

In recent years, citizens throughout the country have resisted such attempts to cover up bad news. They have confronted those who deny them crucial data and have rejected pressures toward conformity and silence. Among the most vocal are grassroots environmental activists who demand government and corporate responsiveness and accountability. These environmentalists rebuff any suggestion that they should allow the experts to handle thorny problems without consulting local residents. The activists know all too well that they, their families, and their communities can easily become victims of decisions made by government bureaucrats or corporate managers focusing only on the demands of political expediency or the requirements of the bottom line.

This book focuses on individuals and groups in the United States, Israel, and the former Czechoslovakia who encountered serious ecological problems and determined to pursue a safe environment and an open, responsive, and accountable society. These women and men confronted firsthand the threat of ongoing nuclear contamination, chemical waste and pollution, exposure to garbage and industrial refuse, untreated sewage, or other dangers. Drawing upon 140 interviews, we examine the personal transformation that occurs as leaders and core group members move from a position of uninvolved residents harboring personal disquietude to major actors collectively working to affect the quality of social life. This transformation is integral to a larger process in which individuals and families join together when an environmental hazard threatens their community.

We argue that faced with a serious environmental hazard and a bureaucracy that seems indifferent or incapable of addressing community needs, citizens often develop a profound sense of betrayal. They realize that they can no longer rely on experts or bureaucrats to protect them. Perhaps most alarming are man-made nuclear and toxic disasters intimately linked to the high technology of modern societies. While nuclear or toxic accidents, compared with traffic accidents or earthquakes, may not cause the greatest number of deaths, toxic contamination creates profound fears and a deep sense of uncertainty. Unlike most disasters, toxic accidents often have a vague beginning and an unknown end. No one knows for sure how long the water or soil has been contaminated, but the invisible presence of radiation or other contamination may inhabit the body or the environment for decades or much longer. Sociologist Kai Erikson has analyzed the impact of such exposure, concluding that it leads to a sense of feeling "dirtied, tainted, corrupted."[1] The subjective impact is very great. "Radiation and most other toxic substances . . . slink in without warning, do no immediate damage so far as one can tell, and then begin their deadly work from within—the very embodiment of stealth and treachery."[2] As a result of these fears and lack of trust in officials who attempt to minimize the damage and concern, activists transfer their trust to their own groups and resolve to be part of the resolution of their community's problems. In this process, they develop a culture of solidarity, which is accompanied by an increasing confidence in their own personal potential and in their collective ability to forge strategies to demand responsiveness from recalcitrant officials.[3]

This emerging culture of solidarity gives the activists the wherewithal to move forward, often under trying circumstances. They soon find, however, that to be effective in the political arena, they must also form strategic alliances with other citizen groups, with sympathetic political officials, with public-interest organizations, and with others who can assist them in achieving their goals. Together, these allies form an alternative network of power poised to resist powerful and entrenched officials who often subordinate environmental concerns to other economic and political interests.[4] We emphasize throughout our discussion that activists are involved in a dynamic and complex process of personal transformation, in creating a culture of solidarity, and in building an alternative network of power. Personal and collective courage are essential ingredients as activists develop and nurture a belief in their ability to require attention to their problems and to change the future for themselves and their children.

In launching a national campaign to expose and end the dangers of dioxin releases, Lois Gibbs and her colleagues at the Citizens Clearinghouse for Hazardous Waste were explicit about the essential link between the struggle for a safe environment and democratic participation.

> Organizing to stop dioxin exposure is fundamentally organizing to rebuild democracy. . . . Our campaigns must not be only about the danger of dioxin, but also about the dangers of a society where money buys power. To create the equality and justice of a true democracy, our organizing must restore the people's inalienable right to govern and protect themselves. . . . When people organize themselves to protect their communities from further dioxin contamination, they're also fighting back against the alienation and isolation that destroys the promise of democracy.[5]

Gibbs is reclaiming what one student of activism has called the "commonwealth" component of democracy. In linking the toxic protests to democracy, Gibbs is highlighting actions in which ordinary citizens work together for the common welfare of the community. This view of citizen rights and obligations balances a contemporary emphasis on individual rights, which focuses on competition and freedom from interference. In contrast, grassroots activists can be moved by a larger concern for the public welfare and the common good, and they are willing to battle for it. At their best they learn to tie their own self-interest to larger possibilities of revitalizing citizen engagement on a local level in ways that represent more than simple voluntarism. They want to share knowledge and power so that they will gain a serious voice in policies that affect the health, well-being, and safety of the community.[6]

Without the decades-long persistence and investigations of thousands of grassroots groups, we would have remained ignorant of dangerous nuclear facilities, hazardous waste sites, contaminated meats, unsafe cars, neglected nursing-home patients, and other threats to community health and safety. Courageous and determined Americans, both on the job and in their neighborhoods, refused to be silenced even in the wake of strong pressures to back off. They continued to believe that in a democracy one could and should fight city hall. They understood that silence meant acquiescence to dangerous risks to health and life.

The Rise of the Grassroots Environmental Movement

Historically, the prevalence of environmental problems did not necessarily generate a locally based grassroots environmental movement. The assault on natural ecosystems and the deterioration of finite resources were evident at least since the onset of industrialization. More often than not, political leaders and citizens alike defined factory pollutants, mining wastes, and the petrochemicals associated with industrialized agriculture as by-products of progress, necessary components of affluence and modernity. Economists, public-policy experts, and government officials all sought ways for less developed countries to imitate the success of the United States and other Western countries in developing a strong industrial economy, with little attention to environmental costs.

Some prophetic observers, like Henry David Thoreau in the 1850s, attempted to rouse public sentiment against unrestrained industrial development because of its cruel consequences to nature. Subsequent organizers fought for national parks and wilderness protection throughout the twentieth century. Not only were they successful in es-

tablishing large areas for nature conservation, they also succeeded in
founding the initial environmental organizations that went on to become major lobbyists for environmental protection in Washington and
in some state capitals. These groups largely focused on protection of
wilderness. Then, in the 1960s, a small group of writers began to call
attention to new environmental problems. Rachel Carson and others
pointed to the hazards of too many chemicals, but their work rarely in-
spired local citizens to mobilize and demand accountability for the
costs of progress to the general population.[7] Criticism remained sporadic and was limited to exclusive circles of naturalists.

By 1970, the environmental movement had become much more established and much more diverse. Until the early 1960s, national organizations, such as the Sierra Club, National Audubon Society, and
Wilderness Society, remained small in membership and focused almost
exclusively on conservation issues. A decade later these same organizations had been professionalized, employing lawyers, scientists, and
lobbyists to advocate for new legislation and regulation of the environment. Fund-raising and membership grew geometrically as public support for environmental protection became much more widespread. By
1990 the ten leading lobbying organizations claimed a membership of
more than three million and combined budgets surpassing $200 million.[8]

As the established environmental lobby became increasingly devoted to Washington politics and the necessary compromises involved
in building support, other more radical organizations and small grassroots groups became increasingly critical of "the nationals" for their
willingness to accommodate industry and its government supporters.
In response to the criticism, another group of national organizations
emerged that deliberately avoided lobbying activities and focused on
direct action, campaigns against waste sites, litigation, education, and
research. By 1990 there were eleven such national groups, including
Earth First, Greenpeace USA, World Wildlife Fund, Rainforest Alliance, and the National Toxics Campaigns. They addressed both domestic and international issues, sometimes used radical tactics such
as tree-spiking, and often promoted grassroots activity. Combined
memberships in these organizations totaled about four to five million,
with budgets of more than $200 million.[9]

In the last two decades, there has been a striking rise in the number of small groups of grassroots environmental activists and their allies, who have dedicated themselves to addressing environmental concerns.[10] In general, the grassroots groups arose in response to increasing revelations of environmental problems threatening to the health of family and friends. They were less moved, at least initially, by ecological and conservation concerns. As reports of the existence of thousands of toxic-waste dumps became public, more and more people found themselves impelled to become involved. Although some believed this local phenomenon would peak and then decline, the 1980s and 1990s saw rapid increases in the growth of such neighborhood groups, both in the United States and elsewhere, sometimes spurred by news of a disaster or by the attacks or neglect of the Reagan administration on many environmental issues.[11] These groups included a much broader cross section of race, social class, and gender than was represented in the established national environmental organizations. Women, often including those with little prior organizational experience, were very strong in both leadership and membership positions. Many groups joined alliances that provided assistance, technical information, and educational materials.

Instead of descending into a period of decline, these groups have become the bedrock of a social movement to expose and respond to threats to their communities. They are crusaders who believe they can petition and pressure their governments to act responsibly. These activists maintain their belief that citizens who band together, who count on each other, and who devote their time, energy, and resources to their cause can make a substantial difference. While they are not ignorant or naive about the decision-making prerogatives of those with power, they insist on citizen participation to maintain a viable democratic system. They reject both indifference and passivity. They emphasize deep involvement and sustained commitment to their beliefs and to their goals. These activists do not demonize their opponents, but understand that officials are often acting from positions of vested interests. Grassroots protesters rely heavily on generating public pressure to change the status quo and are unrelenting in their opposition to policies that they consider harmful to themselves, their families, their neighbors, and their communities. They are not at all reluctant to picket an offending adversary's home or to embarrass those government or corporate managers who ignore them.

Currently, there are literally thousands of grassroots environmental groups scattered throughout the United States. For example, the Citizens Clearinghouse for Hazardous Wastes alone has about eight thousand groups affiliated or registered with the national office. Scholars have estimated that there are about one thousand local groups working on issues related to the protection of the forests. Some of these groups may be short-lived or have only a handful of members, while others are more established working groups, with newsletters, offices, and a more durable membership. Given this diversity of activist organizations, it was not possible for us to study a representative sample of grassroots activists. Rather, in our eighty-six interviews in the United States, we focused mainly on environmentalists addressing some of the leading issues facing the movement—hazardous wastes, radiation exposure, incinerators and landfills, and protection of the forests. This approach enabled us to examine the background, motivation, goals, and methods of the activists confronting a variety of issues at the end of the twentieth century.

A Comparative Perspective

In this study we compare the characteristics, goals, and accomplishments of American community activists to those in other societies where environmental problems were serious but where activists operated under different social and political circumstances.[12] Although we knew that in other parts of the world, particularly industrializing societies and the former socialist countries of Eastern Europe, environmental sensitivity had been defined as a luxury for wealthy, economically developed nations, there was substantial evidence that a new, citizen-based environmental awareness was emerging there as well. We decided to focus on one former Communist country and one democratic society where the environmental movement was in a far earlier stage developmentally. We chose Israel as an apt representative of a country with an incipient environmental movement and Czechoslovakia as one where environmental activism was strongly tied to dissident politics. Such a comparison would enable us to specify the challenges surrounding the early stages of an environmental movement's formation and to test our theory that the crusade for a safe environment entails a multilevel process of citizen response with courage as a central component.

In Israel security issues, economic development, and absorption of immigrants have been the prevailing concerns since its founding as a state in 1948. The hostile relations with its Arab neighbors for the first five decades of its existence created a strong emphasis on defense. Extensive migration and resettlement of Jews from other Middle Eastern countries, and more recently from the former Soviet Union and Ethiopia, further demanded national attention and taxed the resources of the society. Economic transformation became a high priority as the original cooperative settlements founded before the creation of the state began to emphasize high-technology agriculture, and as urban economic leaders focused on large-scale industrial development. As a result, in past years Israelis rarely made the environment a central political issue.

Nonetheless, concern about water pollution and shortages has been growing recently. A five-year drought in the late 1980s and early 1990s heightened awareness of the need to conserve water and pay attention to the pollution and overpumping of one of the major aquifers supplying water to the nation. Similarly, the growing amounts of waste materials produced by an industrial society emerged as a national problem, with illegal dumps filled with rusting cars and rotting garbage spotting the countryside. A small group of early activists were joined by recent American immigrants who brought environmental consciousness to their new homeland, and by a growing number of community residents who refused to breathe locally generated factory dust that caused asthma and other respiratory problems in their families. According to the Ministry of the Environment, Israel currently has eight organizations devoted exclusively to environmental issues.[13] These groups work closely with affiliated organizations that have more general missions but devote some of their resources to environmental causes. The individuals interviewed for this study are drawn either from this small dedicated environmental network or from one of the five to ten local groups that organized to address immediate issues in their communities. (A fuller discussion of the groups interviewed can be found in the Methodological Appendix.)

Increasing awareness and activism by Jewish Israelis had its counterpart in the Israeli Arab community. As Israel's most important minority, the Arabs in the Galilee and elsewhere sought to tie their incipient environmental interests to other social needs. They wanted to address issues of equality that ranged from better health care to modern sewage treatment for their densely populated towns. Although there is now only limited interaction between the two environmental movements, we sought to understand and document the origins, goals, accomplishments, and frustrations of both Jews and Arabs in Israel.[14] To this end, we interviewed Arabs in the Society for the Protection of Nature (SPNI), in a governmental ministry, and in the most significant Arab environmental organization in Israel, the Galilee Society for Health Research and Services. The total number of our interviews in Israel was thirty-three.

To complement our investigation of community-based groups in the United States and Israel, we decided to study a former Soviet bloc society. The impact of environmental dissidence in Eastern Europe represented an excellent case where organized citizen efforts had resulted in dramatic social change. In Czechoslovakia, environmental activists were instrumental in bringing down the Communist government in 1989, making this a prime opportunity to document revolutionary environmental action in a period of national upheaval. Once again, as in the United States and Israel, we hoped to ascertain the contribution of a grassroots insurgence in forging democratic institutions. For decades, the Communist countries in Eastern Europe had a quintessential antidemocratic experience built on a Stalinist ideology that tolerated no criticism from its citizens and allowed no independent access to any adverse environmental information.[15] By the late 1970s and 1980s, slow economic growth and serious environmental problems surfaced despite all the attempts at secrecy, and several Communist governments responded by recruiting scientists to provide classified research strictly for governmental use. Although they wrote critical reports, the data remained secret and the scientists understood that they were to have no serious input into public-policy decision making. That privilege continued to belong exclusively to the bureaucrats. Censorship became the official mechanism to ensure secrecy and a "facade of order." One Polish reference manual explicitly detailed the taboo against sharing important findings, a taboo that pervaded most of the Communist countries. "Information on direct threats to life or health caused by industry or chemical agents used in agriculture, or threats to the natural environment in Poland, should be eliminated from works on environmental protection."[16] Most of the Communist governments in Eastern Europe shared the view that the public did not have the right to know.[17]

During the 1980s, deteriorating conditions led environmental groups to insist on some disclosure of the scientists' findings. Secret contacts with environmental activists in the West offered encouragement and externally validated data. In some countries, independent organizations began to emerge. In others, environmental critics joined state-sponsored nature societies to protest from within. Although the organizational opportunities and strategies varied from one country to the next, by the late 1980s environmental groups in several Eastern European countries had moved to the center of the dissident movement.

In Czechoslovakia, as in most of Eastern Europe, these dissident groups sought to counter the government's repeated claims that the country suffered no serious environmental problems. Despite the dangers of secret-police harassment, arrest, and violence, the protesters, who were small in number, informed the public of the rampant environmental damage that pervaded the country, and linked it to the lack of human rights and to a serious deterioration of public health. As activists in the Velvet Revolution, environmentalists pointed to the excessive pollution that had resulted from decades of burning inferior, soft brown coal and from a general lack of monitoring or enforcement of laws that were designed to protect the air, water, and soil. The activists embodied resistance to an oppressive state bureaucracy. They were particularly successful in challenging the Communist insistence that Czechoslovakian citizens lived in paradise and that environmental problems existed only in capitalist countries and in the imaginations of unregenerate dissidents. By gathering incriminating data and boldly presenting it to the public, the environmentalists helped undermine the legitimacy of a forty-year reign of Communist oppression.

Furthermore, we point out that once the Velvet Revolution ended the authoritarian government in 1989, the environmentalists faced a new challenge. The Communist enemy had been defeated, but the ecological degradation continued. After the initial revolutionary euphoria subsided, many obstacles to change surfaced. The transition to democracy was difficult. Four decades of authoritarianism left a legacy of little faith in the government's ability to solve serious social problems. At the same time, the long history of dissidents operating in secrecy meant that few groups trusted each other any more than they trusted the government. For years most Czechoslovakians had responded to the regime with conformity and passivity, hoping to be left alone to conduct their private lives in peace. Now, in the transition to democracy, no one knew who was a friend or who had been an informer to the secret police.

Although a tight culture of solidarity had been crucial to the activists during the Communist years, they were less clear in the post-Communist period on how to expand their circle and include new recruits. All of these factors surfaced as privatization threatened employment and social security. Many Czechs and Slovaks focused on the need for stability and the desire for a more consumer-based society. In this context, environmental activists wanted to address a myriad of issues, ranging from dangerous pollution levels to continuing construction of nuclear reactors. They hoped to convince their fellow citizens to resist the development of a consumer society that imitated the West in defining all resources as available for exploitation.

According to a 1991 report prepared for the Center for International Environmental Law, there were approximately fifteen environmental NGOs (nongovernmental organizations) in the capital city of Prague. These ranged from small friendship-based groups to the Czech Union of Nature Protectors (CSOP), with "several regional offices and hundreds of local clubs scattered throughout the country." We interviewed members of six of these groups. In addition, there were a series of small environmental centers throughout the Czech Republic. In Slovakia, there were five separate environmental NGOs. The Slovak Union of Landscape and Nature Protectors (SZOPK) was the main nature society, with numerous local clubs and regional offices throughout Slovakia.[18] We interviewed leaders and members from two of the groups. In total we interviewed twenty-five environmental activists in Prague and Bratislava.

The Contents of the Book

In the chapters that follow we examine the circumstances under which grassroots environmental activism flourished in the 1980s and 1990s in the United States, Israel, and the former Czechoslovakia. Chapter 1, "Maintaining a Democratic Society," identifies our major themes. In it, we analyze grassroots activism as a critical component of the environmental movement, and examine the ways in which activists promote democracy in each of the countries in which they operate. By insisting on active citizen engagement, by demanding a right to know about the hazards and risks in their communities, and by asserting that they are entitled to participate in all levels of decision making, these grassroots groups promulgate an ideology and a strategy of democratic participation.

The remaining chapters present case studies in which grassroots activism flourished in different locales. Chapter 2, "Breaking the Bands of National Security Secrecy," emphasizes the centrality of a changing political culture that followed the end of the Cold War era. Such a major shift provided the opportunity for citizens to challenge previously sacrosanct government policies. Indigenous leaders had to arise, however, to expose the problems and undermine the official stance that none had suffered from earlier policy decisions. Chapter 3, "Marching Along with Mothers and Children," focuses on circumstances that lead women to organize to protect family, neighborhood, and community.

Gender becomes a crucial factor when dangerous chemicals or pollution directly threaten the health and lives of children. Nonetheless, to launch a successful protest women have had to expand maternal roles and forge alliances with other strategically placed allies. Chapter 4, "Preserving the Farmland from Contamination," highlights activists who believe that their communities face imminent environmental damage. Unlike the crusaders presented above, these American wheat farmers, Israeli kibbutzniks, and Czech and Slovakian townspeople feared the incursion of incinerators and landfills that might bring potential economic advantage to some but almost certain environmental degradation for all. While often labeled NIMBYs, after the phrase "not in my backyard," their attitudes and action reveal a far more complex reality. Chapter 5, "Protecting the Precious Natural Resources," draws upon all the threats detailed earlier but goes well beyond the harm to human beings. Here, activists and scholars promulgate the centrality of the natural environment and its right to survive and thrive despite humans' desire and need to exploit their natural surroundings. Chapter 6, "The Courage of Ordinary People," details the essential qualities of boldness and willingness to assume risk in the cause of a safe environment. Drawing upon examples from all prior discussions, the cultural, emotional, and social supports for courageous behavior are emphasized. Courage is a potent resource when citizens face powerful government and corporate bureaucracies.

All the case studies presented throughout the book highlight the experiences of some of the leading activists. Their lives and struggles, however, are representative of many of their peers who have long been at their side. In addition, all the activists have thousands of counterparts engaged in long-term battles. The environmental crusaders no longer stand alone.

The photos in the following pages introduce a few of the many activists deeply engaged in the battle for a safe environment throughout the world.

Penny Newman was a young housewife when a nearby toxic dump, the Stringfellow Acid Pits, overflowed into her community. Years of grassroots leadership catapulted her into regional and national leadership roles. Here she stands with a fellow activist, Morning Sunday.

Lisa Crawford was transformed when she learned that her family's water supply had been contaminated by radioactive wastes from a nearby nuclear bomb factory. She joined the Fernald Residents for Environmental Safety and Health (FRESH) and became devoted to her work as an environmental activist.

Lynn Stembridge is the executive director of the Hanford Education Action League (HEAL), which gathered extensive government documents establishing firm proof of the Green Run—the deliberate release of radiation in 1949 on to civilian areas of Washington State.

Tom Bailie, a farmer in Washington State, calls himself a storyteller. He began speaking about harmful effects of the Hanford Nuclear Reservation when few others were willing to do so.

Judith Jurgi and Don Carter (below) grew up near the Hanford Nuclear Reservation. When they realized that their serious health problems had resulted from radiation exposure as children, they channeled their anger into active participation in the Downwinders.

Harold and Dorothy Clinesmith were the driving force behind the wheat farmers' organization against the building of a toxic-waste dump. They bitterly opposed those who wanted major waste-management companies to build in their area of eastern Washington State.

Susie Van Kirk goes to endless hearings about proposed logging plans. "Somebody has to speak for the trees and often I am the only person to do it." She often has to go up against the purchaser and his road crew who are anxious to cut the big trees of northern California.

Tim McKay is the director of the North Coast Environmental Center in Arcata, California. He is passionately dedicated to saving the Headlands Forest and protecting local watersheds.

Florence Robinson and other members of the Louisiana Environmental Action Network/LEAN hold a news conference to protest the health risks resulting from policies based on environmental racism.

Eilon Schwartz is trying to persuade the Israeli public to look beyond immediate contamination problems and think about the value of open spaces and the need to preserve animals, plants, and open land.

Alon Tal, founder of the Israeli Union for Environmental Defense, confers with his assistant, Irit Sapir, about an upcoming hearing.

Lynn Golumbic, shown with husband and one child, was shocked at the level of air pollution that affected her family when they moved to Haifa, Israel. Years of active involvement have brought some improvements.

Reuven Bezner has devoted years to preventing the construction of a garbage dump at a neighboring kibbutz. He believes such a facility will pollute the water, contaminate the land, and destroy the pastoral communities built over the past seventy years.

Lev Fishelson, a longtime environmental activist and a biology professor at Tel Aviv University, convinced top Israeli military leaders of the importance of saving a great coral reef.

Dr. Hatim Kana'aneh is a founder of the Galilee Society, an organization dedicated to environmental and social justice for Israeli Arabs.

Devorah Ben Shaul emigrated to Israel from the United States. As a biologist and science writer for Israel's English-language newspaper, she became acutely aware of environmental problems in Israel.

Juraj Zamkovsky had high hopes for an environmental movement in his hometown of Budmerice, Slovakia. Despite bitter disappointment when the citizens rejected his ideas, he continues to devote himself to new initiatives.

Jan Budaj was a major figure in the Bratislava Nahlas movement, which exposed massive environmental problems in Slovakia, just prior to the Velvet Revolution in 1989.

Pavel Sremer (left) and Josef Vavroušek (right) were active dissidents in
Czechoslovakia and leaders of the environmental movement in the first post-
Communist government. Vavroušek was the federal minister of the newly
formed Environmental Ministry and Šremer served as his deputy minister.

Ja'ra Johnova signed the charter 77 Declaration of Human Rights in 1977. After more than a decade as a Czech dissident, she joined with a small group of women, Prague Mothers, to protest intolerable levels of air pollution. Their public demonstration was one of the first in communist Czechoslovakia.

Ivo Silmav'y was a young activist in Prague working with Children of the Earth. He subsequently became the executive director of the Prague chapter of Greenpeace.

1

Maintaining a Democratic Society

 Social connectedness, or social capital, is an indicator of the health of society, and a powerful predictor of the quality of public life. Citizen involvement in maintaining public activity and concern for the common good is one of the hallmarks of modern democracy. In the last two decades a wide range of new grassroots groups have dedicated themselves to addressing common community problems. As neighbors and friends have encountered toxic-waste dumps, incinerators, radioactive releases, and contaminated water and air, they have banded together to confront the businesses and government agencies that have exposed them and their children to health and safety risks. These new neighborhood organizations may not resemble the fraternal or civic associations of previous generations, but these recently born groups have proved to be dynamic, effective communitarian sources of social change. Some students of community organizing have referred to this new phenomenon as "civic innovation," which they argue is

most important for enhancing democratic vitality and increasing the capacity for solving public problems.[1]

Robert Putnam's recent writing on the decline of civic engagement in the United States provides a contrasting view. His work has spawned a major debate about social capital. Putnam, in "Bowling Alone,"[2] has argued that contemporary Americans are less likely to participate in voluntary activities, ranging from church groups to bowling leagues, than their counterparts a generation ago. The United States has historically exhibited a high degree of civic engagement, but the level of participation has fallen substantially in the last twenty-five years. This tendency to shy away from membership in community groups, Putnam asserts, limits the opportunities for people to build relationships and form the trust that creates the social glue necessary for citizens to come together to solve common social problems.

According to Putnam and other social capital theorists, the level of civic engagement in a society influences everything from children's school performance to economic development and the quality of government. For these reasons, declining membership in churches, parent-teacher associations, and fraternal organizations is a source of major concern. Survey results show that lower levels of participation in civic organizations have been correlated with a populace that is less likely to trust others, less likely to vote, and less willing to believe in the beneficence of government. "In America, at least," Putnam asserts, "there is reason to suspect that this democratic disarray may be linked to a broad and continuing erosion of civic engagement that began a quarter-century ago."[3] Comparative studies indicate that the problem is equal or worse in other countries. The former Communist countries are struggling for ways to reconstruct civic institutions that had been carefully controlled under Communist administrations. Elsewhere, developing countries are striving to build strong voluntary networks that will empower and assist citizens engaged in economic development.

Submerged Dangers

According to Putnam and others, the period of the fifties and sixties was the heyday of voluntary associations in the United States. Positive as that may have been, we believe that it was during this same period of high social cohesion that serious problems were percolating under the surface. The rapid industrial expansion that followed the end of World War II, the nationwide construction of suburbs, and the unprecedented spending on defense production in the atomic age all contributed to growing environmental dangers that were largely ignored. Government and industry both sanctioned unlimited dumping of toxic wastes into rivers and landfills, release of radioactive materials into the air, extensive destruction of forests, and the creation of a consumer culture that failed to anticipate the long-term costs of producing and disposing of petrochemical wastes and other hazardous products.

These threats did not remain hidden indefinitely. Eventually, local residents smelled noxious odors, drank foul-tasting water, and read about growing scientific concern over incipient environmental disasters that seemed to be sprouting everywhere. Some communities were affected more immediately than others; by the late 1970s newspapers carried stories about the high incidence of birth defects in Love Canal, New York; the mysterious leukemia clusters in Woburn, Massachusetts; and the terrifying toxic spills in Glen Avon, California.[4] And these problems were not limited to the United States: among other instances, Agent Orange was the source of extensive damage in Vietnam and other parts of Southeast Asia during the Vietnam War, and a plant explosion in Seveso, Italy, in 1976 exposed thousands of people to a toxic cloud that made headlines throughout the world.[5] Within a decade, many other countries found themselves facing the unhappy results of excessive pesticide use, or confronting unprecedented levels of pollution caused by unrestricted coal burning or the growing number of cars spewing carbon monoxide into the atmosphere. Eventually, a growing awareness of the magnitude of these and other environmental problems created new forms of activism, and, in our view, resulted in dynamic and tenacious forms of social capital.

Our research in the United States, Israel, and the former Czechoslovakia raises serious questions about the assertion that there has been a recent decline of citizen involvement in community issues. While the figures describing American participation in PTAs, scouting organizations, and Rotary clubs may show declining membership, citizens have responded to a new and distinct kind of community organization.[6]

There is evidence that the growth of grassroots environmental activism is more than a local American response. While there are distinct cultural variations, the phenomenon of collective response to the environmental dangers of industrial society has occurred repeatedly in developing countries, in former Communist states, and in advanced industrial societies.[7] Theories emphasizing the decline of social capital must take into account the salience of this rapidly expanding social phenomenon, where small groups of citizens band together to mount grassroots political campaigns to improve environmental conditions.

Many grassroots groups do not have charters, constitutions, or offices in Washington, making it difficult to count their members. Typically, these groups arose spontaneously to meet glaring local needs that could not be accommodated in traditional organizations.[8] Often, when local residents confronted a major local or regional environmental problem, they had nowhere to turn. Not infrequently, they felt betrayed by the very government agencies that they had relied on to protect their best interests, and eventually came to believe that these agencies were actually undermining their health and safety. Whether it was the Nuclear Regulatory Commission, the Environmental Protection Agency, or the local department of health, threatened citizens in the United States often felt that officials were offering them deliberate misinformation and false promises about the safety of radioactive releases or chemical contamination. Often, corporations doing business in the affected area were no less culpable. In fact, it was frequently their actions that had led to the poisoning of the water, air, or land in the first place. These corporations' close connections to government regulatory agencies often allowed industry to conceal dangerous practices and policies. Concerned citizens came to believe that the corporations and government agencies were joined in a cozy partnership that was virtually impossible to penetrate. Residents who questioned existing policies found themselves excluded and patronized by bureaucrats who assured them that they could not possibly understand the complex technical data, the economic pressures, or the needs of national security.[9]

The new social movements that arose from these circumstances often drew participants from across race and class lines. Many activists saw themselves as victimized because they lived in vulnerable communities, unprotected by the bureaucracy that should have been more alert to the dangers surrounding nuclear facilities, hazardous-waste sites, and polluted waters. Often inexperienced in politics, these men and women came together determined to defend themselves. But this effort, they would soon learn, required them to move into uncharted territory and to undertake a long-term, sophisticated battle against powerful and often vindictive opponents. These grassroots activists emphasized that they represented "the people" or "the community," while their adversaries were part of an undefined "other," who stood in opposition to the community. To underscore the strength of the people, the activists called on common experiences, shared beliefs, and a strong investment in the significance of family and land. This common culture was to bind together the protesters and to define a common purpose. They rejected class analyses as a way of viewing their conflict, although they understood that power is often tied to wealth. They preferred to focus on the commonalities of culture that characterize activists and their potential supporters, submerging any conflicts over differences of race, class, ethnicity, and gender as much as possible.[10]

To persist in their struggle activists first had to overcome their fears, their inexperience, and their lack of technical knowledge. They had to possess the stamina and the courage to chart new ground, whether in testifying at legislative hearings, collecting convincing data, or demonstrating public support through large-scale protests at crucial events. They learned not to be intimidated by corporate and government officials, who often disavowed the activists' claims by denigrating their competence.

It is remarkable that so many citizens responded to the environmental challenges during the last several decades. Repeatedly, we found individuals who developed confidence in their ability to organize, determined to force the social system to be more responsible to the needs of the community. What were the cultural and social supports for such commitment? These courageous activists drew on a reservoir of social capital that allowed them to join with neighbors and friends in moments of fear and anger. As they came together, they reinforced each other's belief in the rightness of their cause and made a shared vow to undertake united action. Perhaps most impressive was the ability of a core group to stay together for the "long haul," accumulating the necessary evidence and expertise to win sufficient public support in order to press their case. None of this would have been possible without a strong belief in the democratic process and a faith that justice was on their side. Social capital was at the core of their courageous response, and their bold actions reinforced their reliance upon one another.[11]

The Betrayal of Trust: The Catalyst for Personal Transformation

There are many instances of this potent mixture in which breach of trust, determination to organize, and faith in the democratic system led local groups to protest against the existence of environmental dangers. In the profiles detailed below, we introduce several women who typified the civic innovator. Each identified a crisis in her community and took responsibility to build a focused campaign to seek redress from responsible government and corporate agencies. In so doing they sparked a form of civic engagement unlike any these communities had ever seen.

Lisa Crawford is a prime example of a citizen who was catapulted into new roles when her world was shaken in 1984 by information that threatened her and her family. A secretary with a civil service job in the state of Ohio, Lisa was the mother of a two-year-old and the wife of a General Motors automobile worker. Preoccupied by the demands of a toddler, two jobs, and the construction of their new house, Lisa and Ken Crawford rarely read the newspaper or watched the news. They were vaguely aware that there were rumors of radioactive dust coming from the Fernald uranium-enrichment plant across the street, but they assumed that the complainers were antinuclear activists and did not pay much attention to the growing local concern.

All of that changed dramatically the day that Ken Crawford called his wife at work and told her that their landlord had informed him that their well was contaminated. They were to stop using the water until they had more information. They remembered that the local newspaper had reported cases of three contaminated wells in their neighborhood, but no names or addresses had been released. Lisa Crawford never dreamed that she and her family had been drinking contaminated water: "I left work early and picked up my son at the baby-sitter's and went home to meet my husband. We were sitting in the kitchen, scared, knowing nothing. I called the landlord and told him we needed more information. He told me that he had some letters from the DOE, but he didn't know if he was allowed to give me copies. I began to get very angry."[12]

Lisa Crawford was not satisfied when the landlord's sons told her that the Department of Energy (DOE) was testing the well and that there was nothing to worry about. If that were the case, why couldn't she have copies of the letters? Her growing sense of anxiety turned into rage and a sense of betrayal a few nights later, when she attended her first public meeting. All the reassuring talk in the world could not soothe her when she and her husband officially heard that their well was one of the three that had definitely been contaminated, and that the United States Geological Survey had discovered the contamination in 1981, almost three years earlier. "I did something I had never done before. I stood up in public and spoke. When something like this touches you, it makes you think that there was something wrong with the system and the system had to be changed. That very night Kathy Meyer, the organizer of FRESH, the Fernald Residents for Environmental Safety and Health, came up to me. 'I know you are upset; call me tomorrow and we'll talk; come and help us with FRESH.' And that's how I got involved."[13]

Lisa Crawford became an activist. She devoted endless time and energy conferring with neighbors, attending meetings, learning to speak in public and to chair a meeting. She enjoyed the work and had a sense of satisfaction in pursuing industry and government officials, urging them to remedy the dangerous situation in the Fernald community. This process did not happen automatically.[14] When Lisa Crawford and her neighbors in FRESH first met to address the radiation problems caused by the Fernald plant, they were unsure how to proceed. They first had to convince each other that they were entitled to act in the name of the community. Then they had to create leaders and a core group of activists willing to enter uncharted terrain.[15] In the process, several of them, including Crawford, experienced a profound personal transformation: "A lot of folks in the beginning said, 'You can't fight city hall. You are never going to get anywhere.' And we finally said, 'Let's just do it.' We did demonstrations and marches and all the things other groups did. And then I was asked to come and testify before Congress. I had never flown on an airplane before in my life. My husband almost had to put me on that plane. I was terrified."[16]

Lisa Crawford confronted her terror. She was to embark on a bold and groundbreaking journey. Crawford did board the plane, flew to Washington, and testified before Congress. In overcoming her fears, she did not act alone. She was encouraged and coached by congressional staff members, who told her exactly what to expect and how to react. Her personal transformation was accelerated by active assistance from members of Congress, who depended on firsthand testimony to achieve their legislative goals, and by her work with other grassroots activists who were seeking admission of culpability from both government and industry contractors, and who wanted commitments to remedy the contamination of their communities. She and her friends at FRESH were beginning the process of building an alternative network of power.

Public testimony was but one tactic among many that they tried. After initial trial and error, the group learned to turn up their pressure on the government. Their strategy for building alternative networks of power included developing a coalition with plant workers who could provide the inside information so crucial to the battle. These workers knew in what ways the plant was unsafe and how the contamination affected employees and residents alike. This alliance with the workers gave Lisa Crawford the information she needed, as well as the confidence to approach and even counsel top federal administrators. The former fearful and anxious resident had become an articulate and forceful spokeswoman. She could build links to unions, speak to the media, and convince cabinet officers that she was a force to be reckoned with. Crawford spoke not only for herself but also for her friends and neighbors. The group developed a clear division of labor. Someone kept the records. Another made the phone calls. A third focused on understanding the technical material. Crawford spoke and negotiated for all. She was emboldened by the faith and trust of her group. For her, it was a totally new experience. Her confidence was nourished by their success. The Fernald plant was shut down, and the residents won a multimillion-dollar lawsuit. This result confirmed their view that grassroots organizing and applying collective pressure could lead to greater government and corporate accountability.

> We launched a campaign that we have done for ten years now. And it can actually be a little bit of fun. We made friends with some of the workers on the inside. . . . We forged a very good relationship between the community and the workforce. When you put those two together, I will tell you that you have a very powerful force. If you stay at it long enough, you work your way into the system. By now when I go into D.C. every year I meet with Hazel O'Leary [in 1995 the secretary of energy]. We light fires under every politician that we can find. It's nothing for us to call them when we need something.[17]

Their coalition with the workers, their success in retaining a major law firm, and their links to the nationally based Military Production Network enabled the activists to overcome the disrespect of government and industry officials, who were quick to claim that the local people did not have adequate information and were reacting emotionally without all the facts. The confidence that came from working with friends and neighbors for the welfare of the community was crucial to FRESH's effectiveness. Grassroots activists learned to redefine their roles as mothers and homemakers. Now security for their families came to mean a safe environment in addition to a clean house and homemade brownies for the school's PTA sale.

As small, neighborhood-based groups began to transfer their trust from the government and local industry to their own newly formed alliances, they also developed the ability and courage to reach out for assistance beyond their own regions. They would no longer be dismissed as uninformed worriers unable to master specialized vocabulary. They taught themselves to read technical reports and to be conversant with the options available for remediation. There are many documented examples of this process of growing sophistication.[18]

When Christina Cocek first decided to take action against Norit Americas, a Dutch-owned corporation in Marshall, Texas, that had applied for a special permit to burn millions of pounds of hazardous waste within a mile of her home, she never thought of herself as scientifically inclined, but it did not take her long to realize that self-education was crucial to effective action. The first time she and a few colleagues met with the head engineer from Norit and asked him a question, he responded, "I'd like to answer that but, unfortunately, I think this is all a little too technical for y'all to understand." She described her mental response as "You wanna bet?" Cocek spent the next few months reading, checking with experts, making contacts with environmental groups, and generally educating herself. The pleasure she experienced when Norit withdrew its application for the permit to burn the toxic waste was made even sweeter when she spoke again to the head engineer at the plant about wastewater discharges. This time her confidence and knowledge quickly became apparent: "As I pointed out discrepancy after discrepancy in what he was saying, it suddenly dawned on me that he was nervous because I knew too much. He knew that I had done my homework, and that he could no longer use that 'too technical for you to understand' routine to tiptoe around the truth." Transformed by her newfound ease with technical materials, she realized the power of the network she had joined, "a battalion of compassionate and intelligent human beings who have pooled their skills, resources, and hard-won wisdom to educate people."[19]

Challenging Environmental Racism

The personal transformation that began with an overpowering sense of betrayal and developed into effective political action occurred in groups facing environmental disasters throughout the United States. Margaret Williams and her neighbors in Pensacola, Florida, confronted a bewildering array of health problems in their neighborhood. They attributed the high incidence of cancer, birth defects, and other illnesses to toxic wastes from a local wood-treatment company and a fertilizer factory. But they also believed that the neighborhood's problems were more than just a product of environmental degradation. The Pensacola citizens were convinced that they were also the victims of pervasive racism. Margaret Williams, a retired school teacher, described the double sense of betrayal that she felt. As an African-American, she worried that her community had not been given top priority by political decision makers: "I think if this had been a white neighborhood living between two Superfund sites, and once they found out the levels of contamination here, we wouldn't have had a problem."[20]

Margaret Williams and other Pensacola residents organized a grassroots group, Citizens Against Toxic Exposure. They were not satisfied with the response from the Environmental Protection Agency, which excavated 250,000 cubic yards of contaminated soil and left it in a pile that stood sixty feet high right on the site. Such actions did not win high regard from local groups, who had previously assumed that government agencies were there to protect them. The half-finished job and neglect merely served to convince local residents that they had to take a more active role in controlling the outcomes of such community problems. Margaret Williams voiced her profound disappointment with the EPA: "The reckless nature of EPA's activity was almost as frightening as the contaminants themselves. No measures were taken to protect nearby neighborhoods. Choking fumes and poisonous dust have caused respiratory distress, persistent skin rashes, burning eye irritation, and made existing health problems even worse."[21]

Because so many toxic dumps are located in poor rural communities, the antitoxic grassroots movement has spawned a number of activist leaders in communities of color. Florence Robinson lives in Alsen, a small, predominantly African-American community just north of Baton Rouge, Louisiana. She became deeply involved in community affairs after her health was adversely affected by a neurotoxin released into the air by the petrochemical industries in the area. When she realized that other people in her area were also experiencing bouts of dizziness and nausea, "well that's when a movement gets born." Robinson understood that this movement could not be just an effort of the directly affected. An articulate and forceful professor of biology, Robinson explains to young people around the country why active engagement is so important: "Now, it's an unfortunate thing that so many of us who are activists had to be personally touched before we really took on that role. I would hope that all of us would come to realize that we are a part of society and we can't turn our backs on a problem just because it affects a small group over there."[22]

Robinson worked closely with her neighbors, building a culture of solidarity among those who were similarly afflicted. They all believed that their skin color had played a significant part in their victimization. She quickly learned, however, that local action was not sufficient. She was determined to reverse environmental injustice, which occurs, she said, "any time any person, group of persons, or community of people is forced to bear the adverse impact for the greater good of society." Robinson led her neighbors in forging national connections with others in the toxic-waste movement. She attended conferences around the country, testified four times before Congress, and served on the National Commission on Superfund as well as other organizations. She was convinced that adequate knowledge, preparation, and contacts were essential ingredients of local activism:

> We work together, we demonstrate, we've learned a lot of the tactics of the Civil Rights movement. We march. We sing. We demonstrate. But we also go much beyond that. We go to hearings. We have to learn the jargon and the facts. Yes, I'm a biology teacher. But when I came into this environmental movement, I came just like any other woman. I didn't know what was going on out there and I had to educate myself, just as all the other wonderful women activists did. They had to educate themselves on the issues and had to learn how to fight this power.[23]

Florence Robinson's group, like Margaret Williams and her African-American neighbors in the Citizens Against Toxic Exposure, represented more than one small neighborhood responding with anger to toxic waste in their midst. Rather, these groups defined themselves as part of a larger movement for environmental justice that has emerged throughout the country. Because so many toxic-waste dumps have been found in poor neighborhoods, often inhabited by people of color, the 1980s brought forth an alternative network of power that tied earlier civil rights experience and ideology to the environmental movement. Small, local grassroots groups gained additional support and influence by coming together in 1993 at the People of Color Environmental Leadership Summit, where they issued a statement on the "Principles of Environmental Justice." Their opening words encapsulated their culture of solidarity and their intention to tie local concerns to a larger quest for social justice:

> We the people of color, gathered together at this multinational People of Color Environmental Leadership Summit, to begin to build a national and international movement of all people of color to fight the destruction and taking of our lands and communities, do hereby re-establish our spiritual interdependence to the sacredness of our Mother Earth; to respect and celebrate each of our cultures, languages and beliefs about the natural world and our roles in healing ourselves; to insure environmental justice; to promote economic alternatives which would contribute to the development of environmentally safe livelihoods; and to secure our political, economic and cultural liberation that has been denied for 500 years of colonization and oppression, resulting in the poisoning of our communities and land and the genocide of our peoples, do affirm and adopt these Principles of Environmental Justice.[24]

Penny Newman, a leading California grassroots environmental activist who led her local battle to clean up toxic contamination (see Chapter 3), has worked with communities of all races. She believes that social-class factors play a central role in the victimization of many communities—whether black, Latino, Native American, or white. Her trenchant firsthand observations are supported by the findings of many social scientists who have studied other sites.[25]

So many affected communities are blue-collar or poor. One of the reasons these communities have the pollution to begin with is that they are not on the same social level as decision makers. It's easy to pollute people one never encounters. They can be treated as faceless numbers, many times de-humanized—as one of "them." I've even had a state official say to me, one time when discussing the siting of a dump in the deserts of southern California, that he didn't understand why I cared, since all that was out there were a bunch of ignorant wetbacks.

It's more difficult to pollute people one encounters at the country club, dinner parties, church or, more importantly, fundraisers. When the proposed victims are part of one's social sphere, those that are a part of one's daily personal life, there are few callous enough to pollute them.

The communities targeted for contaminated sites don't have the personal access to these decision makers and therefore have to find different methods of getting their voices heard. That is why the tactics they use—picketing, demonstrations, media, etc., are utilized. They can't simply call up Joe the Decision Maker and chat or corner him at a dinner party and shame him for even considering such an idea. Our phone calls rarely get through, and we certainly don't get invited to such affairs.[26]

Appalled by the treatment they received, angered residents of communities throughout the United States and elsewhere did not retreat. Rather, they quickly understood that the amelioration of their problems could only occur through persistent and united action. While many had no experience in politics or social movements, they were able to analyze their situation, build grassroots organizations for environmental justice, and join regional and even national coalitions that frequently crossed race and class boundaries. In doing this, they transferred their trust from government and corporate organizations to a new belief in their own collective wisdom and potential. This significant cultural shift may have begun with very tentative actions, when neighbors met to share their anger, fear, and sense of betrayal. But initial expression of emotion provided the necessary foundation for building personal confidence, group cohesion, and belief in their ability to confront powerful authorities. Subsequently, they developed organizational skills, ideology, and resources to move their program onto the political and social agenda.[27]

This process of forging personal transformations, creating a culture of solidarity, and then building new, alternative networks of power occurred repeatedly in the United States. Activists used their anger and sense of betrayal to change from victims to knowledgeable and assertive participants. We will see in the case studies that follow detailed accounts of neophyte, nonpolitical residents learning to challenge local, state, federal, and corporate officials. Most significant in their transformation was their ability to organize with neighbors and others victimized by environmental hazards. We cannot overestimate the significance of the bonds they developed. This culture of solidarity impelled them forward, consoled them in times of discouragement, and allowed for sharing of tasks and common interpretation of events.[28] As the process evolved, the neighborhood groups joined alternative networks of power linking their local groups to statewide and national coalitions fighting similar battles, and these coalitions in turn identified lawyers, reporters, and public-interest organizations willing to assist them.

Environmentalists in the Land of Battle

This phenomenon of personal and political transformation was not limited to the American experience. It also occurred in Israel, a country that did not have a strong tradition of voluntary participation in nongovernmental organizations. The citizens of Israel were often preoccupied with issues of national security, warfare, and absorption of immigrants. A high premium was placed on developing a modern economy and using new technologies "to make the desert bloom." But, as the intensive use of fertilizers and pesticides and the overuse of scarce water resources all began to take a toll on environmental quality, small groups of citizens responded by organizing to overcome government and industry neglect.

Devorah Ben Shaul is a prime example of the immigrant transformed into a committed environmentalist, a person who came to believe that Israelis' future could only be secured by a policy of determined concern for land, water, and air resources. She had grown up in a small town in Texas and went to Israel as a teenager in 1947. During her first two-year stay, she fought in the Israeli war of independence. Until that time, she had had little Jewish background, but the experience of fighting alongside recently released concentration camp survivors forever changed her worldview. She watched several newly arrived immigrants meet their deaths in the battle for Jerusalem, just months after they came off the boat as survivors of the Holocaust: "Of course it changed me. I could no longer fit in with a bunch of teenagers in Texas. It made a Zionist of me—that goes without saying. The horror of the Holocaust convinced me that this cannot happen again, and whatever you have to do to make sure it doesn't happen, is what it has to be. I had no doubts and don't have any doubts about that."[29]

Her profound commitment to the state of Israel did not prevent her from developing a very critical attitude toward the absence of sound environmental policies when she returned from the United States more than a decade later to live in Israel permanently. As a Ph.D. in biology, she began working as a research assistant at Hebrew University. Her research and her reading of Rachel Carson and other environmental writers awakened her to the threat in Israel, where pesticides "were being used like water" and "birds were dying by the tons." In the 1970s Ben Shaul began writing a column for the English-language newspaper, the *Jerusalem Post*. As she became more outspoken, her views on profound environmental dangers did not sit well with the government authorities: "At one point the minister of agriculture actually accused me of transplanting American problems to Israel in order to make a name for myself. I was writing about polluted rivers, which they claimed we didn't have, but all of our rivers were an open sewage channel by then."[30]

It was not easy to stand up to a cabinet minister and to serve as a lone voice in the English press.[31] Ben Shaul could have confined herself to less controversial articles. But she was convinced her issues were important, and she had the courage to continue in the face of official attacks. Within a few decades after Israel's independence in 1948, Ben

Shaul and others from the United States and Europe were blowing the whistle on emerging environmental problems. Israel was now their land, and they were no longer content to remain silent. They refused to abandon their dreams for an environmentally safe country and to place all responsibility in the hands of officials overburdened by the perceived requirements of national security, immigrant absorption, and economic development.

They knew that they were building on the work of a few biologists and visionaries who had earlier banded together to conduct a census of existing animal species and had then lobbied for wildlife protection. As soon as the state of Israel was founded, these devoted naturalists succeeded in having the new government institute a series of wildlife-protection laws. Professor Heyedrich Mendelssohn, a wildlife biologist who immigrated from Germany in the 1930s, became an early leader in the nature-preservation effort and worked fervently to establish national parks and protected lands. "We have," he argued eloquently, "a very small country, and we have to do everything in our power to protect it."[32] Well into his eighties, Professor Mendelssohn remained a devoted fighter for preservation of the natural ecology of Israel.

There was also an early effort to organize nature societies, particularly the Society for the Protection of Nature (SPNI), which has long been one of Israel's most popular organizations. From the 1950s on it sponsored educational programs and field trips to acquaint the public with the beauty of the country and to instill a love of the land; yet their efforts were limited in scope and goals. While they embarked on an ambitious and successful campaign to educate the public against picking and destroying wildflowers, they did not encourage environmental activism around problems of pollution, pesticides, or hazardous wastes.

By the 1970s and 1980s, Ben Shaul, Mendelssohn, and a few of their dedicated friends had built strong bonds of solidarity as vocal and uncompromising environmentalists. They kept pushing at the more difficult problems of pesticides, sewage treatment, nuclear energy, and more. Ben Shaul joined with other activists, including Shirley and Herschel Benyamin, to found Econet, an organization that would raise public consciousness by sponsoring actions and by issuing a newsletter to educate the public about the dangers associated with radon gas, lead in gasoline, and dumping untreated sewage. Eventually they raised funds for community-based environmental groups and for the first environmental legal-defense organization. The process of building viable alternative networks of power was now underway. They were determined not to be bullied by the government's desire to justify environmental neglect by calling it a necessary cost of national security. According to Devorah Ben Shaul: "There is no security problem involved in most of these environmental issues, but they can always call it that. The same thing was true after Chernobyl, when our radiation level went up very high. The minister of health would not release the statistics on how much radiation there was, because it would 'confuse' the public. Israeli-grown herbs were returned from Europe for having too high a radiation content, but then they were sold here on the local market. When I wrote about it, they said I was giving Israeli agriculture a bad name."[33]

Criticizing the government's insistence on security issues defied all social norms in Israeli society. Security bound together all Israeli Jews no matter how they differed on other political questions. Ben Shaul and her colleagues exhibited personal courage when they insisted on separating real security issues from other matters that needed political airing. They were vulnerable to condemnation for not being sufficiently loyal to the state. Despite the many frustrations and setbacks that Devorah Ben Shaul experienced, she is convinced that she and her small group of colleagues and friends have made a difference: "The fact is that over a thirty-year period, there is a difference. At least people have become aware. Today, if I talk about this to the average Israeli, at least they know what I'm talking about and have some idea. In 1982, I couldn't get fifty people to a meeting, and today I can get five hundred or a thousand in Tel Aviv. It means something happened."[34]

Israel, we shall see, did not have an elaborate infrastructure of environmental laws, agencies, and nongovernmental organizations. Devorah Ben Shaul and her activist friends were building organizations and developing a vocabulary for public discourse. Many, like Shirley Benyamin, brought know-how and experience from the United States, but they were determined to join with others to create a movement that spoke to Israelis and fit with their Zionist predilections. It was to be a long and challenging struggle.

Confronting an Oppressive Regime

A comparative investigation of grassroots activists highlights many similarities across cultures. Virtually all industrializing societies have experienced rapid increases in the contamination of air, soil, and water, and as a result, most countries have found themselves burying or burning mounting piles of garbage and toxic waste. The rapid depletion of forests and other natural ecosystems has worried naturalists throughout the world. As the consequences of this environmental deterioration have become manifest, small groups of citizens have emerged to articulate the problem and to demand changes that would slow or halt damage to human health and natural resources.

Despite these similarities across national boundaries, there have also been profound differences. The historical precedent of environmental groups existed in some places, but was totally absent in others. In the United States, there was a long-standing tradition of voluntary organizations that encompassed every cause, from better schools to safer highways. In other societies, neighborhood political groups were often defined as subversive. The threat of prison and the repression of environmental advocates sometimes served to keep activism under wraps, but it could not suppress dissidence forever. Even in the most oppressive situations, small groups of citizens met to address their worries about breathing smog-filled air and drinking foul-tasting waters. As they considered their possibilities for making a public impact in the face of government intolerance, they recognized that there was no way to separate their environmental demands from a larger engagement in political dissidence and from a public stand for social justice. Their challenge lay in creating a culture of solidarity and building alternative networks of power in the face of a secret-police apparatus that could easily ensnare the outspoken critic.

Nowhere were environmental activists more sensitive to broader political issues and potential dangers than in the former Communist societies. Since the early 1970s, the Communist Party in Czechoslovakia had sponsored several official nature organizations that had attracted environmental activists as members. There, under the watchful eye of party officials and secret police, young nature lovers engaged in activities ranging from planting trees to restoring overgrown meadows. But the government did not allow these groups to have a social or political agenda that might question public policies or challenge the costs of industrialization. Only in the 1980s did some of these nature-loving enthusiasts transform themselves from supporters of nature education into dissidents willing to challenge the government's claim that there were no serious environmental policy issues. Initially, they were observers when representatives of Greenpeace International demonstrated against acid rain and the dangers of nuclear power in Czechoslovakia and seven other European countries in 1984. Other demonstrations followed in subsequent years. Many Czech environmentalists privately supported this effort, but living in a state that imprisoned political dissidents, they could not bring themselves to be actively involved at that time.

Increasingly, however, these activists began to define the environmental problems facing them as larger than simple issues of nature conservation. In the course of the 1980s they became bolder about raising the questions of pollution, acid rain, and the destruction of forests, risking the price of stepping beyond the boundaries of acceptable political behavior. Those who were determined to develop contacts with environmentalists outside the country and who continued their organized activities even behind the scenes were often visited by the secret police, who threatened their futures. Nonetheless, as dissidence grew in the late 1980s, environmental activities became a magnet, attracting increasing numbers of citizens who wanted to participate in the rising protests.

Ivo Silmav'y was a young activist in Prague who worked with a grassroots group, Children of the Earth, in the late 1980s. This small but persistent group of young people was interested in many issues from the dangers of air pollution to nuclear power to road-construction projects. They were profoundly influenced by the Greenpeace antinuclear protests, their first contact with an international organization imported from the forbidden West. Silmav'y and his friends learned a great deal from the information provided by Austrian and other Greenpeace activists. As they became committed environmentalists, they realized that they were engaging in a growing movement of political dissidence. When the authoritarian government weakened under the weight of Gorbachev's perestroika in the Soviet Union and a debilitated national economy in Czechoslovakia, formerly passive citizens began to join with leading dissidents, who had demonstrated for human rights since the signing of Charter 77 more than a decade earlier. Silmav'y and his friends saw the appeal of environmentalism to an ever-growing public: "All environmental actions before 1989 were an expression of political opinion. That's why so many people came to the environmental demonstrations. The government was very hard on participants—there were arrests and judgments, but the people still came."[35]

Although Silmav'y and his friends initiated some militant protests right after the Velvet Revolution, most Czechs and Slovakians found it harder to sustain grassroots activity after the immediate threat of political reprisal was removed. It became more difficult to mobilize support for environmental activism in the postrevolutionary market economy of the 1990s, although the more committed activists recognized that the environmental problems had not disappeared and would continue to have a critical impact on public health and safety. Yet, the recent social and economic upheavals were disorienting in a country where people were accustomed to receiving direction from the government. Their initial concern for environmental improvement gave way to more immediate worries over job security and the demands of living in a free-market system.

As executive director of the Prague chapter of Greenpeace in the early 1990s, Ivo Silmav'y was determined to rebuild Czechoslovakia's commitment to environmental protection. Despite his full awareness that issues of pollution and toxic wastes had receded to secondary importance in the public imagination, Silmav'y himself did not retreat at all. He gave up his position as a scientist in the Czech Institute for Nature Conservation and became wholly committed to environmental activism. He and his friends rededicated themselves to a form of grass-roots organizing that would ultimately have a positive impact on the community. Their personal transformation was not just a temporary expression of dissidence. Their small groups worked together to continue to push the environmental agenda as much as possible:

> We are in the situation where people are very interested in their economic and social situation, worried if they will lose their jobs or not. So environmental problems have dropped to a lower priority. But we have to solve the problems quickly, because they are so big that we cannot wait for our economy to improve to deal with them. We have increasing allergies, cancers, declining life expectancy, problems of breathing and more. We have to conserve the possibility of life first. We have to develop a special strategy, be more positive, and explain the importance of the situation to the people.[36]

Like many activists, Silmav'y felt a sense of frustration that the environmental cause had receded in importance in Czechoslovakia. Yet he and his friends continued to push forward with as many programs as they could muster, relying on the mutual encouragement that came from their long-standing bonds of solidarity and seeking support and assistance from a vast network of activists throughout Europe. International connections remain as important at the end of the century as they were during the dark, repressive days before the fall of the Iron Curtain. Now the international networks no longer have to operate in secret, and they are an important source of statistical data, organizational strategies, and funds for programs and initiatives. These networks remain a significant resource for small grassroots groups trying to establish themselves in periods of profound social and economic change. Silmav'y acknowledges the critical advantage his group gained from its association with the international Greenpeace organization.[37]

Like their American and Israeli counterparts, the Czech and Slovakian activists organized to respond to serious environmental problems that had emerged from unrestrained industrial production and wanton abuse of the natural environment. These activists, who had matured under a repressive state and had the courage to organize under the eyes of the secret police, had depended heavily on a small group of like-minded dissidents. In the new post-Communist society, they often lacked some of the basic networking and communication skills that were so central to winning public support and sustaining long-term engagements. They found it difficult to compete for public attention in the face of mounting nationalism, accelerated privatization, and escalating demands for consumer goods. The recognition that they were operating in new and unfamiliar forms of organization left some of the earlier activists frustrated but nevertheless committed to involving their friends and neighbors in activities that they regarded as life sustaining.

The Requirements of Courageous Behavior

The growth of grassroots environmental groups in the United States, Israel, and the former Czechoslovakia has generated a potent force for citizen action. Once they defined the problems as central to the health and well-being of their families and their communities, they would no longer turn back. Unwilling to accept explanations about the inevitability of environmental degradation as a result of industrial progress or national development, these activists have determined to join together to demand remediation from government and corporate bodies. The environmentalists refuse to retreat into apathy or seek escape through private manifestations of their alienation. They are now significant players on the national scene who are determined to push their demands for a safer environment as far as they possibly can. These activists have experienced personal transformation, have created cultures of solidarity, and have built alternative networks of power. Their links to each other and to other organizations, both national and international, have given them an ever-expanding base of actual or potential influence. While they face many frustrations and suffer serious periodic setbacks, they have succeeded in placing their concerns on the public agenda and repeatedly alerted local, regional, and national powerholders that they are prepared to fight over the long term.

In the chapters to come, we will meet many others and learn of their dreams and continuing involvement in a wide array of controversial issues. We will demonstrate that the activists are enmeshed in the most heated environmental debates of their day. We first turn to several case studies of citizens who are caught in the volatile mixture of national security decisions and strict government secrecy. When they learn of the resultant environmental degradation and their own victimization, they must decide whether to protest vocally and organize with their neighbors, friends, and colleagues. By taking courageous action, they would end a long tradition of remaining silent, and they would risk the wrath of government agents who have been quick to define environmental criticism as disloyalty and community organizing as potential rebellion.

2

Breaking the Bands
of National Security Secrecy

 For almost fifty years, the national security state has dominated political decision making, national ideology, and the parameters of resistance in the United States, Israel, and the former Czechoslovakia. Actions that otherwise would never have been tolerated in democratic states like the United States and Israel have been widely accepted as necessary and normal by politicians and ordinary citizens. Secrecy has become a crucial component of many decisions, and even well-informed residents have been unable to learn much detail about activities in their own communities when such activities revolved around industry or government operations closely tied to national defense. For example, in the United States, respected scientists conducted secret experiments that exposed unwitting and unconsenting people and whole communities to dangerous levels of radiation.[1] Israeli leaders neglected serious environmental problems that resulted from poor water policies, disregard for Arab communities, and the ab-

sence of adequate plans for disposing of toxic and radioactive wastes. In the Communist bloc, matters were even worse. State-dominated ideology justified national policies from strip mining to weapons production as a response to the aggression of the West. Countries like Czechoslovakia suppressed all unfavorable environmental information, regularly lied to their citizens, and created institutions of repression that punished even mild dissent. Deception developed into a cultural art.

In this chapter we examine several case studies of citizen response to environmental threats to community health and safety that were directly linked to Cold War decisions. Each case—the Downwinders around the Hanford Nuclear Reservation in eastern Washington, the Union for Environmental Defense and the Galilee Society in Israel, and *Bratislava Nahlas,* an environmental exposé by dissidents in Slovakia—illustrates both common and culturally specific challenges for those who sought to shift national priorities from a total emphasis on national security to a greater focus on environmental problems. Each case represents an instance of a local environmental group that developed in the 1980s to respond to issues that had previously been ignored because of Cold War constraints. In the United States, affected citizens living near the nuclear-bomb factories faced a wall of silence that the established environmental organizations had never sought to penetrate. The grassroots activists had to generate public debate if they were to have any possibility of government response to their concerns. In Israel, activists faced a weaker tradition of concern about the environment, as well as widely held cultural assumptions about the necessity to focus resources on military preparedness and immigrant absorption. In Czechoslovakia, security concerns were also paramount, but penalties for organizing were more severe and could even be life threatening. In addition, local organizers faced government control of access to media and a political regime that often resorted to undercover police activity and informers.

In the 1980s the waning of the Cold War provided an opportunity for individuals who now believed that they had been deeply affected by years of environmental neglect to frame environmental concerns, to mobilize others in the community, and to propel these issues onto the national agenda.[2] These citizen crusaders were at the forefront in discovering that Cold War policies had created serious damage in their immediate environment, and they undertook distinct forms of organization in their communities to demand recognition and remediation for long-submerged and unspoken problems. While the relaxation of national and international tensions was necessary for the success of activists' efforts, it was not sufficient. The changing political environment did provide opportunities for local groups to emerge, but little would have been accomplished without the activists' willingness to take bold and effective actions and to put themselves and their families at risk in their effort to spearhead a new social movement. Courageous activists were crucial in articulating the problems and moving them onto the political agenda.

When the appropriate historical conditions were in place and the activists sensed that a political shift might increase concern about environmental hazards, they launched their initial foray into the community. They knew the local culture well and could employ a vocabulary that spoke as neighbor to neighbor. They could not easily be dismissed as outside agitators or troublesome radicals by those defending the status quo. In the most successful cases, whether in the United States, Israel, or the former Czechoslovakia, these emerging leaders moved beyond the initial stages of local organizing to pursue assistance from allies in strategically placed institutions. Activists developed ties with the press, regional and national environmental groups, sympathetic political leaders, and public-interest law firms or NGOs, to secure much-needed publicity, expertise, legal representation, funding, and legislative action. Where such allies were weak or unavailable to local groups, success was limited. In such cases the state was much more likely to contain the protests and prevent them from developing into a broader-based movement for social change. In essence, appropriate political and cultural circumstances as well as local activists in alliance with strategically placed supporters created the crucial combination to facilitate new dialogues and build alternative networks of power. These networks of power were essential for sustaining a long-term struggle against government and corporate officials, who had previously been unencumbered by the demands for public accountability.

Environmentalists Open a Nuclear Curtain

The Downwinders around the 560-square-mile Hanford, Washington, Nuclear Reservation live in an area of the country that is contaminated by severe pollution and radioactive wastes that have accumulated from fifty years of nuclear-bomb production.

Perhaps most disturbing were the revelations from the Department of Energy (DOE) in 1990 that the plant released unprecedented amounts of radiation, affecting hundreds of thousands of area residents, in the 1940s and 1950s. Most vulnerable were the twenty thousand babies born in the region from 1944 to 1960.[3] Even before the official public admission, area residents, particularly those who lived within a few miles of the reservation, were convinced that their area suffered from inordinately high rates of cancer and other diseases. One couple collected data on illnesses and fatalities and produced "a cancer map." Others, suffering from a variety of debilitating illnesses, met in small groups, put out newsletters publicizing their concerns, and invited neighbors and more distant residents to join in efforts to organize about their plight. Despite their small numbers, these activists, who called themselves the Downwinders of Hanford, won some significant local support for their determination to expose this deadly social problem. Of course, many other area residents refused to believe they lived in any danger, and dubbed the activists troublemakers.

One individual embodies many of the characteristics of the local citizens who have asserted in recent years that environmental damage has become a major threat to the health of the entire community, and his experience is worth examining. Tom Bailie's roots are deep in eastern Washington State, where he was born in 1947. He can do a day's work on his farm and also haggle with local bankers over loans to keep his operation solvent. His six-foot stature and strongly built appearance belie the fact that he has suffered from polio, sterility, and other serious medical problems all of his life, which ultimately led him to raise deeply troubling questions.

Like most conservative farmers in eastern Washington, Bailie had been an enthusiastic supporter of American defense policy. Virtually everyone who lived near the Hanford Nuclear Reservation knew that

Communism was the implacable enemy, and they supported the nuclear-weapons production that dominated their regional economy. Beginning in the 1940s, the area around Hanford had been transformed from a rural, sparsely populated region with a large Indian reservation into a modern urban complex employing thousands of engineers, Ph.D. scientists, and skilled workers.[4]

Yet in the last decade, Tom Bailie has been transformed into a strong critic of earlier policies. He is now a "storyteller" dedicated to reconstructing the way the community around Hanford interprets its history.[5] Bailie's stories are not pleasant to hear and have been the subject of local controversy. In fact, his own family has stridently rejected his new role and has warned that his tales will spell the economic ruin of their family. His wife is very angry about his activities, and his father refuses to sit with him at the local coffee shop. Other wheat farmers in the area have told him point blank to keep his mouth shut, lest their crops become unsalable. His bank has threatened to foreclose on his mortgage.

This storm of criticism would have silenced a less determined man. But Tom Bailie is a pioneer propelled by his own history and by what he believes is an epidemic of illness among his neighbors. He uses his personal history and the experiences of his fellow protesters to challenge a long-accepted version of the Hanford story. He began his mission in 1984, before most people gave him or his interpretation any credence. Bailie described childhood memories and his vague sense even then that something was terribly wrong. At the time, he had no idea that these early experiences were part of living downwind from the Hanford Nuclear Reservation:

> I was born in 1947. My first memories as a child are of spacemen-like people walking by my house and waving. I remember seeing deformed animals and watching my parents dispose of them. . . . Men in suits and ties would come into our school and pass Geiger counters around the classroom and over the children. We would wonder why one day all the jackrabbits would be lying around kicking and dying in the sagebrush, when just the day before they were all right. We always believed it was be-

cause we had done something wrong. We accepted a lot of guilt. Grandma always explained that it was *God's will*.

Early on in life one of my jobs was to shoot the deformed kittens and calves—because my father didn't like to do that. Seeing all the sick people and the handicapped children around us, I guess deep inside I knew something wasn't right, but I didn't have anything else to compare it with.[6]

Well into the 1980s the nuclear culture dominated the tri-city area around Hanford. All politicians, Republicans and Democrats, lauded the extensive defense contracts that helped develop their communities. But along with these contracts came secrecy. Elaborate clearances and security checks were part of life. The interests of national security made it reasonable not to explain deformed animals or special Geiger counters in the school. One former resident of the Hanford region, Judith Jurgi, who later became a leader of the Western Washington chapter of Downwinders, could hardly believe that she and others had so readily accepted the secrecy:

Everyone's father worked at Hanford, so you didn't think much about it. But I did not know—I honestly did not know—that Hanford was the place that made the plutonium that went into the Nagasaki bomb. How could I live there all those years and not know? It's still astonishing to me. Workers weren't supposed to talk about their work, so I suppose their families could be completely sheltered. I know we were. . . . And if you had family members, like I did, that worked at Hanford, you just had this fear that if you criticized Hanford or said anything negative at all about it, that somehow it would lead to bad consequences.[7]

The impact of the culture of secrecy was so pervasive that family members seemed to know nothing about the work of the nuclear facility. But at the same time, they understood that speaking up or asking questions was forbidden and dangerous. By the mid-1980s this uninformed acceptance began to unravel. The large-scale nuclear buildup ordered by President Ronald Reagan had pressed the structural limits of the aging plant. In the nearby city of Spokane, just about the same time that Tom Bailie began telling his stories, speakers at a major health conference alerted the public to the dangers of nuclear contamination and exposure to radiation. In May 1984 Dr. William Harper Houff, a Unitarian minister who also held a Ph.D. in chemistry, delivered a strongly worded sermon awakening his congregants to the radioactive dangers in their region. As a result, a local public-interest group, Hanford Education Action League (HEAL), was formed to conduct research and educate the public. This event was an important step in breaking the code of silence. Criticism of Hanford was no longer considered anecdotal information that could be dismissed as the views of a crank or peacenik. Systematic inquiry over a period of years would later uncover some of the history and give a larger context to the stories of Tom Bailie and others.[8] The disclosure of a major and devastating new social problem began in earnest, as strategically placed allies came forth to validate the claims of local activists and to help them transform their personal problems into a national issue.

In 1985, Karen Dorn Steele, a reporter for the Spokane *Spokesman-Review,* ended the silence and complicity of the local media when she reported on the deformed animals and on the high disease and death rates among the local population. Tom Bailie was one of her significant informants. In 1986 a government auditor, Casey Ruud, blew the whistle on missing plutonium at Hanford and on the discharge of radioactive wastes into the nearby Columbia River. His revelations were kept in the public eye through months of extensive press coverage by Eric Nalder and others at the *Seattle Times,* which finally led to a congressional investigation and an indictment of Hanford's safety practices.[9] Hanford was no longer beyond criticism, and all of these corroborating events gave increasing credence to Bailie's stories.

The demands of national security and the fear of Communism no longer sufficed to silence all questions. With the aid of some key congressional staffers, such as Robert Alvarez in Senator John Glenn's office, and the use of the Freedom of Information Act, in 1986 HEAL and the Spokane *Spokesman-Review* acquired critical, formerly classified government documents, from which they learned of several decades of off-site contamination.[10] The documents established the authenticity of the secret Green Run—the deliberate release of radiation in 1949 into civilian areas so that the government could learn how to track possible releases from the Soviet Union.[11] The information shocked local activists and broadened the base of concerned citizens. Under pressure, the Centers for Disease Control acknowledged for the first time that residents of the area suffered a higher risk of thyroid cancer.[12] Bailie's stories now had the imprimatur of public documents that admitted to policies that helped undermine the health of the local population.[13]

This explosive information brought together previously isolated individuals into a culture of solidarity that underscored their victimization at the hands of government and corporate officials and the necessity of their banding together to demand attention and remediation. In July 1989 Tom Bailie called an initial meeting of twenty people who had grown up in eastern Washington in the 1940s and 1950s, all of whom were suffering from serious medical problems. Most were just learning that the origins of their illnesses might well be traced to their exposure to high levels of radiation decades earlier. Their initial reaction was one of rage. One Downwinder, Don Carter, born in 1945, discovered that he had radiation-induced thyroid cancer. He described his reaction: "The anger is overpowering, it is overwhelming, it consumes you. They can't do that to me . . . dammit, they can't do that to anyone. The Constitution says that they can't. To me this is a rape—a physical and mental rape."[14]

Like so many other affected citizens exposed to environmental dangers, their rage against government secrecy and duplicity drove them forward. Carter described his and others' anger as "so frightening that [their] ultimate activism was a way of trying to do something with all that rage." The anger was fueled by a sense of betrayal and breach of trust.[15] They turned to each other for solace and united action. They would no longer turn away and suffer in silence.

The Downwinders called meetings, issued a newsletter, reported on their health problems, and shared childhood memories of strange events. Youthful doubts of people like Bailie were reexamined in the face of growing questions about deformed animals and cancer-stricken neighbors. Their stories now took on greater meaning. The Downwinders had achieved a personal legitimacy for their unsought position as victims. Their anger served as emotional capital in building support for their campaign. They were determined to extend the government recognition that radiation increased the risk of thyroid cancer, and to prove that many of the cancers, multiple sclerosis, sterility, and other medical problems resulted directly from their exposure as children.

As the Downwinders proceeded to organize and develop a strong culture of solidarity, they met condemnation from those in the communities around Hanford who feared the upheaval that would be caused by reinterpreting the history of the last fifty years. Some cautioned about the destruction of the local economy; others could not accept that the government had done anything wrong, and were convinced that the dangers from exposure to radioactive iodine were grossly exaggerated. The battle was now on. A community long tied together by Cold War ideology was now torn by vastly different interpretations of reality.

Despite attacks on their loyalty and emotional stability, the Downwinders' newly founded organization enabled them to cope with a sense of psychological and communal isolation. Solidarity emboldened them and allowed them to resist the social control mechanisms that had silenced them for so many years.[16] The Downwinders had a specific set of goals. Like those in other communities contaminated by hazardous waste, they wanted to inform others of health information they gathered, gain public recognition of their victimization, and secure government funding for medical services. One of the group's founders, Lois Camps, herself twice a victim of cancer, felt empowered as she spent hours on the telephone every day talking to people who thought they might have been affected as children.[17]

As a new group without much experience in political or community organizing, the Downwinders suffered from a lack of organizational leadership and from divided opinion about the most appropriate means by which to pursue their goals. Some victims of radiation wanted to sue the government for compensation. Others sought to concentrate on building a broad-based coalition dedicated to public education and to negotiations with federal agencies in charge of health issues and cleanup programs. Their inability to develop processes for resolving conflict resulted in a split into two groups, one headquartered in Seattle and the other in eastern Washington.

The Downwinders' most significant contribution remained as vocal witnesses attempting to convince a reluctant public and the national government that there had been systematic damage to people in eastern Washington. To move beyond the testimonial stage, the Downwinders allied themselves with other environmental groups around Hanford. The local Native Americans, the Yakima, whose reservation had been partially expropriated for the building of Hanford, were deeply involved in the regional coalition of activists. Like the Downwinders, the Yakima suffered high rates of cancer and, according to their representative, Russell Jim, the highest rates of rheumatoid arthritis in the country. This exacerbated a long-standing feeling of resentment that their land had been expropriated fifty years earlier, weakening their ability to practice their traditions and continue their heritage.[18] The Yakima joined the Downwinders in a regional coalition, which also included the public-interest research group HEAL and allies in the press, in congressional offices, and in national antinuclear groups, to carry the battle forward with Congress, the Department of Energy, and the Centers for Disease Control.

Without HEAL, effective public pressure might not have survived. Initiated as a community group dedicated to research and pressuring the Department of Energy for more information, HEAL became an influential organization in eastern Washington. By the late 1980s, the organizational structure had become more professional, supporting a paid staff from a budget financed by foundation grants and individual donations. HEAL executive director Lynne Stembridge and research director Jim Thomas have represented the public on important advisory committees that oversee government research and cleanup efforts. As a member of the Military Production Network, a national organization of groups combating contamination from nuclear-bomb factories, and the tri-state Hanford Health Information Network, HEAL is an integral member of a national coalition to lobby for continued government accountability.

The presence of HEAL illustrates the significance of strategic allies for local leaders and smaller community-based groups like the Downwinders. HEAL has access to technical advisers, funding, public-education outlets, and national lobbying efforts that can sustain the

Downwinders' goal of reaching a wider public in order to bring pressure on the DOE for continued health monitoring, compensation for victims, and adequate cleanup. The Downwinders themselves remain the authentic voices of victims, poised to serve as witnesses to the dangers of a half century of government nuclear policy.[19] At the same time, some of the Downwinders remain suspicious of national networks and the competition among competing groups for scarce resources. As Downwinder Lois Camps expressed it: "I understand the need to keep in touch with those who share our concerns on an international level, but not by costly conferences. A grassroots approach that keeps the people (NOT THE 'EXPERTS'), in charge of the data collecting and actual facts concerning geographical areas, health effects, etc., will be the only way we can be absolutely certain the information is untainted by political influence."[20]

In late 1988, as a result of extensive pressure, the DOE reluctantly admitted that there were enormous problems of contamination, requiring years of cleanup and the expenditure of billions of federal dollars. Apparently, the government had known of the seriousness of the problem for some time, but little had been done. In a remarkable admission, a high-level official stated: "The reports said a crisis was coming, but nobody said a crisis was coming next year. It is obviously of greater magnitude than we thought."[21] After several years of protests and congressional investigations, the government planned for cleanup programs and for more stringent safety standards.[22] Old reactors were decommissioned, plutonium production ceased, and officials began planning for decades of remediation. With the realization that large defense appropriations could be replaced by equally lucrative cleanup contracts, many more local residents became receptive to the call of the Downwinders and their allies.

The fight for compensation for victims continues. In the spring of 1994, Hazel O'Leary was the first secretary of energy ever to acknowledge that the government might have to bear responsibility for those who were victimized by radiation experiments.[23] But claimants are still finding it difficult to prove a cause-and-effect relation between the contamination and many illnesses. Thus far, courts throughout the country have not supported claims of cancer from environmental exposure, because of the difficulty of proving that the radiation specifically caused the cancers and other medical problems. The Centers for Disease Control has responded by launching epidemiological studies, but Downwinders and their allies remain very skeptical about government intentions. They want government and the private contractors who ran the Hanford facility to accept liability. The activists are totally unsympathetic to arguments that their victimization was an unintended consequence of a legitimate national security program. They do not believe that the release of radiation occurred at a time when less was known about radiation damage at low levels. The struggle to penetrate veils of secrecy and to sustain public support continues, but as political priorities shift, there are no guarantees that it will remain an item high on the public agenda.

There are several lessons to be learned from the Downwinders. Their experiences teach us much about post–Cold War environmental activists in particular and about protest groups more generally. The activists helped to define a social problem that earlier had been perceived as a normal and acceptable cost of economic prosperity and national security. This redefinition of local circumstances required changed political circumstances, local leaders with the courage and vision to mount a major organizational effort, and the establishment of a broad-based coalition to demand attention from the Department of Energy, Congress, the state of Washington, and Rockwell Industries, which had served as the managing contractor of the plant. To succeed, activists had to break the code of silence and secrecy that obstructed their access to crucial information. They drew on the possibilities of a democratic society, where, as an opposition group, they could recruit the expertise and assistance of political leaders who shared their concerns. They could take advantage of the checks and balances in the political system, which had severely narrowed during the Cold War but had then reopened with the passage of the Freedom of Information Act, Right to Know laws, and Nuclear Regulatory Commission provisions. All of this legislation offered the possibility of using federal procedures to challenge the existing, established policies.

To ensure continued progress in an era dominated by cost-cutting and deregulation rhetoric, the activists and their strategic allies will have to remain steadfast, never assuming that the battle has been won. Some of the means for continued participation are now institutionalized. Grassroots activists are represented on various government advisory committees. HEAL remains an active monitor. At the same time, the danger of individual burnout is great. Local activists often feel they must take a break from the unrelenting pressures of participation in a grassroots effort to undo fifty years of damage. Individuals' need to withdraw for personal reasons can easily threaten the viability of a core group of local activists if care is not taken to replenish the group on some regular basis.

Environmentalists Gain a Footing in the Land of Battle

Until very recently, most Israelis considered concern about pollution, pesticides, and overdevelopment to be a Western luxury. Although there has always been interest in nature protection, as noted earlier, most Israelis believed their country had to focus first and foremost on security, then on economic development and absorption of immigrants. There was a strong consensus that these priorities superseded all other social and environmental issues. For Israelis, national security has meant a focus on the ever-present tensions in the Middle East and on the intermittent wars with Arab nations. Even in times when there have been no active battles, Israeli society has been organized around military requirements to combat terrorism and control a hostile Palestinian population.[24]

Despite these cultural and political limitations, a very small group has long been determined to press for a broader set of priorities. These environmentalists never challenged the national security culture, but they did define preservation of the land, the air, and clean water as essential goals in Israeli life and were determined to make this part of Israel's political and social agenda.

A disproportionately large number of these activists are former Americans who migrated to Israel in recent years with sophisticated concerns about the environment and some strategies for organizing local movements. They joined a small cadre of older naturalists and academics who remembered the beauty of the land in the 1930s and 1940s. All of these activists have tapped into a deeply rooted Zionist tradition of love of the land. Nonetheless, they lack a strong environmental infrastructure for regulating and monitoring the quality of the air, water, and soil. They have set out to raise consciousness and build the necessary structures to promote greater accountability.[25]

Historically, the lack of legislation or adequate enforcement of environmental protection meant that the responsibility for preservation of natural resources fell to individuals who had the influence and access to make occasional gains, despite the popular notion that environmental concerns should be subordinated to other national needs. For example, Lev Fishelson, a biology professor at Tel Aviv University and a long-standing analyst of environmental degradation, described an experience that captured the ongoing struggle in Israel between ever-present concerns with security and the preservation of precious environmental treasures. In 1975 Israel controlled the Sinai peninsula, which was under the military jurisdiction of Ariel Sharon, the hawkish and powerful general. Professor Fishelson learned that Sharon planned to build a soft sand road around the perimeter of the Sinai. That way if terrorists crossed into the Sinai from the sea, the army could track footsteps in the sand. Since there are some places in the Gulf of Eilat where the mountains come up from the seashore, the plan was to destroy the mountains and cover them with sand. Giant bulldozers began working from the north and the south. Appalled by this decision, Lev Fishelson and Azeria Alon, a colleague from the Society for the Protection of Nature (SPNI), the country's largest nature-protection organization, went into action and arranged a meeting with General David Elazar, then the commander in chief of the armed forces and a powerful figure in national politics. Fishelson explained to Elazar about the ecology of the Red Sea, pointing out that one of the world's most beautiful coral reefs and its abundant wildlife would be destroyed. Several military experts were ordered to meet with Fishelson and Alon. Professor Fishelson argued his point. According to him, Sharon's deputy shouted, "If you stop the bulldozers, how then should I prevent the infiltration of terrorists?" General Elazar interrupted, "Don't ask the professor. It's his job to explain how we will destroy this valuable coral reef. Now you figure out how to prevent infiltration—without the bulldozers." And they did. In the late 1980s and early 1990s, Fishelson lamented, no one was available to stop Sharon when, as minister of housing, he leveled whole areas of undeveloped land to build Jewish settlements in the West Bank.[26]

Reliance on the ad hoc decisions of sympathetic individuals in power could never guarantee more than sporadic interest in the environment. Fishelson and his colleagues recognized that their movement required institutions that were positioned to confront ongoing environmental degradation. The failure of governmental involvement is crucial, for there is no strong tradition in Israel of nongovernment voluntary organizations equivalent to the Wildlife Federation or Greenpeace. Grassroots environmental organizations are of recent origin and are still small and mainly dependent on funds from abroad. Environmental activists know that most citizens expect the government to take the lead in any issues of national concern. It is the government that involves itself with schools, housing, health, and immigrant absorption. Most voters assume these issues, which have historically been the focus of government responsibility, take priority over the newer questions about toxic wastes and garbage dumps, developing open spaces, or air and water pollution.

Despite all these historical, cultural, and structural limitations, there are countervailing trends. The Society for the Protection of Nature, which is partially government supported, has tens of thousands of members. For years it has emphasized love of nature and outdoor education and has focused on hikes to acquaint Israelis with their natural heritage.[27] Significantly, the organization has recently begun to incorporate some political organizing for environmental protection.[28] Other organizations, such as Life and Environment, have joined the SPNI in securing national parks and nature-protection laws. But the role of grassroots organizations remains weak.

One environmental activist, Alon Tal, saw the contradiction in Israeli life and hoped to do something about it:

> There is a tremendous paradox in Israel, where, on the one hand, it is a nation which is incredibly tied to the land. People are familiar with the flowers and the birds and all these natural

things which their contemporaries in the United States would not have any sense of. At the same time, there is a tendency toward massive negligence in regard to the illegal dumping of trash. It is particularly disturbing driving through the Land of the Bible and seeing cars junked and all kinds of debris on the beaches. Actually, it has gotten a lot better in the last ten years. A decade ago, you would end up with a lot of tar on your feet when you went swimming at the beach, which you had to wash off with kerosene.[29]

A transplanted American with an Israeli law degree and a Harvard Ph.D. in environmental policy, Alon Tal began taking important steps in institutionalizing nongovernmental activity on behalf of the environment. His energy and vision so impressed the heads of Econet, a small environmental foundation, that in 1990 they funded him to start the Union for Environmental Defense (UED).[30] The organization, built on the model of the United States Natural Resources Defense Council, mobilized young people, many of them directly out of the army, to join the board of directors to ensure that the UED would not become another one-person crusade. The organization, which has garnered substantial financial support in its first few years,[31] joins a growing movement that is questioning the monopoly of defense priorities in the national consciousness. Tal and the UED have begun to mobilize previously isolated activists, have given legitimacy and assistance to community-based environmental groups, have led the way in using the courts to fight egregious environmental abuse, and have introduced environmental law into the law school curriculum. Alon Tal is a pioneer and visionary with a determined commitment to influence Israeli life. All who know him speak of his boundless energy and willingness to take on the most challenging issues. He is adept at forming new organizations, focusing on long-neglected problems, and yet not alienating the few members of the Establishment who have been deeply involved in the effort to draw greater attention to the environmental crisis that affects many sectors of Israeli life. Uri Marinov, for example, long a major government figure, named Alon Tal and his UED as the most significant contributor to the environmental struggle in recent years.[32] While often on the opposite side of a legal action, Marinov respected Tal's imagination and hard work. Others have labeled Tal as one of Israel's most impressive "pioneers" for his willingness to move into uncharted waters. Forsaking a safer path, Alon Tal exhibits a major characteristic of the courageous. He has been willing to take risks in the cause of his environmental principles even when this entailed directly confronting the government and its explicit definition of the paramount needs of the national security state.

Thus, with the waning of the Cold War, residents in the Arava desert region, where Alon Tal's own kibbutz is located, the Union for Environmental Defense, the Society for the Protection of Nature, and others tested their political effectiveness. The issue was the building of a Voice of America communications tower in the Negev at the request of the United States, which wanted to broadcast its programs to Eastern Europe with a stronger signal.[33] This coalition of environmental activists opposed the tower, arguing that it might have made sense during the Cold War, when broadcasting to Eastern Europe was a high priority. But with the demise of the Communist states, there was no justification for building a structure that threatened the desert environment. The radiation emitted would be particularly destructive to the millions of birds that migrate across the Negev en route from Europe to Africa each winter. Large parts of the Negev were already given over to the air force for training, so reducing this natural resource even further was anathema to thousands of Israelis, who participated in protest hikes. American environmental organizations helped by lobbying Congress, while local activists vigorously lobbied Knesset members.[34]

Earlier, the Israeli government had been anxious to oblige the Bush administration, but intense environmental pressure in both countries led President Clinton to drop the plan. This fight against the Voice of America tower was a major campaign for the newly politicized Israeli environmental groups, and their success spurred them to continue. They began a campaign to promote public transportation over highway building and high-rise apartments over single-family houses to preserve limited open space and minimize pollution. They have been careful, nonetheless, never to create the impression that environmental activists are unpatriotic or unsupportive of defense and immigration concerns. Alon Tal, the leader of the UED and a resident of the contested Arava desert region, serves in the military reserves like all other men his age, and works hard to show that environmental concerns can be responsibly integrated into other national priorities.

Yoav Sagi, the president of the Society for the Protection of Nature, described the tension for Israeli environmentalists:

> Living in this country, you cannot take the same approach as some of the environmental organizations that claim or act as if conservation and the environment were the most important things in the world. The situation here makes you more humble. You are involved in all the problems, particularly those including Israel's wars. Environmental issues are very, very important. But these are not the *most* important issues. If it comes to the very existence of the state, we cannot afford only to consider the environmental side of it. No one would pay attention to us if we put the environment as the most important thing. This leads us to study the whole picture in order to find the right solution.[35]

Clearly, unlike Tom Bailie and other Downwinders in the United States, Israeli activists do not attempt to reinterpret their history and the policies that stemmed from national security concerns. Many American Downwinders feel duped and betrayed by their government. They are incredulous that they could have been so abused by institutions in which they had placed their highest trust, whereas Israeli activists are far too involved in continuing hostilities to harbor such intense feelings. Instead, they have attempted, with some significant success, to add new issues of environmental reform to the political agenda and to balance the legitimate needs of national security against the fragility of environmental resources.

A very different style of activism can be found in the Israeli Arab community, where once again issues of security directly conflict with maintenance of a healthy environment. Local Arab reformers condemn the government's security policies as a threat to community health, and are determined to use environmental reform to achieve greater equality for Arab communities within Israeli society. Unlike their Jewish counterparts, Arab activists identify Zionism, with its focus on security for the Jewish state, as the ideological system that has relegated them to second-class status in Israel.[36] For them, the environmental struggle is one component of a larger quest for economic and social justice, and they have little patience when their requests are denied "for security reasons." A major figure in this battle is an American-trained physician, Hatim Kana'aneh.

Dr. Kana'aneh cares deeply about Arrabe, the Galilee village in northern Israel in which he was born, where he was raised, and where he and his large extended family still live:

> From the time I was a child I was told I was going to be a doctor because I was smart. In rural Arab communities, there usually was no doctor in the village. I lucked out, being the youngest of five boys, so that my brothers could earn an income and help support me through high school. When I was attending high school in Nazareth, we would go out and sell pieces of the cross to tourists, among other things trying to get contacts. Because I had this idea of wanting to study in the United States, I latched on to a childless couple who were actually interested in supporting someone like me. They assisted me with the paperwork and also in sponsoring my studies.[37]

After he completed his medical education and his master's degree in public health at Harvard University, Dr. Kana'aneh chose to return home to Arrabe, rather than accept a lucrative offer to remain in the United States. He insists that he has never been interested in being a doctor for its own sake. For him, the goal has always been to improve the health conditions of the Israeli Arab community.

> When I finished my training, I had several extremely lucrative offers to stay in the United States, including an offer from the Harvard School of Public Health to run a big experiment in nutrition. It was a very attractive offer to do research and to work with my mentor, who was a famous nutritionist at Harvard. It

was good money and high prestige, but I kept telling myself that was not what I came here for. I would lose the reason for becoming a doctor if I did not go back to my village. In my mind that is what I wanted to do. Go back to the Galilee and improve the lot of the Arab population in Israel.[38]

The return was not easy. He and his wife described living conditions in the village that were far simpler than what they had been used to in the United States, yet they were happy to be home, where he assumed his new position. In 1970, Dr. Kana'aneh began working for the Ministry of Health and became the subdistrict health officer for the Western Galilee, one of the highest positions held by an Israeli Arab at that time. The ministry position provided him with the opportunity to press for change in health-care delivery, such as the training of young Arab women to work as nurses and paramedics. He began to make his mark as a physician who wanted far more than simply to treat his patients. He wanted to change their living conditions. His years of intensive study in the United States had changed him. He was no longer the provincial boy who had left northern Israel to study in the United States. The experience of college, of medical school, of research projects, had transformed him into a physician with a vision of how his people could live. That did not include unsanitary conditions, chronic illness, and a high infant mortality rate.

The death of several young villagers as a result of Land Day in 1976 had also been traumatic. Demonstrating against government confiscation of village land, six young men had died in a confrontation with the army. Dr. Kana'aneh and his family left the village for two years to live near his wife's relatives in Hawaii. Despite the attractions of their life there, they decided to return once again to Arrabe. They disliked the American commercial life and firmly believed that their two children would have the safest and richest upbringing surrounded by his large family in the small village in Israel, where the local doctor was among the most respected residents. Yet, Dr. Kana'aneh wanted more than a secure retreat for his children. He returned even more committed to change health conditions. His opportunity soon arose.

In 1978, he encountered an outbreak of typhoid in his village and found that sewage had contaminated the water supply. This episode galvanized Kana'aneh's commitment to environmental medicine. He became convinced that the lack of adequate sewage-treatment plants was the number one problem in Arab communities, and a symbol of their unequal treatment in Israeli society. The government had channeled major resources toward building Jewish communities in the Galilee in order to create a Jewish majority in a heavily populated Arab area.[39] Israeli political leadership rationalized the neglect of Arab villages as a necessary by-product of ensuring the security of this northern region of the state. In addition to very limited municipal services, Arab communities were not allowed to expand beyond their original borders despite rapid population growth. As a result, most villages experienced increased density, and received little help in planning for the disposal of sewage. Bureaucratic obstacles made it difficult for the local municipal officials to raise sufficient funds or to obtain the twelve separate approvals from national officials that were required to upgrade the sanitation system.

Dr. Kana'aneh, like most Arabs, found government reluctance to place Arab and Jewish communities on an equal footing objectionable. In the years since the founding of the state in 1948, Israeli Arabs had slowly gained increased civil rights, but remained economically and socially disadvantaged. Military administration of the Israeli Arabs ended in 1966, and subsequent decades saw increased freedom of movement and education. As Israel became more confident about national security in these areas, Israeli Arab groups were allowed to organize more freely. Kana'aneh and his associates seized the opportunity for organizing to promote environmental and health improvements. For them, one of the most significant measures of public health has been the infant mortality rate, which remains twice as high for Israeli Arabs as for Jews.[40] Infant diarrhea is the enemy, and prevention is Kana'aneh's concern.

Dr. Kana'aneh's work took an important new turn in 1981 with the formation of the Galilee Society for Health Research and Services, an organization founded by four local physicians (three Israeli Arabs and a European doctor working in the Galilee): "When we got together, we said, What are the issues? What are we talking about? We identified environmental health as the first priority, specifically sewage and garbage disposal. Then we identified health education and, third, 'special risk' groups, including the mentally handicapped. None of us really knew anything about sewage, but we knew health hazards because we live with them. As you leave my office now, you step over a little ditch with sewage flowing in it. It is a relevant daily life experience. It is foul smelling, and you can't miss it."[41]

Dr. Kana'aneh served as chairman of this voluntary organization[42] from its formation and became its full-time director in 1991. The Galilee Society represents the first such organization totally dedicated to work on behalf of the Israeli Arab community. All voluntary organizations must have funding to ensure continuity and long-term mobilization. Those that can afford some paid staff are usually at a substantial advantage in coordinating volunteers, sustaining ongoing connections to other groups, and financing travel, technical advice, and publicity to further the cause. The Galilee Society has been fortunate in that respect. Although the local community has little surplus cash, the Galilee Society has been able to procure stable funding from American and European foundations and especially from European churches, which have provided an annual base to the budget. This enabled the Galilee Society to employ Dr. Kana'aneh as its director, to fund programs, and, most important, to retain its independence from the government.[43]

From its inception, the Galilee Society has focused on the key environmental problems that affect health among Israeli Arabs. It has addressed the high infant mortality rate among Israeli Arab children; confronted the central problem of sewage disposal, which affects the drinking water and thus the health of the entire village; obtained an increase in financial support from the government for services to Arab communities, which now receive about one-half of what Jewish communities get; provided health education; and prevented overdevelopment in Arab areas of the Galilee.[44]

Dr. Kana'aneh's crusade for a safe environment—for appropriate sewage disposal, safe drinking water, controlled development, and the maintenance of clean air—is part of the larger picture of his quest for social justice for Israeli Arabs. He wants Israel to live up to its promise as a democratic nation. He wants what he feels he is entitled to as an

Israeli citizen. His anger at the conditions of the Arab villages is balanced by his ongoing commitment to the idea that common sense and goodwill will prevail, although he recognizes that his goal of a secular, non-Zionist state of Israel may not occur in his lifetime. Yet like Alon Tal and many others, he has faith that change can come about within the system. He has sought to push the government beyond its own limits by demanding far greater attention to the health of the Arab communities. He has had the courage to campaign for change rather than to escape into private concern or to fuel political alienation or to nurture paralyzing cynicism. Dr. Kana'aneh and his colleagues at the Galilee Society embody the commitment to building a democratic nation where all sectors, all citizens, are equal in their ability to call upon the country's resources for their welfare. In their actions they have drawn upon their substantial social capital, which derives from their long-standing and deeply entwined relationships with members of the area's communities.

Environmental activists in Israel, whether Jewish or Arab, can only be effective if they are able to persuade influential members of the Israeli public that environmental issues do not threaten national security but have an urgency that must be addressed. Alon Tal and Dr. Hatim Kana'aneh know that activists must develop alternative networks of power to help them pursue their causes. Grassroots activists need accurate information to press any pollution case. They must develop legal precedents and procedures to empower them to use the courts. Political parties and candidates must incorporate environmental issues into their platforms, and must be held accountable for their actions. National and international environmental groups have to offer advice and technical assistance to local communities that feel threatened by the failure of the government to respond to excessive pollution, inadequate sewage or garbage disposal, toxic-waste buildup, or other forms of environmental degradation. All of this is slowly beginning to happen. Although there is still no equivalent to the American EPA or organizations like the National Wildlife Federation or Greenpeace, which lobby for stronger environmental protection, concern about water, pollution, and open space is now part of Israel's national dialogue.

Many of these issues will continue to be deeply entwined with national security and the ongoing peace negotiations. Water is one of the most contested resources in the region, and a multinational group continues to work on that issue. If such international efforts produce an agreement to protect scarce water, it might provide support for domestic activists advocating greater protection of clean water. Similarly, Israeli Arab sanitation and environmental protection will thrive if the Israeli government is able to turn its attention and resources from security to a wider array of national issues. Only in a less tense political atmosphere will Arabs achieve full environmental and social rights and will the environment in general become a major focus of Israel's still embattled population.

Environmentalists Confront a Police State

In Czechoslovakia, where secrecy had been the most extreme before the fall of the Communists in 1989, human rights activists initiated a dissident movement in 1977 and subsequently identified environmental advocacy as legitimate, if dangerous, protest against a despised government. Many dissidents believed that the environmental degradation that plagued so much of the country was a direct outgrowth of the policies of the Communist government, which had emphasized the development of heavy industry and the use of soft, sulfur-rich brown coal to meet its growing energy needs. By the 1980s a majority of citizens no longer believed any of the government rhetoric about security needs or Cold War interests, but they feared internal repression and potential jail sentences for engaging in public protest or dissent. Only small groups of dissenters organized around environmental and political dissidence.

This disenchantment had a two-decade history, but there was little opportunity for public expression until the decline of Soviet influence opened some possibility of dissent. When Soviet tanks invaded Czechoslovakia during the Prague Spring of 1968, few of the critics believed that the Soviet-installed government would remain in power for more than twenty years. The alienation of many intellectuals and workers was forcefully expressed in the Charter 77 petition, but this demand for human rights, published in Prague in 1977, resulted in jail sentences for the leaders and harsh repression for many of the signatories.[45] As a result, the Czechoslovakian government faced no expanded protest until the waning of the Cold War, when human rights and environmental groups challenged the government and called for accountability. During those difficult dark years of the 1970s and 1980s, the small underground groups of environmentalists were nourished by connections to their Polish and Hungarian counterparts and by hard-won contacts with a few Western scientists and environmental activists, who kept them abreast of worldwide developments and concerns. This transnational movement rejected the strictures of Cold War ideology and projected a global view of the world's most pressing needs.[46] In addition, Czechoslovakian environmentalists benefited from the Western mass media that penetrated the Iron Curtain. In particular, Slovakians were able to watch Austrian television and its coverage of a referendum against nuclear power plants and new dams.[47]

Like its Eastern European Communist neighbors, the Czechoslovakian government had paid little attention to the environment despite its own official regulations on air and water pollution. As a result of neglect, its cities suffered from air pollution so serious that children were periodically sent to the countryside to breathe fresh air when the atmosphere was particularly foul. In addition, more than a third of the country's forests were destroyed by pollution, and 70 percent of the rivers were so badly polluted that half of the nation's drinking water did not meet minimum standards.[48]

One dramatic example of environmental activism and of the successful attempts to create viable alternative networks of power occurred in Bratislava in the last years of the Communist government, where a group of concerned activists worked in the city branch of the Slovak Union of Landscape and Nature Protectors (SZOPK). This organization was one of two officially sanctioned nature societies that had traditionally had many Communist Party members and secret-police infiltrators observing its activities. Its membership also included environmentalists who despised the government but had no other outlets for their political opposition. Sociologist Martin Bulora, himself a member of the Bratislava environmental movement, described the small environmental groups as "islands of positive deviation."[49] Unlike Prague, with its dissident Charter 77 movement,[50] Bratislava had been a quiescent city. It had few known activists and had experienced less severe repression by the government.[51] A small and dedicated group in the SZOPK had begun organizing against the proposed Gabcikovo and Nagymoros dams, which were joint Czechoslovakian/Hungarian projects with serious potential for environmental damage.

But by the late 1980s, Bratislava was poised for a broader protest. Gorbachev was in power in the USSR, and the forces for change in the Communist nations intensified as a result of glasnost and severe economic pressures. There were splits within the Czechoslovakian party leadership, with some segments willing to entertain reformist ideas. When they realized that few party representatives were actually attending the meetings of SZOPK's Bratislava city district group, the environmental dissidents of SZOPK seized the opportunity to extend their activities beyond their normal nature-protection work. Although dissidents could never be sure there were no secret-police informants infiltrating their group, in 1987 the leaders of the city committee of SZOPK decided to take the risk.

One significant figure was Jan Budaj, who had been involved with the cultural underground in performances, films, and happenings that were condemned by the regime. He worked as a coal stoker, the only job open to those labeled as dissenters. As an emerging dissident leader, Budaj decided to join with other environmental activists, such as Mikulas Huba, Fedor Gal, and Pavel Šremer, several of whom had sacrificed safety and careers because of their earlier resistance. Šremer, for example, had been arrested as a young university graduate when he protested the invasion and the Soviet occupation in 1968. He spent more than two years in a high-security prison, where his surroundings consisted of gray walls with almost no view of the outdoors.

> From the windows I could occasionally see a tree in the distance, and I realized and appreciated how important is the relationship between man and the natural world. When I got out of prison, I was not allowed to do any work in my field. Like so

many others, I had to become a manual laborer. Given my past training and my prison experience, I became acquainted with others of a similar mindset and became involved in nature protection work.

The situation gradually changed with the arrival of Gorbachev on the scene. It became possible to become active in a wider framework of environmental activities. It is important to understand that environmental information had been kept secret by the regime. Most people had no idea about environmental information, and we wanted to publicize it and make the public aware of how important it was. Our organization was made up of scientists and journalists and others. It was based on friendship and on being able to trust one another.[52]

Together, these friends and colleagues decided to ferret out hard data to inform the public of the serious environmental deterioration that plagued their city. Although it was taboo even to talk about air pollution, the SZOPK group planned an integrated report, *Bratislava Nahlas,* to address the dangers of polluted air and water, untreated waste, nuclear energy, improper urban planning, poor traffic control, and more. They wanted to produce a readable document so that the general public would realize that these issues were all directly linked to the political and cultural situation that dominated Slovakian society.

Like Tom Bailie and Judith Jurgi in the United States, and Alon Tal and Hatim Kana'aneh in Israel, these Slovakian environmentalists sought to highlight a set of issues and persuade the public that a serious social problem existed. To do this, clear and readily understandable evidence was essential. This was their challenge. Courage and care were required ingredients in this effort. For in this case they had to act in a highly repressive atmosphere. The planners of *Bratislava Nahlas* were determined not to have their publication immediately denigrated as a dissident document, which might frighten the public and undermine its broad educational purposes. At the same time, the title, which can be translated as *Bratislava Aloud,* revealed their intention to speak out and break the silence that had blanketed Slovakia for decades. They embarked on a dangerous mission that, if misunderstood or mislabeled by the authorities, could result in their imprisonment.

Under the guise of collecting information for their other publications, each activist approached government officials to secure statistics about one particular topic that did not immediately appear to be too controversial. As Jan Budaj explained:

> It is important to remember that at that time environmental organizations were not illegal. So there was the possibility for our organization to go to government offices and ask for some official cooperation. It is also very important to realize that Slovakians did not feel a sense of fear in looking for information which would help improve the quality of life for ourselves and our children. The fear of oppression was not connected with environmental activities. If, on the other hand, members of Charter 77 had come along and had introduced the idea of an environmental report, nobody would have cooperated, because of fear. The Communist system had created a huge fear among the public for any political dissidence. This was very different when it came to an effort associated with environmental improvement.[53]

At times, the activists found officials who gave them more than the standard party response. Some of the officials were reflecting the growing splits in the party; others were feeling the winds of perestroika and were willing to leak previously secret information. The researchers were scientists, lawyers, architects, and other professionals. In addition, several journalists helped with the writing and editing, and about fifty people checked and corrected the facts. In the end the network of friends expanded to mount the necessary campaign for public recognition of environmental problems. Twenty-three people produced and signed the report, which took six months to complete and which was written in secret to avoid detection and possible arrest.

One thousand copies of *Bratislava Nahlas* were printed. Since the writers did not have the required official permission to distribute such a document, they published it as an appendix to the minutes of the meeting of the city chapter of SZOPK, the nature society. The report opened with a strong declaration:

> In our city, the basic conditions of life have become problematic. Contamination of the atmosphere is threatening the health of virtually all inhabitants, particularly the aged, the sick, and children. . . . The degradation of values, waste, the damage to human health, and the mass problems which will impact upon future generations are immoral; nevertheless, they occur daily before the eyes of the citizens, no one is ever called to account- ability. . . . The moral dimension of the Bratislava situation is, we believe, just as serious as the public health or economic viewpoints.

They ended their courageous introduction with a call to action that had never been heard in Communist Bratislava: "We expect that the public discussion (which this document would like to introduce) will not only articulate the interests of the citizens of Bratislava, but will mobilize their forces and renew the relationship of the citizens with re- spect to their city."[54] To facilitate a widespread public discussion, the environmental leaders sent copies to Communist Party officials, to ex- pert groups, and to working groups within various ministries, calling upon all of them to embark on a discussion of the troubling issues raised in the report.

When the regime's functionaries recognized the significance of the document, they declared it illegal and tried to seize all known copies. They attacked the report in the press, labeling it as untrue, anti-Com- munist propaganda, and resorted to the Cold War national security rhetoric that had worked so well in past decades. But by this time Bratislavans acting independently had reproduced thousands of copies, and confiscation was impossible. The document became the subject of intense discussion and the government's condemnation only served to enhance the impact of the publication. One contemporary ac- tivist, not involved in the *Bratislava Nahlas* movement, described the public reaction:

I was twenty-one years old when *Bratislava Nahlas* was published. The Communists' reaction to the publication was probably the best advertisement for the environmental movement. Everyone knew that the Communists were lying when they said that the facts put forth in the publication were not proven, were not based on reality, that things were not nearly so bad, and that the document was written by anti-Communist activists. It was the best beginning for social change. It was clear to everyone what was going on, especially when the Communists confiscated all the copies and prohibited the making of additional ones. At the same time, thousands of illegal copies were circulating, everyone was reading it, and everyone was aware of what was going on. It spread among the public, and I was very attracted to the action that the environmentalists had taken.[55]

At the same time, a representative of the Voice of America obtained a copy and publicized it, which gave *Bratislava Nahlas* more notice and increased fears that there would be retaliation against the organizers. The police questioned and harassed the leaders repeatedly, but these leaders refused to repudiate their work, as most earlier protesters had done when threatened by police retaliation. Maria Filkova, the secretary of SZOPK, described the most serious incident, when a bullet came through the window of their offices. "If I had not been bending over to say something to one of my colleagues, they would have shot me in the head. It was at a meeting of our city board, and the authorities knew that we would be here, because our phone was tapped. I was not afraid. I just did not feel fear."[56] Filkova and the other SZOPK leaders were convinced that the regime could no longer suppress all dissenting evidence with impunity. In the end they were proved right. Knowing that several of the signatories were well-known public figures, involved with popular nature-protection activities, the police were reluctant to imprison them. These environmental activists had a form of legitimacy that gave them protection for a more far-reaching dissent than Slovakians had ever known.

Bratislava Nahlas was a significant watershed in mobilizing opposition to the government, for it broke the silence and quiescence that had long been a major Communist tool. Budaj, like his colleagues, was proud of their victory. Their culture of solidarity had held despite threats, harassment, and even bullets:

> It was fantastic that during this time, when the attacks on us were rising rapidly, no one denounced or blacked out his signature. Slovakia, until this point, was represented mainly by political timidity. There were many cases where, for example, some well-known actor signed something and then afterward had to cancel his signature. We felt it as a shame. This was the first action in which nobody retracted his or her name.
>
> Like Charter 77, *Bratislava Nahlas* publicized the people who were not afraid to act. It made them visible to the public. Second, people experienced for the first time how it feels when you don't lose. It was an unusual experience. And people formed a sphere where they were willing to act; even though they might lose their professional careers, people were willing to act in the name of environmental ethics. It was a chance to stand in the center of the creation of a new value system for the entire country.[57]

The production of *Bratislava Nahlas* reveals in stark terms the components of courageous behavior that may come to the fore when an oppressive regime seeks to invoke the requirements of national security to combat a challenging document. The environmental protesters believed that the long-denied problems were so serious that they were required to act on behalf of their fellow residents of Bratislava and the rest of Slovakia. They drew legitimacy from their deep ties with the millions of their compatriots who were denied access to vital information about conditions that daily had a detrimental effect on their health. They were convinced that if they acted in concert, they could have a significant impact on the system of decision making that for decades had vaunted secrecy, manipulation, and threat as the highest values of the state. The environmentalists relied on their culture of solidarity, on their belief in one another and in their trust that no one would betray the others to ward off the fear that had paralyzed so many earlier efforts. Without a formal declaration of any kind, they had given allegiance to the ideal that united, collective action directed toward the careful accumulation of evidence could sway a still-cowed public. The activists acted on their faith that they were on the crest of a major social upheaval. The time was ripe for bold yet carefully planned and orchestrated action. This time they proved right in their assessment. Their bravery placed them on the forefront of a historic change.

Like many of the United States communitarian activists, the *Bratislava Nahlas* group addressed their publication to "the people" of Bratislava. They appealed to all citizens who had been abused by state policies. In this moment of reaching for unity they assumed that they spoke for a broad community of interest with no ideological divisions. Only later did those differences surface.

The organizing effort became a proving ground for the revolutionary leadership. When the Communist government fell two years later, these environmentalists emerged as important Slovakian leaders.[58] Many organized against the building of a nuclear reactor in the center of the Bratislava university campus. They helped mobilize several hundred students, who marched on November 16, 1989, the eve of the Velvet Revolution, shouting "We want freedom!" and "We don't want a reactor!" Later several of the *Bratislava Nahlas* participants were elected to the first transitional parliament. Others, like Pavel Šremer, went on to important positions in the Federal Ministry of the Environment and other areas of the government. The public recognized their leadership role in exposing the lies of the government, which had repeatedly insisted that there were no major environmental dangers in the region. The courage of the *Bratislava Nahlas* participants was extraordinary. Their determination to break the silence of forty years played an important role in raising environmental consciousness and in consolidating political opposition.

Although significant at that historic moment, the movement was unable to sustain the environmental improvement they hoped the revolution would initiate. First, some of the leadership was discredited when Jan Budaj and several others were named as one-time informants for the hated secret police.[59] As new political parties emerged and nationalism became a central issue in Slovakia, divisiveness grew among the activists. Budaj himself became chair of the Slovakian National Council, while others, like Huba and Šremer, founded the Green Party, with a more committed focus on environmental politics. Some of the most experienced leaders left for Prague to assume new roles in the democratic government. Within a short period of time economic development and Slovakian separatism superseded the urgency of the environmental issue.[60]

Those who remained dedicated to environmental reform found few institutions to assist them in their ongoing efforts to ameliorate air, water, and soil pollution, address the dangers of nuclear and toxic wastes, reverse the destruction of the forests, and stop the building of the controversial Gabcikovo dam between Hungary and Slovakia. There were no environmental organizations with fund-raising capacity, few procedures for taking violators to court, limited press coverage, and sporadic research and monitoring groups to contribute to public debate. Those who continued to work relied on the newly emerging Environmental Ministry and some small activist organizations largely funded by foundations from abroad like the German Marshall Fund. Activists found themselves challenged once again to rebuild the environmental movement in a new political context that emphasized a free market and economic transformation over environmental protection. Public fear under the Communists was replaced by nation building and a desire for material goods.[61]

The Centrality of Leadership

The emergence of citizens' groups required the transformation of highly motivated individuals into grassroots leaders with the ability to create a culture of solidarity and to obtain support from strategically placed allies in order to build viable alternative networks of power.[62] Concerned neighbors, whether in the United States, Israel, or Slovakia, relied on effective spokespersons like Tom Bailie, Dr. Hatim Kana'aneh, or Maria Filkova, who were willing and able to articulate the communities' goals. These leaders redefined their neighbors' experience so that long-standing unspoken problems could become public grievances demanding redress.

The leaders had the personal charisma, the willpower, and the tenacity to mount a long-term battle. They were not cowed by threats or attracted by promises of personal gain if they would compromise. They had a vision of what was possible and of the world they wanted for their children and a value system reflecting what they hoped to achieve. In addition, the leaders were among the first to seize upon changing cultural ideas about national security, secrecy, prerogatives of the state, and the rights and responsibilities of local communities. They publicized new findings about environmental hazards and promoted environmental health and safety over exclusive concern with jobs and national security ideology. They rejected what they considered to be the false claims of patriotism and reinterpreted the meaning of democracy, Zionism, and socialism. In all three cases, their new interpretation generated profound debate and mobilized others in the community to step forward and work for a redress of local problems.

As we have demonstrated, the development of new community leaders did not occur in a neutral political context. The change in the Cold War atmosphere profoundly enhanced leaders' ability to mobilize grassroots groups, which depended on government cooperation or, at a minimum, acquiescence. Groups like the Galilee Society in northern Israel had to have a legal right to exist, which they had not had earlier in Israel's history. Although nominally independent, grassroots groups normally required some financial assistance from the state, either in the form of tax-exempt status, the right to collect money from international donors, or, in some cases, a direct subsidy. To be most effective, community groups needed to secure accurate environmental data. They benefited from a judicial system that could provide institutional routes for redress.

While the Slovakian environmentalists represented the most alienated of the citizens' groups, they too had to use the cover of the state-supported nature-protection society and to rely on information and leaks from government functionaries. Their success, like that of the Downwinders or the Galilee Society, would not have been possible ten or fifteen years earlier. Similar grievances may have existed, and individual dissidents may have spoken up, but the culture of secrecy in the national security state was too pervasive and powerful to allow leaders to emerge and grassroots groups to organize. Only as the Cold War atmosphere abated and state control became less enforceable were leaders and core-group members able to lift the veil of fear that had long precluded such actions. They were now willing to take risks for goals that increasingly seemed legitimate and attainable.

In addition to the emergence of grassroots leaders and a more receptive political culture, citizen crusaders also had to tap into a national infrastructure that could assist them in their struggle to redefine priorities. These new activists had to use whatever resources were available to them to mount a campaign for recognition and influence. They needed to convince an interested mass media to publicize their ideas and, better still, to mount independent investigations. Positive publicity was at the heart of all the movements. In Slovakia, where this condition did not exist, sympathetic journalists willing to assist the *Bratislava Nahlas* group in creating its own "press" wrote and edited articles for the group's publication. This broadly distributed report was crucial if the *Bratislava Nahlas* group was to have any hope of pressuring the state by appealing to broad public sentiment.

Many activists, particularly in the United States, also depended on public-interest groups, which provided guidance, expertise, research, and important contacts. Some of these nationally based groups, like the Clearinghouse for Hazardous Waste, grew out of earlier grassroots efforts and were distinct from the more established environmental organizations, which were often more enmeshed in the compromises of national politics. Where the national movement was weaker, as in the former Czechoslovakia and Israel, the activists had to call on a worldwide environmental movement like Greenpeace or the World Wildlife Fund to help them to launch their activities. Even in the most repressive period of Communist history, small openings to the West enabled Czechoslovakian leaders to contact well-known environmental activists and learn of trends in environmental legislation. These contacts were crucial in sustaining Czechoslovakian environmentalists and in preparing them for a time when they could develop an environmental advocacy movement. At the present time, several international groups

ing assistance and training in financial and organizational
ment of nongovernmental organizations. In Israel, activists
ied on the United States not only for information, training, and
funding, but also to set standards that could be demonstrated to the Israeli public. In both Israel and the former Czechoslovakia, this crucial
assistance from abroad propelled the environmental movement forward. As in the United States, activists saw their opportunity and
grasped it.

While both men and women were deeply involved in grassroots
activism, under certain circumstances women undertook roles of central leadership. This occurred particularly when mothers believed
their families were directly threatened by unforeseen hazards to their
health. Under such circumstances, women invoked their roles as
mothers, proclaimed a special responsibility, and sought legitimacy as
protectors of their children. This mantle gave them special recognition
and protection as they moved into new terrain. It also often led to a
crescendo of criticism from those who labeled them as naive inter-
lopers into political territory that extended well beyond their traditional sphere of home and school. The next chapter examines the role
of mothers as organizers and leaders in promoting environmental
health and safety.

3

Marching Along with Mothers and Children

In recent years, mothers' groups throughout the world have won public recognition for initiating movements on behalf of important social causes. From the Madres de Plaza de Mayo, who regularly marched to protest the disappearance of their family members in Argentina, to the United States–based Mothers Against Drunk Driving (MADD), mothers' groups have surfaced to demand attention for serious social problems. Scholars have referred to these activities as maternalist or motherist movements, meaning that women in these groups have claimed the special nurturing and caring qualities of mothers to justify their public roles in causes associated with children and families.[1] While some applaud women's ability to use their status as mothers to move beyond the private sphere of the home in order to engage in public discourse, other scholars are critical of women's tendency to define themselves as inherently different, possessing unique qualities limited to women.[2]

This essentialist argument, as it has come to be called, always runs great risks. While using the mantle of motherhood may initially garner support for women's entrance into political arenas from which they have traditionally been excluded, an emphasis on difference, the critics argue, also reinforces notions of inequality because it places women on a plane different from that of men. Further, this focus on mothers' special roles and qualities overlooks important differences between women of divergent class, race, or ethnic backgrounds, and ignores the fact that mothers can be found on both sides of any controversial issue. In addition, an overemphasis on the unique role of mothers can have the effect of excluding men, and even women who have no children, from their movements. Perhaps most challenging is the critics' observation that, even where successful, most of these mothers' movements are a flash in the pan, arising in periods of crisis and disappearing as soon as the immediate crisis ends, leaving men in the dominant political structures to continue business as usual.[3]

Despite these serious charges, feminist scholars who have looked most closely at the history of mothers' involvement in social movements have not denied the significance of women's attention to public activity that grows directly out of their maternal concerns for peace, child welfare, and elder care.[4] These scholars point to a long history in many countries of significant political activism by mothers. Antiwar organizations, rent and bread strikes, and other militant actions all began out of maternal concern, but proceeded to politicize women and take them into the complex public arena. Some women activists use their maternal role because they believe it is the only one that the predominately male media and government officials will recognize. These men are willing to show women defending their sick children, but rarely invite them to meetings to discuss serious analyses of the technical and political issues at hand. Recognizing this reality, feminist scholars like Sara Ruddick and Ann Snitow argue that women must be careful not to accept oversimplified ideas about mothers' special qualities. While continuing to draw on their concerns for nurturing and caring, women must avoid a tendency to rely solely on their maternal role for legitimacy. They must not see a contradiction between their special experiences as mothers and the need to seek social justice based on equality for all people.

The community-based environmental movements from which women have protested dangerous health and safety conditions highlight both the advantages and limits of organizing as mothers. Since the 1970s women in the United States, Israel, and Czechoslovakia have expanded their traditional activities as wives and mothers when they believed that local and national policies endangered their families and communities. To fulfill their roles as caretakers and guardians of husbands and children, these women have overcome deeply ingrained cultural practices that limited their public activities to more traditional settings such as the school, the church, and benevolent associations. They had not been part of the feminist movement that encouraged women to move into nontraditional roles, but they were prepared to broaden their definitions of appropriate behavior for themselves and others concerned about health, safety, and the quality of life. They came together as neighbors and friends in comfortable and familiar settings to articulate shared problems and to force their issues onto the political agenda of their respective governments.

Relying on the sense of their unique vantage point as mothers, these new community activists developed initial confidence, and eventually won acceptance for activity that might otherwise have been considered brazen or foolish. Yet as they created effective networks, women confronted questions from others about their ability to take care of their children. At times, initial approval from husbands, relatives, and friends turned sour as increased involvement took the women away from their traditional homemaking tasks. Accusations of child neglect or inadequate housekeeping often vied with earlier approval for their actions as concerned mothers. Women also became the target of criticism from government and corporate officials, who wanted to minimize their effectiveness in seeking remediation for environmental damage. For example, one consultant for the organization representing the industries that were being sued by a California group of environmental activists graphically described his ambivalence in dealing with Penny Newman, a determined and competent woman organizer whose case is described in detail later in this chapter. For her adversaries, every acknowledgment of Newman's effectiveness was offset by a question about her integrity or her "real" motives for threatening the status quo. The industry representative believed that there were two reasons that nearly all activists were women—the very reasons that made them vulnerable to severe criticism: "First, their home is threatened. I grew up in the cattle business, and if you really want to have your hands full with a mad cow, mess with her calf. But also, here was a chance for a woman to assert herself as an equal. And what we have discovered is that there are a lot of Penny Newmans in this world that are maybe just as competent as Governor Wilson [of California]. And they've discovered it. So you are not going to shut them up."[5]

The industry spokesman's grudging respect for Newman's competence was nevertheless compromised by his insistence that she was like a "mad cow"—irrational, insistent, and adversarial. He trivialized her political and environmental insights by reducing them to mere psychic tensions when he suggested: "As a matter of fact, Penny has made quite a career for herself here, but the problem is that these activists can't be reasonable. They have to be adversarial because, if they start being reasonable, industry will pat them on the top of the head and tell them to go home. So they really raise hell, and it turns out that it's a lot of fun to do that. It's very gratifying because suddenly people listen, but then you get to be a problem because, once people start taking corrective action and you are still screaming wolf, they want to skin the wolf."[6]

Mothers' groups, whether in the United States, Israel, or Czechoslovakia, had to confront this patronizing level of opposition in meetings, in the local media, and on the streets of their communities. They heard complaints from relatives as well as adversaries, in words that could be painful and stinging. To overcome the ridicule and put-downs, successful community groups had to go beyond legitimizing their actions as an extension of their traditional activities, because this simply provided ammunition for those who were attacking them for their naive approach to social problems. Would-be activists had to prove their seriousness by finding one or more committed and knowledgeable leaders and by developing a working core group, a cogent ideology, political savvy, and the resources for processing technical information. The central figures in the core group had to become sophisticated community organizers, able to build broad-based coalitions and develop strategies to negotiate with political leaders in their city or their nation's capital.[7]

Local mothers' groups sought and often received essential assistance in their endeavors from national environmental organizations. Where the neighborhood groups were able to create or join a broader-based political coalition, they had the greatest success in forcing officials to take remedial action. When they remained isolated, they could not sustain the ongoing effort necessary to prevent the issue from slipping onto a back burner.

why ?

While there are important political and cultural differences among the United States, Israel, and Czechoslovakia, all these women undertook new commitments as grassroots activists when they perceived serious environmental threats to their families. In this chapter we highlight the personal transformation of several mothers whose experiences in their three societies exemplify varying degrees of transition from the private sphere to the public arena. They changed from concerned neighbors to formidable environmental activists, from devoted mothers to nationally recognized figures. Some retained this new identity only until an immediate crisis ended, while others never left the arena of political and social change.[8] They were captured by the enormity of the environmental and social problems facing their region, and by their own ability to function effectively in the political sphere.[9]

As in earlier cases, we emphasize their strategy of creating a culture of solidarity that provided them with meaning to undergird their fight and with emotional support to nurture and soothe them in moments of despair and dread. They also sought links with other groups engaged in comparable struggle, with journalists who could provide the necessary publicity, and with government officials willing to give them encouragement, credibility, and information. All of these groups and individuals helped the women form alternative networks of power, which carried them or their messages from their homes and small group meetings into high-level government offices or corporate boardrooms. As they pursued their cases and made contacts with others working on public-safety issues, the women began to define their work as more than an isolated project. They came to believe that they were contributing to the democratic process, in which citizens help to shape the political agenda and to force accountability on their elected officials.

We underscore that this commitment to reinforcing or actually building democracy differed in the countries under study. In the United States, California activists fighting the terror of chemical wastes defined their organization as a reaction against the blatant disregard of government and corporations for the safety of their children and community. The residents organized as a form of self-defense and to secure their rights as American citizens. They insisted that as taxpayers they were entitled to the same services and concern for their health and property as others living in more affluent communities. These ideas were at the foundation of their understanding of democracy. Equality under the law also meant that all people were entitled to protect their homes from toxic wastes generated by powerful industries. They passionately believed that the system had failed them, and they were determined to reverse that by using every legal means they could find.

In Israel, activists based in Haifa, Israel's third largest city, demanded acknowledgment from responsible public and business officials that serious air pollution existed and that residents were at severe risk from daily exposure. As they organized for a long-term battle, they came to believe that their actions went well beyond concern for a local problem. They believed they were making a significant contribution not only to their city but also to their country at large. The leaders articulated this ideology by asserting openly that their time, energy, and financial contribution to their cause was a worthwhile investment in the future of their country. In an era when the vitality of early Zionist ideology in motivating citizens was fading, they reasserted and redefined its importance. They believed that their Zionist dream could best be realized by enlarging the issues to be addressed through Israel's democratic institutions. For too long, they argued, serious environmental problems had been ignored as the government attended to other priorities and citizens accepted the premise that the issue was "out of their hands." In building a grassroots environmental organization that challenged this passivity, these activists were true "civic innovators";[10] they drew on extant groups in the community and persuaded them to enter a new terrain to fight for cleaner air and better health.

In Czechoslovakia, the women who focused on environmental problems had long been political dissidents. Unlike their counterparts in California, they had no illusions that under the Communist government there was any right to protest against environmental degradation. Their actions were more akin to those practicing civil disobedience against unjust authority. They were willing to take the risk of state punishment because they believed in their cause and in an ideal of democracy that entitles citizens to act on behalf of the larger community. Unlike the women in Haifa, Israel, the women of Prague had no interest in strengthening either the ideology or the actuality of the existing state. On the contrary, they were harkening to a democratic tradition in Czechoslovakia that they believed the Communists had tried to destroy.

In all three countries, the mothers had to exhibit courage not only in confronting their environmental adversaries, but also in overcoming the subtle and obvious challenges to women assuming leadership roles in protest politics. As they engaged seriously with the problems that they identified, their roles expanded into hitherto forbidden and foreboding areas of public life. They were easy targets for criticisms that they were just ignorant housewives, on the one hand, or neglectful mothers and wives on the other. Either explicitly or implicitly, critics raised questions about women's participation in public, male-oriented debates; ridiculed their political style; called into question their experience and technical competence; and emphasized their "emotionalism." Sometimes these coded comments were delivered with humor; in other cases the criticisms were purely vindictive. But in either case, the critics mounted an insidious attack on ordinary women's attempts to challenge established authority and traditional roles in the community, just because they were mothers concerned about their children's future. Their critics appealed to long-standing, if unspoken, assumptions that mothers had a prescribed arena in which they should operate—school, home, church—an arena that was not supposed to accommodate their roles as lead challengers demanding attention from the highest authorities.

The women activists did not always respond directly. In most cases, they insulated themselves against such attacks by building an identity that gave legitimacy to their new roles. Beyond defining themselves as mothers entitled to protect their families, they mastered all the technical vocabulary; they never missed an important public hearing or meeting; they learned to use the media and techniques of public demonstrations. They self-consciously articulated the issues in ways that could be easily understood by a larger public, whose support they needed. Whether they used folksy methods or sophisticated analyses, they understood the importance of building a sustaining organization that could push their agenda forward, no matter what the stance of the opposition.

The cases profiled below are representative of a widely noted phenomenon. Small women's groups have appeared throughout the United States to confront local environmental threats. The Citizens Clearinghouse for Hazardous Waste works with hundreds, if not thousands, of such groups. Our own interviews with dozens of women confirmed the finding of other scholars that women are heavily represented in membership and leadership of grassroots groups.[11] Although there are fewer such groups in Israel and Czechoslovakia, the Israeli and Czech women discussed in this chapter embodied a growing concern by citizens like themselves about environmental problems. Dozens of women in all three countries told us that they believed they must interrupt daily life as they knew it in order to demand action and remedy for serious problems of pollution, radiation, and other toxic hazards.

From Community Volunteer to Citizen Activist

Penny Newman of southern California is a prime example of a shy housewife permanently transformed into a successful leader whose influence continues to permeate an entire region of the country. When Penny Newman and her family arrived in Glen Avon, California, in the early 1970s, she knew nothing of a site called the Stringfellow Acid Pits. Although it was located just a few miles from her new home, she, like most residents, had no idea that in 1956 the state of California had persuaded local landowner James Stringfellow to let them use a high, arid plot of land as a depository for the growing industrial wastes in southern California. Neither Penny Newman nor her neighbors could have known that since then the accumulation of toxic chemicals had filled the pit to such a point that a period of heavy rains would send them overflowing into the community of Glen Avon just a few years later.

There were several long-term residents in the community who did express concern that they were living at the edge of a potential disaster. As president of the local PTA, Penny Newman felt obliged to look into the allegations that the pits posed a threat to the children of the community. Newman approached local and county water-quality and health officials, who assured her that the site had been closed recently and that everything was under control. She trusted their competence and their integrity.

> And so I dismissed my concerns. I figured these people were the experts. They knew what was going on, and their job was to protect us. It was not until several years later, in 1978, when we had heavy rains, that I saw for myself there was foam in the water. And then the newspaper reported that the state had decided to release some of the chemical waste onto our town. There was a part of me that just could not believe that the state would release a million gallons of toxic chemicals into the community. They just let it flow with the rain water in the areas where our kids were playing, into the school, which six hundred children attended. It seemed impossible, but from everything I could see, it was happening.[12]

Government officials claimed that the chemicals had been diluted by the rain water, and that this kind of deliberate release was preferable to the potential danger of uncontrolled flooding. Newman was most profoundly disenchanted with what she felt was a breach of trust on the part of school officials. They were not faceless bureaucrats from Sacramento, but men and women with whom she had worked for years, first as a teacher's aide, then as a volunteer, and finally as PTA president and special-education teacher. When she learned that the superintendent had decided not to inform parents that chemicals had leaked into the schools and that he had unilaterally decided to keep the school open, Newman was transformed into a bitter critic: "It was like having my best friend turn on me. Everything that I had believed all my life was just turned upside down."[13]

Newman's reaction captured the disenchantment that affected many of the women who were caught between the desire to believe that government and corporate officials knew what they were doing and direct evidence that their children had been endangered. Their daily lives reminded them that they were living with contaminated water, poisoned by toxic chemicals. At first, activist Sally Mehra explained, the mothers thought the problem was limited to the poisoned water that had run through the school. Then they realized that every rainy day might bring more chemicals onto their streets, and they felt they should keep their children home in bad weather. The final insult occurred when Mehra learned that her well water was contaminated; she had to rely on bottled water until the local residents could convince the state to develop an alternative community water supply: "I had a year-old daughter and didn't want to expose her any more than necessary to the chemicals and radiation. I bathed her in bottled water, washed her clothes out of the area, and had a diaper service for a year so that she wouldn't be exposed."[14]

This sense of daily danger led Newman, Mehra, and their fellow residents to form Concerned Neighbors, an organization to monitor events at Stringfellow Acid Pits. Newman's PTA and Junior Women's Club leadership led to her selection as cochair of a meeting at which residents expressed their concerns and fears about Stringfellow. A dozen years later, she was still chairwoman of Concerned Neighbors, which had grown from a small neighborhood organization to one that sued state, county, and corporate officials on behalf of thousands of persons who claimed to have sustained harmful effects from the chemical releases.[15] Their significant social capital—membership in PTAs, service as Cub Scout den mothers, and other voluntary service—provided initial motivation and a social network to draw on. But the experience as concerned neighbors created a whole new set of opportunities and challenges that transformed the group into sophisticated agents of change, while they still retained their down-to-earth style as mothers and friends.

In part, the organization helped the mothers confront their guilt. Initially, when they saw their children suffer from asthma, skin rashes, headaches, and dizziness, the mothers had blamed themselves. As Penny Newman described it:

> Am I such a bad mother that I can't take care of my children. . . . It was years before we really connected their health problems with exposure to the toxic chemicals. I was feeling those things, along with many of the women in the community. We were the ones who were up all night with the kids. We were the ones taking them to the doctors day after day. On windy days you had kids throwing up everywhere from the chemicals coming down in the dust. All of this prompted the women of Glen Avon to join hands. We didn't know what we were going to do. But we knew we could not allow the flow of chemicals into our community anymore.[16]

The experience of caring for sick children was a classic motivation for neighborhood women to mobilize. Sharing their frustration and guilt was the first communal move, one that has been repeated in mothers' groups throughout the world.[17] When the feelings of pain and despair are converted into determination to do something about a problem, mothers take their first steps toward becoming community activists. At first, women's entrance into the political arena may be viewed as surprising and even refreshing. Historian Amy Swerdlow described the initial response of the media to Women Strike for Peace action when strontium 90 was found in cow's milk after nuclear testing. She quoted *Newsweek*'s shock in 1961 that these mothers were "perfectly ordinary looking women with their share of good looks, the kind you would see driving ranch wagons or shopping at the village market, or attending P.T.A. meetings."[18] But this benign appearance was only one side of the coin. In fact, women had to move out of their ranch wagons and village markets and learn new skills.

Penny Newman's new responsibility as chair was different from anything else she had done. She had to gather and interpret technical reports, organize her neighbors, and confront local and state authorities, all the while balancing her family responsibilities. It proved to be a tough act. Her husband initially approved of her activism, but came to resent the extreme demands it made on her time and energy. Like many women activists, she had to negotiate a set of principles that protected her marriage by enabling her family to maintain some semblance of a private life. It was not easy. Newman's name now appeared frequently in the media, and like many women activists, she had become the butt of local jokes and wisecracks, as well as the object of admiration and affection. Her involvement changed her sense of herself: "When I look back at how I was when I got married versus how I am now, I see two totally separate people. In the beginning I was going to be a housewife and just take care of the kids. I was very shy."[19]

This personal and emotional growth was enhanced by her group's growing political acumen. Initially, the women's techniques involved trial and error, and unlimited determination. They did not like being labeled as hysterical housewives:

> We were consistently underestimated because we were women. The agencies didn't expect us to be able to do anything. After all, we weren't trained scientifically; we didn't have Ph.D.'s. So we began to think about calling on our experiences in running a family and taking care of children. We found that many of our skills fit perfectly into a campaign to influence policy. We found that if you treat bureaucrats like children, it works. We would ask them nicely the first time. If they didn't respond, there was a consequence.[20]

The "consequences," according to Newman, often meant targeting a middle-level bureaucrat and besieging him or her with pickets, petitions, memos, and then moving on to his or her superior.[21] Newman and the Concerned Neighbors learned to use the media effectively. They made sure that the local papers and television stations had pictures of every protest. They befriended reporters and invited them to meetings and demonstrations. As in so many other areas, their use of the media became increasingly sophisticated as they gained experience. One activist recalled the difference. "Our demonstrations have gotten high-tech. It's not like the old days of walking with picket signs in the hot sun. We plan a demonstration and contact the press. We have always had good rapport with press, and they almost always show up if given notice. We do a press packet, walk up and down for the camera crews, pack up our stuff and go home. That way we're on the news and have reached millions of people. It's important to know how to get publicity. You have to have something important to say or the press won't keep coming back."[22]

After a rocky start, the group also formed a close relationship with their congressman and his aides. In February 1983, George Brown promised Penny Newman that he would hold a field hearing so the public could express its views on Stringfellow. By the time of the meeting in April, Concerned Neighbors succeeded in bringing more than nine hundred people to the hearing. When the congressman cut Newman off after ten minutes, a near riot erupted. The crowd so shocked Brown's staff that the court reporter threatened to leave. Yet the public concern was clear. To Congressman Brown and Penny Newman's credit, they had breakfast the next day, cleared the air, and developed a strong working relationship.[23]

Initially, the only source of substantial funds for the Stringfellow cleanup was the state of California. When Concerned Neighbors wanted to lobby for an appropriation for Stringfellow, they had to go to Sacramento to meet with state legislators and officials. It was the first time that many of these women had ever been to Sacramento, and it became an occasion to learn how state politics worked. At first, they did not receive the full $11 million they had requested; nonetheless, they were placed on a priority list for some of the clean-water funds. Most important, they began to learn how to approach state agencies. All of this would serve them well in future negotiations with several California governors and with EPA officials. By working together, Concerned Neighbors figured out how to penetrate the political system. After getting the runaround, they no longer accepted benign expressions of concern that were not followed by concrete actions. Where cooperation failed, Concerned Neighbors sought other means. When, for example, the regional EPA failed to take action after several animals died suspiciously near a test well site in 1991, Newman and her neighbors demanded action. When persistent attempts failed to obtain a safety plan or an investigation of the animal deaths, the exasperated activists raised the ante. They explained their intentions to the regional director in very strong language: "Since cooperation with EPA has gotten us nowhere, we will no longer bother but will find other means for making our concerns known. We will also make sure that everyone knows that EPA does not have the trust, confidence, or cooperation of this community. This will continue until you can come to us with a resolution to the problems. Specifically, that you've developed a community safety plan. . . . EPA, not the polluters, are charged with protecting public health, and we aim to see that you do."[24]

As part of their struggle, the activists developed an ideology that focused on the necessity of community solidarity and empowerment. Penny Newman became an eloquent spokeswoman for the power of community involvement: "It really doesn't matter who's in office. You have to make it an issue that the public can understand and that the public appreciates. The ultimate lesson we learned is that outside help will come and go. But the people that you can count on, and the only people you can rely on, and the people that you worry about are those from the community itself. These are the people who are going to be there come hell or high water, because they all share the common problem."[25]

Although the women in Concerned Neighbors did not initially define themselves as feminists or political activists of any kind, they developed a keen understanding of protest politics. Maybe a small core group would do most of the ongoing work. But it was important to have strong community support, to be able to bring dozens of people to a meeting if necessary or sign hundreds on to a class action suit. Some of the core group continued to be surprised at the transformation of their personalities. Sally Mehra, a member of the steering committee in the suit against the state of California and the involved corporations, noted that "if you had seen me when I was younger, you would never have thought that I'd be in this position. I'm not the type of person to do this type of stuff. I was okay with PTA, Girl Scouts, and Little

League, but this requires keeping up with technologies, processes, changes in government, and more."[26] Many of the citizen crusaders began as traditional housewives, sometimes working as secretaries, teacher's aides, or occasionally as professionals. They were active in community organizations ranging from the PTA to social service clubs. They had fairly traditional views about gender-segregated roles and accepted the major responsibility for maintaining their homes and caring for their children, but as a result of their experiences, they also sought greater impact in community affairs. They met other women who were organizing against environmental hazards, and came to realize that women's roles had to be expanded if the quality of their lives was to improve. They seized the opportunity to control their own destiny by directly confronting powerful government and corporate entities. The most active among them no longer defined themselves exclusively as mothers. They had learned how to use the political process to further their own influence, and they were a substantial force to reckon with.

These deeply involved citizens were also influenced by the growth of a worldwide environmental movement that educated the public about the dangers of the degraded quality of air, water, and soil. Environmentalists reported on growing health hazards and insisted that the public could take action to reverse the discouraging trends. The women in Glen Avon soon had allies and supporters throughout the country. As Penny Newman became increasingly sophisticated in her organizing ability, she assumed the position of regional coordinator for a West Coast alliance, which gave her an office, a salary, and national recognition for her efforts to assist communities suffering from toxic waste all around the country. She developed close ties to her congressman, George Brown, and to his chief aide, Leannah Bradley, who facilitated Concerned Neighbors' participation in public hearings and served as a liaison to EPA and other federal agencies. Later, Newman's group joined with the Clearinghouse for Hazardous Waste, headed by Lois Gibbs, who had led the fight over Love Canal. This enabled Newman to bring her by-then-considerable expertise to parallel efforts on the East Coast.

Newman became an excellent public speaker and led the formation of a community coalition that sued the principal responsible parties, the state, and the county. The formerly shy mother was now a formidable political leader, able to face detractors as well as ardent supporters. After years of participating in every forum, hearing, protest, and citizens' advisory committee, Concerned Neighbors could point to significant victories. The state of California and the Environmental Protection Agency had spent more than $100 million to cap the Stringfellow Acid Pits and to contain the toxic wastes within the pits. The community successfully lobbied the state for money to install a safe-drinking-water system. The activists were also instrumental in the passage of a state Superfund law that phased out the disposal of liquid hazardous wastes into landfills. These victories became models for other communities in the Superfund program. Nevertheless, the local residents continued to worry about underground movement of the toxics, and applied pressure for improved technologies that would continue to monitor and pump out deeply buried dangerous waste materials that could travel along a plume into the water supply of Glen Avon. Nine years of personal-injury trials against the state of California, Riverside County, and eleven private companies that had dumped wastes in the Stringfellow Pits resulted in a series of settlements and verdicts that awarded Glen Avon residents more than $110 million.[27] Although pilloried by the lawyers for the defense, Penny Newman remained a folk hero to many members of her community. She continued her work as director of the Center for Community Action and Environmental Justice and coordinated Communities at Risk, a network of communities at contaminated sites.[28]

In writing about the miseries of the Ojibwa Indians in Canada, Kai Erikson describes them as "a people with a broken culture." He uses the term "broken culture" to capture the bewilderment and social disorientation that resulted when traditional values failed to give meaning and organization to everyday lives disrupted by loss of land and environmental degradation.[29]

In contrast, one might see Concerned Neighbors as "culture menders." Faced with fear and despair over the toxic floods and damage in their small community of Glen Avon, they were able to build new bonds of trust, to invent new political strategies that would allow them to preserve the life they knew and cherished. Their activities were a strange mixture of traditional and radical, of cherishing the past while demanding political change. As mothers, they placed the future welfare of their children above all other priorities. As neighborhood women, they used emotional ties and bonds of friendship and caring to set the political style. One activist explained how important this style was in sustaining the group: "Because you are with these people so much, you're able to talk about things that aren't going well. Maybe somebody's illness has kicked up again, or maybe someone's child is having trouble. There's been a lot of true lasting friendships that have happened over this time that have held the community together to keep the fight."[30]

This gendered form of political action, however, was never exclusionary. In fact, the women wanted as many men to join them as possible, and one local art teacher was a contributing member of the group. "It didn't bother me that I was the only man involved with all those women. They tried to get men involved, but the women have been doing it for years and years. Some don't have jobs; one is an old activist who loves the work. I'm not a member of the core group, but I go to protests, make posters, attend community meetings."[31]

Some men were worried that protests would affect their property values or make their houses impossible to sell. But the women persisted. They called meetings, explained the problems, and critiqued the responses of officials. They worked with lawyers and kept the community advised about the intricacies of their class-action suit. In combining barbecues and local celebrations with this demand for change in the power relationships, they maintained the allegiance and confidence of their followers and persuaded most people that there was hope for Glen Avon and its future.

From Immigrant to Activist

Transformations such as Penny Newman's and the formation of core groups of activist mothers could be found in many places throughout the world. Several years after the toxic floods in Glen Avon, a serious environmental threat mobilized a woman and her neighbors to confront the powerful government and corporate officials of the city of Haifa, Israel. That experience transformed Lynn Golumbic from a recent immigrant absorbed in the daily life of family and work into an activist leading a community-based group that placed the issue of pollution control high on the list of social and political goals in Israel's third largest city.

Lynn Golumbic and her family immigrated to Israel in 1982. This was the fulfillment of a dream she had had ever since college, when she had a spent a year in Israel. Golumbic's husband, Marty, went to work at the IBM research center in Haifa. Lynn, who had an MBA from Columbia University, worked in sales for IBM. They bought an attractive apartment high up on Mount Carmel in Haifa and proceeded to settle in with their two daughters. In addition to home and work, Lynn Golumbic was active in the Association of Americans and Canadians in Israel (AACI), and she and her husband were deeply committed to the country's development. They did not yet realize that their family's health would deteriorate because of Israel's neglect of its environmental problems.

The Golumbics knew that since the formation of the state in 1948, the major focus had been on defense, economic development, and absorption of immigrants, and that issues like pollution were viewed as the cost of supporting much-needed industrial development. They understood that young Israeli adults were challenged by the usual problems of study, work, and family. In addition, all Israelis served two or three years in the military, and after that men served in the reserve forces for at least one month a year for several decades. As a result, citizens and political leaders alike believed that they did not have time for issues like the environment, which they defined as "luxuries."

The Golumbics never intended to challenge these prevailing cultural values, but within a relatively short time after their arrival in Haifa, Lynn and Marty and their two young children were all suffering from asthma. Two more children were born, and they too suffered from unexpected respiratory problems. The Golumbics had been neither environmentalists nor political activists in the United States, but it became increasingly clear to them that Haifa was the most polluted city in Israel, and that its petrochemical industry and oil refineries created constant black smoke that produced serious health hazards. In their first apartment they would be visually reminded of the constant black cloud hovering over the city: "We would face the city of Haifa, and see this black cloud just sitting in the middle of the city. We were in shock and had physical problems as well. We weren't environmentalists, but we knew that breathing black smoke was bad for us. If you look over the valley of industry, you see the problem. We have oil refineries; we have the Israel power plant, petrochemical industries, close to two thousand plants down there. So there is a lot of junk in our air. We didn't know that much then, but we soon got to know more about it."[32]

Subsequently, the Golumbics moved to one of the most desirable residential sections of the city. But even living high upon Mount Carmel no longer shielded the more affluent residents from the effects of the pollution coming from industries surrounding the port. A small group of activists had been trying to fight the pollution problem for decades, yet political and economic realities militated against them. Haifa was a progressive city with strong labor unions, but the issues of health and safety had not become part of the unions' agenda. Many people employed by the electric power company or in the oil refineries were afraid of losing their jobs. Air-pollution data were impossible to obtain from either the companies or the government, so no one could prove that pollution posed a serious health risk to the city's residents. The offending companies were the only ones monitoring the amount of sulfur dioxide (SO_2) in the air, and they were unlikely to define the situation as a health hazard.

The activists' experience with public protest began in 1988. A group of workers from the oil refineries had been told that environmental fanatics were planning to meet and demand the plant's closure. Determined to save their jobs, the workers' committee organized busloads of workers to demonstrate against the environmentalists. When Lynn Golumbic and a few friends arrived at the demonstration to join the activists, they were immediately confronted by the workers and asked which side they were on. Golumbic responded that they were there to appeal for clean air for everyone's children, not to divide the crowd into

us versus them: "After a half hour of vigorous arguing, they understood that we were not going to demand to close down the plant,
merely demand that anti-pollution measures be taken, and then they
decided not to interfere with our demonstration. They also gave us
their megaphone to address the crowd, since no one from the environmentalists had brought one."[33]

Later that year, when the electric company announced that a new
power plant would be built in Haifa, the level of concern and controversy grew among the residents of the city. A citizens' group, Enza,
served as an umbrella organization for local residents. They consistently asked, "If present levels of pollution are unacceptable, what
would a new plant do?" Golumbic, who had ceased working when her
fourth child was born, was at a meeting of the AACI when an Enza
representative urged the group to take advantage of the upcoming
elections. This would be a propitious moment to challenge the existing
pollution standards and the planned construction of a new power
plant. Golumbic and a few friends agreed to devote themselves to this
issue.

Lynn Golumbic was elected chair of the AACI air-pollution committee and formed a coalition with Enza and the Haifa branch of the Society for the Protection of Nature (SPNI). Since 1988 was an election
year, activists believed that they had the opportunity to influence
politicians if they could mount a full-blown campaign to gain serious
attention from the candidates.

First, the activists had to make air pollution an ongoing public issue. Golumbic and her core group used as many appeals as they could.
Saving the children was a popular theme. In one instance, they decided to sit in on sessions of an ongoing court case involving the oil
company. When they arrived at the courthouse, they learned that the
trial was a closed session, so they held a demonstration of mothers and
babies:

> We got there, and they wouldn't let us in because it was a closed
> session. So we decided to have a mini-demonstration right
> there. We bought posterboard and markers and made up five
> signs. We called the local paper and told them we were demon-

strating in front of the City Hall/courthouse. Our signs said things like "You're Choking Us to Death," or "Let us Breathe." The policemen watching us were very uncomfortable with our impromptu protest. We told them, "Let us stay for five minutes, just until the reporter takes our picture." We were six or seven women and some children, so we decided to continue with it.[34]

These experiences were crucial educational opportunities for the women. By negotiating with the police and the reporters, they learned how to plan strategic demonstrations for maximum media impact. Their focus on mothers and babies reflected their understanding that this emphasis on family had an emotional resonance that would further their cause. In addition, the availability of several mothers who were working part-time or not at all enabled the women to devote themselves more fully to the cause. The emphasis on mothers and children was not their only approach. They invited men to join their activities and used the motto "Air pollution is destroying the city." The style they developed differed markedly from that of other longtime Israeli environmentalists, who did not understand or use direct public appeal. Golumbic, like many successful leaders, understood that social movements had changed. They now required a profound understanding and use of mass media. The message had to appeal not just to sympathizers, but to an indifferent and even unsympathetic public. Therefore, effective messages had to be simple, direct, and free of complexity or ambiguity.[35] Despite some serious personality differences, Golumbic succeeded in holding together the loose coalition of the AACI Anti-Pollution Committee, Enza, the original environmental group, and the Haifa branch of SPNI, Israel's largest nature conservation society. Sometimes more energy went into achieving consensus on appropriate tactics than actually went into the struggle with the electric and petrochemical companies, but in the end the coalition held.

Golumbic succeeded in getting her colleagues to take advantage of the forthcoming elections; at political rallies and meetings they questioned all candidates about their positions on building a new power plant in Haifa and on the pollution problem more generally. The activists contacted professors at the university, who advised them on technical issues and pulled together all available studies on the health effects of air pollution. Israel was not accustomed to this kind of focused and concerted effort on any environmental issue, and the novelty of the group's pointed, persistent crusade enabled them to receive good coverage from the local press as well as from radio and television.

When Lynn and Marty Golumbic arrived in Israel, they never thought that they could personally influence developments in their adopted country. In the course of Lynn's active involvement in the pollution issue, both husband and wife came to define her activism as their contribution to Israel: "What did Americans contribute to the struggle? We brought style and technique and a lot of perseverance. We basically came with the attitude that if we went about it in the right way, we would win. It may not be this year, and it may not be next, but if we go for it, justice is on our side. We understand that you need to have an issue, define it, bring it to the attention of everyone in the best way you can, and keep on this issue until something is done about it."[36]

This belief that they were making Israel a better place sustained them. They convinced themselves and others that they had an obligation to interrupt politics as usual. Citizen participation on behalf of the community may have been an American idea, but Israelis quickly adapted these techniques to their politics and culture. Gradually, Lynn Golumbic emerged as a nonpartisan leader who could articulate the growing popular concern about environmental problems. After years of intense effort, which included several lawsuits, Golumbic's coalition could point to serious changes. The electric company and the minister of energy recommended to the National Planning Authority that the new power plant be located elsewhere. The environmental group also initiated a court case in which Marty Golumbic served as the named injured party in an attempt to force lower thresholds for sulfur dioxide in the air. An elaborate legal procedure resulted in a negotiated settlement. The minister of the environment signed into law twenty-one new air-pollution standards, eleven of them for pollutants that had never had standards before. As a result of these agreements, Haifa no longer exceeds acceptable standards for SO_2 pollution; pollution levels are reported every day in the newspaper. These were major and unprecedented victories for the citizens and their allies, although concerns remained about peak days when pollution exceeded the legal limits.[37]

In some ways Lynn Golumbic's personal transformation parallels that of Penny Newman.[38] Never previously an activist in the United States, Golumbic had nevertheless absorbed certain strategic skills in her college years that stood her in good stead as she and her colleagues began to organize a protest movement. As a marketing professional, she knew how to define an issue and mobilize a public effort by using petition drives, demonstrations, door-to-door campaigns, and children's contests in the schools. She learned to write effective press releases and to contact reporters in a timely way in order to maximize the coverage the group's actions would receive in the media.

As in Glen Avon, California, local groups based on neighborliness and a sense of community used their social capital to bring crucial issues to the public, to demand accountability from local officials, and to effect changes in public policy. They acted together when disillusioned by the neglect of health hazards by the established political and industrial leaders. They thrived on strong leadership and the work of a small core group of activists, and they formed coalitions between traditional nature societies and newly formed grassroots environmental groups in order to maximize their influence.

The Glen Avon and Israeli cases also differ in significant ways. Penny Newman and the Concerned Neighbors were not content simply to raise consciousness and turn the remediation process over to the state. They aimed for a redistribution of power in which they would be party to the many decisions necessary to clean up the acid pits and monitor underground contamination of the water. For more than a decade, they continued to attend every hearing, give critical readings to every report, and file objections when they felt that the plans were deficient. They were also involved in a long-term legal suit to recover damages to their health and property.

The Haifa group, by contrast, was determined to stop the new plant and wanted to ensure continued monitoring of sulfur dioxide and other chemicals. But they did not insist on active participation in the monitoring and treatment of air pollutants. They did their service to society, and assumed that the victories they had won would be honored by responsible officials. Lynn Golumbic described them "as a group of women with Western views of democratic participation who used their education and dedication to organize and push for environmental change."[39] They believed that they had successfully demonstrated the power of public participation. Writing in the *Jerusalem Post,* environmental activist and journalist Devorah Ben Shaul applauded the Haifa mothers' victories: "But the real gain here is more than just the lowered sulfur content in Haifa's air. There is also the renewed confirmation that the citizen does have something to say about the quality of the environment in which he or she lives and works, and that ordinary citizens, working together, can bring about change."[40]

By succeeding as agents of change and by proving that citizens' voices do matter, these activists enhanced democracy. They were perfect examples of civic innovators, engaged citizens seeking new strategies to resolve contemporary problems.[41] In both the Haifa and the Glen Avon cases, the mothers' concern about environmental damage spurred the women to move beyond their normal daily lives to confront new challenges. They were not willing to define environmental hazards as part of the natural order or as an acceptable price of economic progress. They believed that dangerous pollutants resulted from the conscious decisions of industrial and government officials, and that these poisons in the air and water could cause irreparable harm to human health. The political and economic order had to be challenged if their children and communities were to grow and prosper.

In the wake of these achievements, these mothers' domain could no longer be limited to the home and child-oriented activities. The traditional boundaries between the public and private spheres no longer made sense. As mothers, they were obligated to confront even the most powerful forces to reverse dangerous actions and protect their families. They were drawn to environmental activism over other political activities because it centered on an issue that directly threatened their families. They described their desire to protect their children as the primary motivation for joining a local group; children provided the essential ideological underpinning for demanding action and lent weight to their cause. They represented a socially acceptable reason for mothers to move outside their conventional roles to engage in sit-ins, stand on picket lines, miss dinner, and leave the house uncleaned. The protection of children was more than a public rationale. In private life as well, it legitimized mothers' new roles for other family members and for the women themselves.

For leaders like Penny Newman, the initial desire to protect their children continued to transform their lives long after their children had grown up. Their commitment to social change and community building remained their central priority. In contrast, Lynn Golumbic was drawn back into the orbit of a job and caring for her family. Although she remained on the AACI's National Environmental Task Force, it was difficult to sustain her previous level of activism once she went back to work. Professional commitments often compete for women's time and attention; in most societies, working women continue to take the principal responsibility for home management and child care, leaving few hours for other commitments. Therefore, many of the most active women in the maternal movements have historically been those who were not working or who had part-time jobs.[42] There is little doubt, however, should the circumstances warrant it, should the environmental problems resurface, that Lynn Golumbic would once again reassert her leadership. She has learned far too much over the years to settle back into a nonpolitical role.

Like many Israeli women and others in the United States and elsewhere, Lynn Golumbic represents that reserve army of women activists who have made a substantial contribution to social and cultural change and then have stepped back to attend to other responsibilities. While they have reduced their day-to-day involvement, they continue to value their activist ideology. They are remembered by their peers and by subsequent leaders for what they attempted, sought, and achieved. They become part of the history and folklore of the movement.

From Dissident to Activist

Ja'ra Johnova became involved in the environmental movement in Czechoslovakia when her deep-seated disenchantment with the Communist government took a sharp personal twist with the oncoming birth of her first child in 1977. Until that time, like many people in Czechoslovakia, she had privately hated the Communists, who had seized power in 1948 in a political coup. They had been kept in power in 1968 when Soviet tanks crushed the popular reform movement known as Prague Spring, which had won public support on the promise of "socialism with a human face." By 1977, Ja'ra Johnova was fed up with the years of political repression. She knew that, at best, anyone who challenged the government faced the loss of a decent job and the right to adequate housing or a university education. At worst, dissenters faced the possibility of a long prison term.[43] Nevertheless, in 1977 Johnova's passive alienation became public dissidence when she decided to act on her belief that the debased environment in Prague was a direct threat to the health of her expected child.

The year 1977 was crucial in Czechoslovakian history. At the end of a decade of repressive rule that followed the Soviet invasion, a few hundred citizens denounced the Communist government for the first time. Led by writer and activist Václav Havel, the dissidents signed a statement calling for an end to government human rights abuses. Johnova and several members of her family decided to sign the Charter 77 document. This was a very courageous act, in which relatively few Czechoslovakians joined.[44] Johnova knew that she risked government censure and retaliation by participating in an open act of defiance. Nevertheless, she believed that officials had to be put on public notice that Czech citizens held them accountable for the lack of human rights:

> In 1977 my daughter Christina was born. That year was important for me because I signed Charter 77. I wasn't really interested in politics, but I wanted to say no to all the liars and all the lies. Many of my friends also signed. They were coal stokers and cleaners, musicians and students.
>
> For the first time, Charter 77 announced that all people had basic human rights. We supported the country's laws, but they were constantly being violated by the authorities. We were opposed to aggression and violence.

I knew, of course, that nothing would happen in the next year or two, but I believed that if we helped to do something, then there would be a long-term possibility of change. At least if I signed it, I would have the right to look my daughter straight in the eye.[45]

For Johnova and many women activists, children embodied the future. Would there be a reasonable society in place for them? Activities that showed no possibility of immediate gain became worthwhile because they might aid the children in the future. Ja'ra Johnova's optimism did not bear fruit until twelve years later, 1989, when the Charter 77 dissenters and hundreds of thousands of other Czechoslovakians forced the downfall of the Communist regime in a bloodless confrontation known as the Velvet Revolution. Yet during the intervening years of the late 1970s and 1980s, Johnova was not inactive. Despite the government's efforts to crush the opposition by severely limiting their employment options and by imprisoning their leaders, Johnova and her friends focused their attentions on the environment.

Johnova knew that the air pollution was so serious that it scarred all the city's buildings. The government exported the best coal, and kept the inferior soft brown coal as the domestic source of fuel, creating pollution that was so debilitating that the residents of Prague suffered high rates of asthma and other respiratory illnesses. The government's practice of removing children from the harsh city air for a few weeks may have appeased some worried parents, but did nothing to alleviate the disastrous environmental conditions. Johnova was even more disturbed by the government's effort to conceal incriminating data, and by its continued insistence that the pollution problem was under control. She and her husband were part of a small group of environmentalists, the Green Circle, that met to discuss a wide range of environmental problems within Prague and throughout the country. Their major goal was to penetrate government secrecy in order to obtain basic empirical data that would have been readily available in Western countries. They wanted information on dam construction, the operation of nuclear plants, soil contamination, and agricultural problems.

Although the Green Circle emphasized many environmental issues, Johnova herself continued to be most concerned with air pollution in Prague. In early 1989, ten months before the fall of the Communists, she met with several women who had organized themselves into a small group called Prague Mothers (Prazskewe Matky). These women were searching for a way to make a statement without going to jail. They were troubled that in the winter, when the pollution was most heavy, their children were chronically ill with headaches, vomiting, allergies, and respiratory diseases. Anna Hradilkova, one of the initial founders of Prague Mothers, described its origins:

> We had many good friends and spent hours talking about the situation. We were concerned about the health of our children, and this led my sister to write a petition in the form of an open letter to the government. We knew that we had to obtain as many signatures as possible, because the more people who signed, the smaller the danger would be. Many people would not sign it, because they were afraid. But, we managed to get five hundred signatures, one person passing it to another. Mothers were more prepared to sign because they were worried about the health of their children. We called it the petition of Prague Mothers because this was an emotional name. We never thought of forming an organization—it did not seem possible at the time.[46]

Anna Hradilkova and her friends circulated the petition to all the newspapers, but only one small environmental journal was willing to print it. The petition, mild by Western standards, defied the norms of Communist society by publicly challenging the government's assertions that there were no pollution problems. The petition demanded vital statistics about pollution and the impact on children's health, and went on to call for conversion from the highly polluting soft coal to gas as the principal means of heating buildings in the city.

In January of 1989 the Prague Mothers submitted their petition to many city offices, including the main pediatric health officer of Prague, the Office of Hygienics, and city hall. The officials responded to their concerns by asserting that the government was beginning to take appropriate steps and that, with the program underway, the air would be more suitable by the year *2010*. The Mothers were disgusted by this response. In their view no one seemed to be accountable for conditions that were damaging to their children in the present. Vague talk of improvement twenty years in the future merely underscored the failure of the government to meet the pressing needs of Czechoslovakian citizens.

After some additional correspondence and a fruitless meeting with local officials, the Mothers decided to organize one of the first environmental demonstrations ever to occur in Prague. This was a particularly daring act in a country known for citizens who held their tongue and kept their disapproval of public policy to themselves. Anna Hradilkova described the atmosphere in Czech society: "We lived in a society that had no ideas, that didn't believe in anything. Our generation just did not believe in community or anything else. People just tried to get the best without harming themselves. There was no responsibility to anything larger than your own family."[47]

Clearly, any idea of civic responsibility or individual responsibility for the common good went against the social norms. Yet, the Prague Mothers and other environmental dissidents wanted to revitalize democratic traditions as much as they desired to protest environmental degradation. The Prague Mothers were determined but not reckless. They carefully chose to hold their protest the day that visiting environmental officials were in town, because they knew that foreign journalists would be there to cover the meeting. This lessened the likelihood of police interference and harassment. About thirty women and their children marched in the demonstration, carrying a banner demanding improvement of the Prague environment.

Many friends and acquaintances accused them of irresponsibility for taking their children to such a dangerous event. Here the concept of motherhood became a double-edged sword. Taking children on the march no longer symbolized nurturance and love of family; marching with children represented risk and a real question of responsible action. Anna Hradilkova was well aware of the danger and the paradox involved in their political activity: "I understand that there is really a question whether to take children to such a risky event, but I think it is a much bigger danger for the children and their parents to remain passive. I think it was especially important for the bigger children who already understood the situation and realized that some things are worth fighting for."[48]

The Prague Mothers' determination to defy societal norms against challenging the authorities, their willingness to risk substantial punishment, was based on a multifaceted concept of courageous behavior. The Mothers had decided that they must act to protect their children from the effects of reprehensible official actions. To remain silent would give tacit support to policies they abhorred. They could no longer be complicit, precisely because so many of their compatriots seemed willing to remain silent in order to avoid any trouble. The Mothers had earlier taken the first steps of protest, and a public demonstration seemed an appropriate follow-up to their petition, which had garnered attention but ultimately had been unsuccessful in evoking a positive government response. They realized that a carefully planned outward show of resistance would be most effective if the children were there to represent all young victims of environmental degradation. While such a presence entailed risks, it also would be a significant learning experience for the children. They would march hand in hand with their mothers and with other children and would imbibe a political philosophy that required citizen participation in public life. Such a socialization experience, the Mothers reasoned, would pass important values from one generation to the next. Courage, the willingness to put oneself at risk for a principle, was a precious social resource that had to be taught to their children. To reinforce its significance required going beyond the mere mouthing of words. In this case, they were willing to expose their children to a short-term risk in order to achieve a long-term benefit for all youth in the city of Prague.

Ultimately, their action was successful. Foreign journalists covered the event, and police followed the protesters, but they did not break up the demonstration or disrupt their protest. An unauthorized political demonstration in a Communist country was so unusual that the Prague Mothers became an object of curiosity. Many bystanders gathered to watch and ask questions. Despite the dangers of participation in any act of dissidence, more than a hundred people in the crowd actually signed a version of their statement, which they delivered to several ministers just as the police arrived to confiscate it.

The Prague Mothers were exhilarated by the success of their public protest. The large number of signatures and interested bystanders reinforced their belief that they were acting on behalf of the larger community. Several women who had organized the demonstration continued to work together, and remained involved in the growing dissidence against the government. In November 1989, things came to a climax when police responded to a student march with massive brutality. By this time the government was no longer able to count on a quiescent population that would look the other way. Hundred of thousands of citizens assembled in the main square of Prague. The Civic Forum, the umbrella group of the opposition, demanded the resignation of the party leadership and free elections. Strikes and demonstrations developed throughout Czechoslovakia to support these demands. On December 10, 1989, the Communist Party leaders agreed to turn over power to the Civic Forum and its counterpart in Slovakia. Free elections were held for the first time in almost half a century, and Václav Havel was elected president.[49]

Initially, the Prague Mothers were thrilled by the realization of their dream. Although it was unclear if long-standing problems would necessarily be resolved, the Mothers decided to pursue their goals and become an official organization. They began to hold regular meetings and to invite others to attend. Both Anna Hradilkova and Ja'ra Johnova were important members of this new effort, but they found that the transformation from a small dissident group to an effective political-pressure organization was not easy.

Ja'ra Johnova remembered the frustration of those early days and their need to refocus: "In the beginning we tried to do too much, and it was a mess. We soon began to specialize, and we decided our main activity would be to focus on air pollution. Nowadays, we have quite a lot of information on it."[50]

Major problems continued to confront them. Even in the new regime, government officials argued that qualified experts should make environmental decisions, not mothers pressing for cleaner air.

They wanted the Prague Mothers to return to taking care of their children. Although they themselves held many traditional ideas about gender roles and family obligations, Johnova and Hradilkova and their friends totally rejected the view that they should be excluded from public discourse about the environment. Their earlier experiences as dissidents and environmental activists had persuaded them that responsible motherhood required them to remain concerned about environmental issues that affected the lives and health of their families and the entire society. They were less sanguine about the means with which to make the most effective contribution in this new regime. The Prague Mothers were disheartened by a raging new public desire for more cars, appliances, and household goods. This yearning for a consumer society only promised more air pollution in an already crowded Prague. The enemy was no longer visible in the form of corrupt, self-serving Communist bureaucrats.

The Prague Mothers found that environmental issues quickly lost the center stage they had held during the first days of the Velvet Revolution.[51] The new government began defending policies that gave priority to economic development over protecting clean air and water. The Prague Mothers wanted to continue fighting for their cause, and believed that their revolution could only be successful if citizens took personal responsibility for the common good. As Johnova explained: "Prague Mothers cannot just organize lectures; we have to engage in serious political activities."[52]

The difficulty encountered by mothers' groups in maintaining their effectiveness during a transition from authoritarian to democratic government has occurred in other countries as well. The Madres de Plaza de Mayo in Argentina demonstrated formidable courage when they marched weekly to protest the disappearance of their children during the military dictatorship of the 1970s and 1980s. The Madres became a symbol of morality, credited with inaugurating a new politics of mothers by breaking down earlier barriers against women's participation and against any form of public protest criticizing the military regime.

Yet the Madres had difficulty remaining effective once a democratic government was elected. Despite their attempts to maintain a unified

moral voice resisting amnesty for military leaders, they lacked the political know-how needed in the new political atmosphere. One student
of Argentine politics described the new requirements that the Madres
seemed to lack: "To be effective, women had to master the Armed
Forces' budget, convince the committee of Defense in the Legislature of
their demands, and analyze the potential effects of any hurried move
on the political chessboard. To be effective in this new environment required more than principled commitment; it required political acumen
and technical know-how."[53]

The Prague Mothers recognized that organizing in a post-Communist society required different organizational strategies and skills on
their part. It was no longer effective to show that environmental
degradation resulted from the corruption of the government and the
bureaucrats' lack of concern for its citizens. Ironically, the end of the
Communist government, which the Prague Mothers had long yearned
for, also brought great difficulties. The enemy of environmental progress became time, money, and concern for economic development.
Former friends and fellow dissenters scattered. People worked longer
hours and had less free time. The Prague Mothers felt caught between
the need to spend time with their children and their fight for a decent
environment, which was so essential for their children to thrive.[54]
There was limited precedent for voluntary organizations and public
participation in democratic politics in the new republic. The emergent
political culture left the Prague Mothers somewhat frustrated, but determined to figure out the next steps.

The Transformation of Mothers

The confrontation between mothers and the authorities in Czechoslovakia was the most adversarial and dangerous of the three cases we
have presented. But in all three countries, women activists came to realize that straightforward appeals to local officials did not result in the
desired actions, and they felt betrayed. They lost trust in the idea that
the established institutions would be able or willing to deal with the se-

rious environmental problems that profoundly and personally threatened them and their children. These women were not moved by officials' explanations that repairs would take time, were too costly, and could threaten local industry. Because they had never had political power, women activists were less invested in the traditional institutions, and were well placed to take on leadership in new groups such as Concerned Neighbors or the Prague Mothers. Angered by the platitudes intended to pacify them, women formed neighborhood networks to confront local conditions that affected their families. These new groups became the archetypes of what Alberto Melucci and Enrique Laraña and others have described as the "new social movements."[55]

As Melucci and Laraña have noted, these mothers' groups did not organize around traditional class issues. While not speaking with a Marxist vocabulary of class conflict and proletarian revolution, they did quickly see their battle as confronting powerful and often wealthy adversaries. The groups emerged in response to a concrete threat and were founded on the belief that conventional authorities overlooked their needs. Their ideology was diffuse, and emphasized grassroots involvement in decisions affecting their communities. The social structure of the organizations was nonhierarchical despite the rise of well-known leaders. Decisions were largely made by consensus, which made sense for women whose primary allegiance had been to the family and the neighborhood. These women crusaders were propelled forward by their strong identity as mothers, and took on new activist roles to reinforce their maternal obligations. But in so doing, those who became leaders and core-group activists permanently changed their own identity and the character of their families. Inevitably some conflicts arose.

Often, what began as a jointly approved attempt to protect the family later produced severe familial tensions. Some husbands and children resented the incessant meetings, constant phone calls, missed dinners, and kitchens filled with organizational literature. The intense level of activity could easily undermine the very family stability and harmony that the women had initially set out to preserve. Some women responded by renegotiating familial expectations and limiting their political participation. They maintained their activist commitments, but agreed to limit calls during dinner, to remove files from the kitchen, or to preserve certain days or hours for uninterrupted family time. Others could not renegotiate, and withdrew from their new lives as reformers when they realized that the disruption of their old patterns was too threatening. In a few cases, particularly in the United States, where divorce is more common, the strains were too deep, and marital relationships disintegrated.

This new form of activism for mothers had some resemblance to mothers' groups formed by earlier generations of women to address a range of crises. But the new grassroots organizers had some critical differences. For one thing, they had the advantage of a worldwide environmental movement that had paved the way by raising consciousness, establishing precedents, and supplying information and advice. Mothers were concerned with the impact of environmental degradation on their children and felt compelled to take action, but they recognized that these problems were political and required more than just maternal concern. They insisted that industry and government acknowledge that environmental and health damage was not the result of an act of God or the consequence of misguided but innocent policymakers. They demanded that officials admit that their policies were responsible for serious problems and that they take appropriate remedial action.

The struggle for changing local and national policies transformed these mothers and their communities. Years of dedication often involved them with officials from the Environmental Protection Agency, the Department of Energy, the Environmental Ministry of Israel, the Czech police, and others whom they had never believed they would encounter. Women learned how to organize their activities for widespread press coverage, and recruited technical advisers to assist them in the face of official criticism that they did not understand the technicalities of the issues involved. They quickly realized that their most important asset was widespread community support backed by a core group of committed workers who made the cause their first priority. In some instances in the United States and in Israel, groups turned to the courts to sue those who were responsible for community damage. These complex, lengthy class-action suits required extensive interaction with lawyers and grueling trial preparation. Even when they were victorious in their legal battles, difficult questions arose about administering the settlements fairly and not allowing monetary gains for some to derail the larger quest for repairing the environmental damage.

As important as the "mother role" was in motivating political action, the most effective leaders knew that they had to learn new skills of organizing, gain mastery over technical information, and reject often painful criticism that they were neglecting their families. A smaller group of leaders went beyond the push for a single neighborhood-improvement goal. For them, the experience of community organizing opened new possibilities for long-term engagement in pursuing social change and environmental safety. To gain leverage in their political systems, they used grassroots methods: building broad coalitions, developing appropriate expertise, and engaging in ongoing negotiations with officials throughout the corporate and government hierarchies.

Those who had to negotiate with the maternal activists understood the power they had developed. One Department of Energy official at the Fernald nuclear-bomb factory in Ohio described somewhat enviously the effectiveness of Lisa Crawford, the leader of FRESH, the community-based Fernald Residents for Environmental Safety and Health: "Lisa's a good leader. She does her homework, strikes good chords with the media. They know they can call her and get a quote. She knows where the sensitive spots are, how to pour salt into open wounds to get action. As a result of all her work, she's nationally known. She can call the secretary of energy and get a response. She's talked to the secretary, while I never have."[56]

This determination to be heard and get results led the mothers' groups to achieve unconventional but formidable power. With unconventional protest strategies and traditional gendered behavior that emphasized close personal relations, they forced attention from officials. By developing a sophisticated understanding of legal and technical issues, the women introduced new forms of civic engagement into their communities. As "civic innovators," they worked hard to maintain widespread public support that gave credence and political clout to their demands. The activists often served as "culture menders" in communities that were threatened both environmentally and psychologically. They demanded attention to hazards that had serious health implications and that demoralized the community. In resurrecting public morale, the citizen crusaders became a driving force for maintaining and building a democratic society.

4

Preserving the Farmland from Contamination

 The battle over garbage has come to typify the struggles of environmental activists throughout the industrial world. Garbage has become omnipresent, a product of modern life that continues to increase with every additional convenience and complexity of contemporary society. The problem of the growing quantity of solid waste has been complicated by the increasing production of toxic wastes that are the hallmark of a high-technology society—batteries, tires, toxic metals, and plastics—all of which are dumped on a daily basis.

During the past seventy-five years few people gave much thought to garbage. As long as the sanitation truck appeared and removed the garbage from their households, most residents believed that the municipal authorities had somewhere to put it. But with the growing emphasis on the environment in the last quarter century, this complacency eroded sharply. In the United States, traditional dumps gave way to lined sanitary landfills in which garbage was covered with soil in an effort to mask noxious odors and prevent leachate from contaminating the neighborhood. But experience soon proved that landfills were filling up rapidly and had a short life, and that it was impossible to prevent pollution of the soil and water as toxic wastes penetrated the ground.

Incineration has had a parallel history. After a period of naiveté in which urban governments believed they could burn anything, officials came to understand that toxic emissions were a serious environmental problem, as was the large quantity of ash produced by incineration. As sensitivity increased and new technology became available, many incinerator operators added scrubbers and filters in an effort to lower poisonous emissions. But while this improved the quality of the air, the residual ash grew more concentrated with toxics that ultimately needed to be disposed of somehow. Products that were used on a daily basis, such as plastic bags, disposable diapers, and Styrofoam cups, became a nightmare for waste-disposal experts both because of their high volume and their nonbiodegradability.

In the 1980s and 1990s the search for new landfills intensified throughout the United States and elsewhere. As land near major cities increased in value, many communities sought to haul their waste materials longer distances to landfills that could be built in sparsely populated areas, where real estate was cheaper and community opposition might be less severe. In addition, garbage disposal was privatized. Municipalities began contracting with private companies, which had purchased some of the latest technologies in Europe and elsewhere, to build and run landfill and incinerator operations. As the per ton costs of disposal skyrocketed, garbage became a big business, dominated by a few major corporations, such as Wheelabrator, Ogden Martin, and Waste Management.

These companies sited and planned the new landfills and incinerators and developed campaigns to overcome community opposition. One well-known report, issued by Cerrell Associates, a consulting firm in California, analyzed effective strategies to overcome opposition to new incinerators and landfills. The report examined demographic and sociological variables and concluded that "rural, low-income neighborhoods, whose residents had limited education, and tended to be older in age," were likely to offer the least resistance to a new waste-disposal site. The report further recommended that the decision to build a garbage-disposal facility in a new area would be most likely to succeed if the company had an experienced public-affairs director and a credible advisory committee who together could manage the public reaction.[1]

By the late 1980s, high-tech waste disposal ran into trouble as community opposition surfaced throughout the United States and soon followed in other countries. These grassroots activists, objecting to the siting of toxic-waste disposals, sanitary landfills, or new incinerators, had a crucial advantage over groups protesting the dangers from bomb-factory radiation or the damage from decades of exposure to industrial air pollution. For activists opposing new landfill and disposal sites, the damage was not yet done. Communities could mobilize to prevent future degradation by keeping Waste Management or Wheelabrator out of their region. Unlike Downwinders, organizers against new hazardous-waste sites could not rely on victimization to play a major role, since no damage had actually occurred yet. But to prevent the construction of new facilities and thus thwart the wishes of waste-disposal companies that had the approval of regulatory agencies, timing was crucial. Most citizen activists understood that the stakes were high and that they would have to reorder their lives if they were to succeed in preventing the storage of garbage in their areas. They often had to sustain public opposition over a period of years. In cases where the leadership was not able to maintain strong public support, communities were not successful in combating business and government interests.

As rural people living in areas that were often conservative or apolitical, activists soon found themselves playing roles that felt very strange. Their world was turned upside down as they found themselves using protest tactics that they had formerly associated with urban radicals, people as different from themselves as they could imagine. Their sense of self was jarred as they built alliances with those whom they would have rejected under other circumstances. Like activists combating different threats, they underwent a personal transformation that was often disorienting. Furthermore, their own communities were often divided between those who feared the damage that would be wrought by a landfill or toxic-waste dump and others who believed that a new industry would bring important economic opportunities. Former friends could easily become bitter opponents. "Far-out radicals" could become new allies. The whole system of modern life, with its emphasis on technological solutions for problems, came in for scrutiny. Reassurances of "state-of-the-art" technologies no longer satisfied their doubts.

The community environmental activists, whose constant refrain was "Not in my backyard," were quickly labeled NIMBYs. NIMBY came to be a pejorative label that described selfish groups who promoted their private interests over the common good. This attack on their credibility forced community activists to develop a broader view of the issues and a more sophisticated approach to the problem of waste disposal. This criticism of NIMBY activities has appeared internationally as well. Critics here and abroad have scorned grassroots efforts to keep waste dumps out of the activists' regions, but others have seen these actions as the building block of a major social movement.[2] Environmentalists have argued that local restraints on ever-expanding landfills are crucial to building support for a system that will depend on waste reduction, recycling, and reuse.

In the cases that follow we describe the requisites for effective local grassroots activism to go beyond simply preserving the immediate environment without regard to the impact on others. When a strong ideology about community responsibility develops and one or more committed leaders emerge, we see a radical transformation of activists' ideas and strategies. In both eastern Washington state and in Kibbutz Mishmar HaEmek, Israel, initial community resistance to a new garbage facility propelled local leaders to develop expertise in garbage separation and treatment, in alternative methods of treating waste, and in legal and political decision making. Armed with a sophisticated understanding of the issues, activists assumed a broader view of environmental problems and thereby resisted the label of NIMBY. Instead, they advocated major changes in social and economic behavior without ever giving up their battle to keep the landfill or incinerator out of their region. These cases are not isolated incidents. They reflect our findings in several other communities in the state of Washington and confirm the conclusions of other scholars and public-interest groups.[3]

But the ability to develop a larger understanding of the environmental issues does not always occur. In Slovakia, the initial enthusiasm for addressing problems of a toxic-waste dump waned when distrust of the leaders and economic dislocation overcame environmental anxieties. The townspeople would have needed greater faith in public dialogue and more experience with the democratic process to develop a sense of solidarity and transform a momentary crisis into a lasting social movement. Without some institutionalized processes that allow serious debate about political issues, the public was easily swayed. In one moment, they regarded the environmental leaders as heroes. Shortly after, they turned on them as enemies. This volatility in public understanding and interest is present in all areas of social change. In Slovakia, it was particularly severe, since the people had to undergo so many radical transitions in so short a time.

Stewards of the Land

A picnic was called for Sunday afternoon at the Benge, Washington, school playground, a small community of less than one thousand people. A couple of dozen folks arrived, carrying casseroles and salad as their contribution to the potluck event. They came from Benge and Ritzville and Lind and a number of other tiny communities scattered in the wheat-farm country of eastern Washington state.[4] They ranged in age from mid-twenties to more than seventy, and they greeted each other with warmth and pleasure. There were old friends and new, brought together by their passionate opposition to the siting of a new toxic-waste dump in the midst of their agricultural region. They were surprised to find some strangers from the East Coast attending the party, but more than welcoming when their neighbors Harold and Dorothy Clinesmith introduced them as researchers who were interested in finding out more about the garbage controversy.

Harold and Dorothy were clearly the driving force behind the picnic. Dorothy oversaw the placement of all the food, thanking the various contributors and monitoring the distribution of food. Harold greeted the newcomers, relaying the last details in the battle with Ecos waste company and with the Department of Ecology of Washington State. In his early sixties, he was cheerful, fatherly, and full of energy as the president of the local grassroots group.

As the afternoon wore on, many of the participants spoke of their commitment to the area. In this region of southeastern Washington, they explained, there were only eight inches of rainfall annually, but there were eighty inches of topsoil. These extraordinary conditions were ideal for growing wheat, and that is precisely what most of them did so well. The toxic-waste companies might have thought that this was a perfect place to dump their stuff, in that the land was high and dry, with hard basalt rock underneath. But cracks riddled the rock, and anyone who thought about it would recognize that the toxics would eventually make their way down to the aquifer.

Friendly and forthcoming, the group thought of themselves as hard-working family folks who had chosen a wonderful way of life. Normally conservative Republicans who never considered themselves protesters, they did not have much patience for a state government that was considering building a toxic-waste dump in an area where it could threaten the food chain. The risk was even greater than it had seemed at first. They also feared that the Japanese government would get wind of the contamination and would no longer buy their wheat. Japan was a major customer, and without these exports, the economic future would be grim.

The controversy had begun two years earlier, in 1989, when rumors circulated that a company had been hired to do land assessment in the area for both a toxic-waste dump and a solid-waste landfill. Initial activity took place in Ritzville, a little further to the north, and soon after that a meeting was called about a possible facility in the Benge area. Harold Clinesmith and several others attended the meeting, although he was quite certain at the time "that the government would not do anything bad to us." Initially, he felt reassured by the waste company's statement that they only planned to use "state-of-the-art technology." Besides, some of the opponents who came down from

Ritzville seemed so radical and had come on so strong. Their style of opposition was alien to a couple who had farmed there for four decades. The technical terms initially seemed confusing and unfamiliar to them, and Harold and Dorothy Clinesmith were not certain what to think. By the end of the evening, however, doubts began to creep in. Was this a risk they could afford to take?

Others were initially even more adamant. Greg Beckley, a forty-year-old farmer with several small children, heard about the land assessment from a friend and responded immediately. Living only an hour away from the Hanford Nuclear Reservation had given him some idea of how land could be ruined: "I knew of what Hanford had done to us, and I knew what other industries could do to us. I simply wanted to protect myself, my heritage, and my children. They were changing our environment; something foreign was coming in, and it was not acceptable to us."[5] Like other environmental groups, the wheat farmers had to articulate a belief system that supported their opposition to the landfill. The mothers' groups in California, Prague, and Haifa sought credibility through their children. Their cries of "Let our children breathe" carried a cross-national message that both legitimized their complaint and explained their sense of urgency. The wheat farmers' overriding concern was the sanctity of the land and the obligation they felt to serve as its responsible stewards. Greg Beckley, like several others, had a long heritage on that land: "I'm a fourth-generation wheat grower; my grandparents and forefathers have been here, and they worked this country for some time. They were proud of what they left to future generations, and I would like to pass the same thing on. It is a beautiful place to live, and I am not going to let somebody take it from me. I guess that's what keeps pushing me along."[6] For the Clinesmiths and several others, the obligation to the land was part of a larger religious sense of obligation. Dorothy Clinesmith described the religious awe that she and Harold felt toward farming: "Well, I feel that the good Lord provided this way of life to us, and it's one that we love, and I feel like we have the obligation to protect it. It isn't basically even ours—He loaned it to us, and we're to be good stewards and take care of it, and pass it on to others, and it should be in good shape when they get it."[7]

The farmers' profound commitment to a way of life and their strong ties to the land clearly had deep roots. Like many activists who found their way of life threatened by intrusions from government and industry, these folks imbued their land with special meaning. For some, the land held religious significance. They believed that God meant for them to watch out for and preserve this precious resource. For others, it was the symbol of their culture, providing work and enabling families and neighbors to thrive in an atmosphere that they defined as healthy and invigorating and ideal for raising families. They never anticipated, however, that their traditional beliefs about land and rural culture would propel them into a life of activism wholly unimagined just a few years earlier.[8]

Unfortunately, the lives of grassroots activists did not always fit easily into their schedules or their sense of themselves. The isolation of their farms meant that every hearing held in Seattle or Olympia represented lengthy travel, in addition to the time spent in the statehouse or at meetings. Phone bills could run as high as $300–$400 a month, since almost all phone calls were long distance. John and Gretchen Harder, a young couple in their thirties, described the physical and psychological toll that so many of the others also experienced:

> It takes a commitment to drop out of your day-to-day livelihood routine and go to Olympia, make the sixteen-hour commitment to five hours over, five hours back, and whatever testifying you do, and blow out of your comfort zones in having to get up there in front of some state legislative panel. I am not the most technically expert member of the coalition. We are up against the developers, who have the monetary interest and the professional public-relations people marketing their program—and they're countered by Farmer John—you've got to be kidding.[9]

For John and Gretchen Harder and the others, such disruption of their work schedules, such disturbance of their "comfort zones," and such confrontation with well-paid and well-trained antagonists were all integral parts of a complex syndrome tearing away at their cultural integrity. On the land where they had been born and raised and had begun their own families, they were secure in the knowledge of their own competence. They knew the obstacles to raising good crops and maintaining an economic balance sheet. But testifying in Olympia or Seattle was different. They were in uncharted waters. As John Harder plaintively stated, they were out of their depth. The people across the room representing major industries were prepared and determined to hold a mirror before the farmers to reflect their awkwardness, lack of knowledge, and naiveté. Yet, despite the anxiety, Harder and the others continued to fight. Their entire way of life, their identification as farmers, their bonds with each other, their determination to preserve their community, and their belief in their cause all fueled their courageous reactions. Their shared culture of solidarity with their neighbors would not allow them to retreat. While their adversaries emphasized their inadequacies, they drew strength from a commonly held belief system and an organization that celebrated their tenacity and integrity. The loss of time for work and children, the fear of lawsuits, and the financial costs were exacerbated by the deep regrets most felt over the divisions in their community. Greg Beckley had high school classmates who no longer spoke with him, because they disagreed so profoundly about the toxic-waste and garbage facilities. Beckley refused to give any business to merchants in Ritzville whom he blamed for initiating the battle by introducing and supporting the waste-disposal corporations: "I haven't spent 25¢ in Ritzville in three years. I never plan to go back to Ritzville. The bunch of merchants up there—they brought these companies in, touted them around like tin gods, and said, 'Hey, this is best for us.' It turned a lot of people off. There's been a total economic boycott in some of these towns, and it has hurt real bad because they can't afford to lose a thing."[10]

After finishing college in Seattle, one recently married couple in their mid-twenties had returned to the area where they had grown up, only to find their town changed. A few years earlier all the residents had gathered to take a big group "family" photo on the occasion of the town's centennial. Now everyone was bitterly divided. Michelle Smith said that "it is just like two separate communities living together. Everybody knows who is on whose side." Her husband Tim agreed: "It's very stressful, just to go into town to get parts or something for the equipment, because you never know if you will run up against someone who is going to make a smart-aleck remark. I always think about it when I go into town, and I have to prepare myself."[11]

The pain of disrupted relationships was clearly revealed by both Greg Beckley and Tim Smith. A once congenial, supportive, and attractive community was now torn by vehemently competing definitions of what was good for the area. Each side criticized the other for a foolish and stubborn allegiance to its own position. The rifts were so deep that once-pleasant encounters in a store were to be avoided. Tim Smith could not readily accept so drastic a change. He was deeply troubled by it. The world of his childhood, of his growing-up years, had been severely undermined. The culture of solidarity built on the common experience of the wheat farmers now had an exclusionary clause. Once-valued neighbors were no longer on the inside. They were now defined as the "other," as people whose businesses should not be patronized, as those whose goodwill could no longer be guaranteed. Beckley, Harder, Smith, and the others also understood that their stress was partly offset by the commitment and by the appreciation of new friends made through this crusade. Young and old had come together to see their project through, and the bonds of solidarity among them were clear. Yet the whole experience was very unsettling for those who had initially been skeptical about or hostile to environmental organizations. Suddenly people were identifying them as liberals, a tag that did not sit comfortably at first. John Harder and his wife, Gretchen, felt the contradictions, and could not reconcile all of them: "We don't want our chemicals taken away. They are our crop management tools. We don't want a bunch of strange urban environmental interests dictating how we manage our resources."[12]

But contrary to the normal Wheat Farmer Association's position, John now began to see "danger in labeling all environmental groups as the enemy." He recalled the counsel of a former wheat growers' lobbyist: "Never trust an environmentalist, because they are going to get you." Yet, that no longer seemed so certain when the Washington Toxics Council, Washpirg, and Greenpeace had given them support and assistance. "I used to be so certain that I was a conservative Republican," Gretchen Harder said, "but now I am just not sure—maybe I am really a liberal Democrat."[13] Unlike many grassroots activists who enthusiastically turned to environmental organizations for help in building an alternative network of power, the wheat farmers often felt ambivalence and conflict. Environmental groups offered expertise and access to other activists equally concerned about the ramifications of toxic-waste dumps. Yet, the political orientation and even the lifestyle of many environmentalists seemed alien to conservative farmers, who had long defined the environmental groups as hostile to their dependence on the use of pesticides in growing wheat. Nevertheless, the crisis in the community fostered strange and unpredictable alliances. While some neighbors no longer spoke to each other, strangers who had once seemed so distant now became dependable allies.

For some, the identity crisis that accompanied these changes led to a feeling of burnout. Yet, many refused to walk away, in part because of their love of the land and in part because of the rage that Ecos Corporation and Waste Management Inc. engendered through what the farmers believed were their distortions and underhanded tactics. Greg Beckley was ordinarily a soft-spoken man, except when he described his views of the company's tactics: "When Ecos first came out with their promotional videotape, it was a slap in our face. Here they had just purchased nineteen thousand acres of prime irrigated land in Lind, and in their promotional tape they are telling us, gee, we won't site it in an agricultural area, not anywhere near farmland. Damnedest bunch of people that ever set foot on the face of the earth."[14]

The Citizens Hazardous Waste Coalition, under the tireless leadership of Harold Clinesmith, spent several years battling the plans to build any toxic-waste dump or hazardous-waste incinerator in the eastern Washington region. Since the Department of Ecology received at least three separate proposals for incinerators in the area, the activists often felt as if they were fighting a moving target, but by the end of 1992 Ecos had withdrawn its application for a waste facility. Although pleased that the much-dreaded plant would not threaten their nearby farmland, the activists quickly realized that peaceful harmony would not immediately return to their region. One letter to the local paper by a severe critic of the environmentalists revealed the deep divisions that remained in the community: "Hazardous waste facilities are the workhorses of our economy. They provide a necessary service for all business and industry."[15]

But those supporting the landfills were not simply disappointed by the failure to build the new facility. They blamed the environmentalists for denying the area new opportunities: "The fate of our project may be cause for celebration by NIMBYs (Not-in-my-Backyard) but what does it do to help solve the problem? . . . Back to the self-proclaimed heroes. For those who think the project's failure had something to do with the location in an agri[cultural] area—it didn't. As for the role of the opposition itself, the claim that prospective buyers were deterred by its ferocity? They weren't."[16]

Knowing that their adversaries remained determined and well organized, the coalition turned their attention to a new proposal, this time by another major company, Rabanco, to build a hazardous-waste incinerator in the next county. The activists uncovered memos between Rabanco and its public-relations consultants that underscored the magnitude of the campaign to persuade the public to accept the toxic-waste incinerator. In one communication to the vice president of Rabanco, the professional public-relations consultant outlined what he thought the company's strategy should be. He began by focusing on the upcoming public hearings, and ended by recommending that the company spend $10,000 per month to preserve any hope of overcoming grassroots opposition: "These public sessions are designed to permit citizens to have an impact on the decision-making process and are good forums for presenting information about the project. However, they are also designed to be an outlet for public dissent, and thereby become media events. . . . The Department of Ecology needs to know that your project is perceived as safe by a significant number of residents, and is important to at least some of the institutions and business interests in Grant County. The media need to have that perception, as well." Recognizing the effectiveness of local opposition to the toxic-waste incinerator, the consultant continued by chastising the company for insufficient work on the public relations and marketing of their product. He continued: "At this stage, I believe it would be very difficult for you to field a team of Grant County citizens willing to speak on your behalf." But, he went on, all was not lost. Companies could rely on expensive professional services that could turn around public opinion and win the confidence of the Department of Ecology in order to acquire the necessary permits. The consultant's lengthy analysis of the situation concluded with the following recommendation: "In addition to your and Linda's present level of personal involvement, I believe you could effectively schedule a person in Grant County two days a week. To send a consultant into the county for two days a week, including time, travel and expenses, would run about $10,000 per month depending on the billing rate."[17]

Harold Clinesmith was shocked when he found this memo in the local library; it had been accidentally included in a folder that contained correspondence between the company and the Department of Ecology. He responded by using the only strategy available to local citizens' groups, publishing it in its entirety in one of the local community papers.[18] By exposing the plans to win over public opinion through public-relations agents, Clinesmith hoped to persuade more community members that they were being manipulated. He wanted to convince the undecided that the activists were acting on behalf of the local residents, while the companies were using hired guns so they could make a profit. Persuading a larger public was one of the most important battles of all.[19]

Beyond that, the activists kept up pressure on regulatory agencies. They learned the technical and legal issues and petitioned the Environmental Protection Agency to designate the aquifer that supplied water to the area as the "sole-source aquifer." Such a designation would require additional regulatory protection against the possibility of any toxic contamination of the area's single water supply. By the summer of 1994, Rabanco had abandoned its plan to build an incinerator in Grant County, and decided to sell the land it had purchased in the mid-1980s. The company's officers would not acknowledge that the opposition had caused them to abandon their plans. "Building an incinerator doesn't seem plausible any more," announced the company's president. "We're looking for offers from people wanting to do something different, something plausible on the land."[20]

As various proposals rose and fell, Harold Clinesmith and his colleagues continued to insist that the state adopt more stringent siting requirements for any hazardous-waste facility. They rejoiced when their eastern Washington water supply was declared a sole-source aquifer, and dismayed when they learned in late 1995 that new rules would now allow certain levels of hazardous waste to be incorporated into a solid-waste landfill. The victories were sweet, and some of the threats to the nearby agricultural lands were diminishing, but the underlying problems would not go away. A significant question remained unanswered. Were the changes in state regulation the direct result of better-designed and -operated solid-waste landfills including state-of-the-art technology, as Waste Management insisted,[21] or were they the result of effective lobbying by the corporations and their lobbyists?

Clinesmith, aided by various northwestern environmental organizations, continued to bombard local newspapers and officials with letters arguing that the problem could only be solved by much more extensive separation of waste material, expanded reuse and recycling, and a limited amount of incineration that should be managed close to the area of production. Their initial NIMBY approach was now replaced by a sophisticated understanding of solid- and toxic-waste issues. The problems they faced went well beyond any particular proposed disposal plan. The solution to their problem meant, as two students of the subject argued, changing from a system in which private industry makes decisions to bury or burn waste matter based on profit-and-loss statements to one in which strategies are developed so that "post-manufacturing, post-consumer 'discards' are potentially reusable and recyclable."[22] The activists had long ago abandoned any NIMBY instincts just to make sure that the waste dump would not be in their area. They had become political activists who insisted on participating in crucial regional decisions. They advocated approaches that would radically change ideas about legitimate manufacturing methods, that would repudiate excessive packaging and disposable goods in favor of a system that demanded reduction of wastes and active programs to reuse and recycle manufactured goods.

The wheat farmers of eastern Washington were white middle-class Americans who had always believed that they had control over their own lives. But maintaining that control required years of commitment from a core group of activists, and substantial support from many of their neighbors. In other areas of the country, the battle is similar, but even more difficult. Frequently, landfills and toxic-waste dumps are built in remote areas where poor residents, frequently people of color, must overcome a history of powerlessness in order to confront their adversaries. Several Native American reservations in the southwest, such as the Cahuilla Reservation in Southern California, were designated as prime targets for urban waste and sewage sludge. Working with several tribal businessmen and their non-Indian partners, the city of San Diego planned to transport its sewage sludge to the Cahuilla Reservation for decontamination. Tribal members, organized as part of the California Indians for Cultural and Environmental Protection, objected to attempts to bribe and intimidate them, and exposed EPA plans to bypass appropriate public hearings. Caught between the EPA and the Bureau of Indian Affairs, tribal council members ultimately could not defeat the political maneuvering that overturned the antidumping and antipollution measures. Determined to fight back, they suffered from small numbers, a paucity of economic resources, and limited leverage on the system.[23] But their battle continues with the assistance of the Citizens Clearinghouse for Hazardous Waste and the absolute determination of a dedicated group of tribal members.

Like other activists, these determined few had to define the problem so the public could understand and support them, had to develop a culture of solidarity to withstand bribes and attacks on their credibility, and had to join a larger network that could assist them in their struggle. For the wheat farmers of eastern Washington, as for the activists on the Cahuilla Reservation, it required courage to forgo the ordinary rhythms of daily life, to engage in sustained, sometimes exhausting activity, and to withstand public accusations. They were willing to do this in the name of preserving a quality of life that had come under attack from cities and corporations that needed a place to dump other people's waste.

You Can't Put That Garbage Here

Israel, a country of 5.5 million people who live in an area about the size of New Jersey, produces about 3.1 million tons of solid wastes each year. The steadily increasing population and the rising standard of living have led experts to estimate that the production of solid wastes will continue to grow at about two percent annually. Until the Ministry of the Environment began to turn its attention to the mounting problem of garbage, virtually all of the country's wastes were dumped in landfills that had been built with little regard for environmental considerations. Illegal dumping, concentration of the population in the Tel Aviv area, and a poorly developed recycling program all contributed to a growing sense that the problem was reaching crisis proportions.[24]

In 1989 the government approved a National Outline Scheme for Solid Waste Disposal. The Ministry of the Environment announced a plan to reduce the several hundred small and twenty-nine large landfills to twenty-five within five years, and to an even smaller number of well-controlled landfills after that. Their goal was to shut down improperly maintained sites, organize a national plan for garbage disposal, and attend to the growing crisis of garbage from the densely populated cities in the center of the country. Despite all the good intentions and revisions of the plan, six years later progress had been slowed, and conflict had emerged between the government experts and community-based groups throughout the country.

Reuven Bezner was born on Kibbutz Mishmar HaEmek in 1930, the year his parents joined with others to found the kibbutz. Located about forty-five minutes from Haifa, in the lower Galilee, the kibbutz has a mixed agricultural and industrial economy. Like many well-established kibbutzim in that area, it looks like an idyllic rural town, with small houses and gardens surrounded by green fields and young forests. Bezner is very much the Sabra (native-born Israeli) and kibbutznik in his love of the land, his joy in nature, and his deep commitment to preserving the rural heritage of pure water and a clean environment, passed on by the pioneers who built the kibbutz. He remembers with pleasure and pride his father's important role in the early days of building the water system, which modernized an ancient viaduct built almost two thousand years earlier by the Romans. The new system carried water from two abundant streams to the settlement of several hundred families below.

Like many members, Reuven Bezner has held many jobs in the kibbutz and is currently a mechanic in charge of maintaining the agricultural equipment in the kibbutz garage. In the past, he served as secretary of the kibbutz, one of the most significant leadership positions, an opportunity that gave him an understanding of the complex issues involved in economic and political decision making in his small egalitarian community. He spent several years in Canada as a representative of the kibbutz movement and has traveled throughout the world. Yet Bezner remains a local person, a modern Israeli devoted to his kibbutz and the quality of its environment.

The routine of Bezner's life was radically transformed in 1990, when he learned that a neighboring kibbutz, Ein Hashofet, was investigating the possibility of locating a large landfill on land between the two kibbutzim. The dump, located just above the two aqueducts built sixty years ago by Bezner's father, would become the principal waste site for garbage from the cities of Haifa and Hadera and from elsewhere in the northern half of Israel. The prospect made Bezner fearful of a precipitous decline in the quality of life in Mishmar HaEmek:

> The place where Ein Hashofet decided to build the garbage dump is exactly at the top of this valley, just where the water comes down to our kibbutz. It is an absurd idea that we are going to drink water coming from the garbage dump, including wastes from hospitals that have been thrown into the dump, radioactive materials from factories. It would be very dangerous. I am also concerned that they want to locate the dump in the middle of the forest, where we walk and look at trees. These are the reasons that we are so concerned and why we or-

ganized this group of people against the dump. I have a very emotional feeling for this place and I think it is very important for the kibbutz.[25]

Like his counterparts in the United States, Bezner was initially motivated by a strong sense of betrayal. How could a neighboring kibbutz imagine assaulting the environment with a garbage dump? After all, they shared the same Zionist ideology about settling the land and living communally in a rural setting that was partially agricultural. Nevertheless, a small group of the economic leaders at kibbutz Ein Hashofet thought that building and running a major landfill offered important economic-development opportunities for the kibbutz, which, like many kibbutzim, was suffering from a decline in agricultural income, high debt, and an inadequate industrial base. Giora Yanai, one of the Ein Hashofet advocates of building such a business, explained his interests:

I know about this waste dump mainly because I was part of the economic committee of the kibbutz. We had a big trucking business and were looking for different markets. About ten years ago [1982], we found out that dumping waste is a very good business. I got all the figures and started to check if there were a possibility in this area. Since that time we have been checking, testing to get permissions and the necessary licenses. We were aware of all the ecological problems and knew that everything had to be done under conditions that would cause no damage to anyone.

The garbage business would, in Yanai's estimation, be an important growth industry that would create significant partnerships between the kibbutz and private industry: "One of the future areas in which the industry will develop will be recycling. This is a universal worldwide problem. I think we have a good chance if we are close to it, working and knowing the problems, to get into this type of business in the early stages. I'd like to get into this area of industry."[26]

When Reuven Bezner learned of the plans at Ein Hashofet, he immediately saw the dangers and the need to educate and energize others in his kibbutz and in the regional moshav and kibbutz council.[27] Bezner went through the process characteristic of so many environmental crusaders. His roots and childhood memories provided the emotional basis for his concern, but he quickly realized that these subjective motivations would never be adequate to convince and convert others. He had to collect the appropriate data and develop technical and legal arguments to counter the pro-business proponents at Ein Hashofet and the decision makers at the Ministry of the Environment who had decided that this area met their requirements and could become a linchpin in their national plan. He spent the first two years of his crusade developing the necessary expertise: "I read books and talked to many people from abroad and here in Israel. I developed many friends who have helped me. I am now an expert in garbage in general and garbage dumps especially. By now I am a doctor of garbage dumps."[28]

Bezner examined and filmed virtually every legal and illegal garbage dump in the country. He used maps, diagrams, and home videos to demonstrate his major points. All the evidence pointed to the inability of Israel to enforce its environmental regulations anywhere, particularly at the per ton price garbage collectors could charge. The graphic pictures of poorly maintained dumps throughout the country confirmed Bezner's skepticism about the promises of "state-of-the-art" technology with little or no danger to surrounding residents. Bezner and his supporters recognized that a negative critique would never satisfy those who had to alleviate the waste-disposal crisis in the country. He convinced his kibbutz to hire engineers to offer alternative plans that would be environmentally more responsible. Like other effective activists, he reached out to experts, scientists, lawyers, and engineers to enhance his expertise and provide him with credibility.

Once armed with knowledge about the dangers of even the most carefully built dumps and with information about the need for a nationwide program for garbage separation and recycling, Bezner organized a nonprofit organization to convince the local regional council, composed of kibbutzim and moshavim in the area, to withdraw their initial support for the Ein Hashofet landfill. He was able to garner support from the entire region and especially from his own kibbutz, Mishmar HaEmek, which was the only settlement directly downstream from the proposed site of the landfill. Despite goodwill and support from many allies, the burden of the battle was fought by Bezner and his wife, for whom it became an all-consuming emotional battle: "Our son thinks it is not a good thing that my wife and I are so impassioned. It is not good for the family. We have seven grandchildren, a big family, and other projects. We spent too much time on this; we took it too emotionally and got too involved."

Despite some regrets about the personal costs of their battle, the Bezners would not rest until they were assured that the garbage was not coming into their area. Supported by a strong coalition of kibbutz members and by other activists in the region, who clearly saw him as their leader, Reuven Bezner went before the entire community of Ein Hashofet and argued vigorously against the ill-advised path that their leaders had taken. Some Ein Hashofet residents were sympathetic—those who held the same pastoral values that had initially motivated him. Itsik Shafran, a member of Kibbutz Ein Hashofet, led the internal opposition to the landfill plans. As the head of the beef-cattle operation in the kibbutz, he spent considerable time outdoors, in the area where the landfill was to be built. "I live there and work there and watch the spring there. And I can imagine how it will look after the project will start and how the plants will be completely destroyed. We can declare that we will protect everything and take all the precautions that will be needed to protect from air pollution, winds, smell, or whatever. But something will happen in the long or short run." Like Bezner, Shafran feared technical inadequacies, and valued the preservation of a pastoral way of life that provided the basis for everything he did:

> We want this area to remain as virgin as it is, not to be involved in a project that would be dangerous. But we also have a principle about how we would like to educate our children. If we have this operation here, we will be like everyone else—factories, garbage operation. It will undermine the unique community we are. We will build it; then we will find an Arab worker to operate

the tractors; the guard there will be Arab for sure. None of us will stay there twenty-four hours a day. Soon it will have no connection with this kibbutz, and nobody will be in touch with the problems or involved in controlling them.[29]

Shafran, like Bezner and like the wheat farmers of Washington State, defined the land as much more than a source of income. The kibbutz members had actively chosen to live in a small rural agricultural and communal settlement. Shafran had not left for the lure of the city as many of his childhood peers had done. To threaten the land was to call a whole way of life into question, and for him it was not worth any potential profit. The Ein Hashofet kibbutz operates on a town-meeting model, with all members voting on major decisions and policies. The membership debated the issue for several nights. At the end only seven people voted to proceed with building the dump; the rest rejected the proposal as too dangerous or too divisive. They preferred to defer to the passionate objections of their neighbors and to pursue other projects.

Despite this major victory in 1992, the battle did not end. While Ein Hashofet had rejected the landfill proposal, they had agreed that if the Ministry of the Environment insisted on building a garbage dump in their region, then they had to be the ones to run and control such a facility. The commitment of the ministry to establishing new and improved landfills and the undying conviction of the economic leaders of Ein Hashofet left the door open to renewed possibilities.

The conflict initially was between those at Ein Hashofet who had pursued the business opportunity and others who had rejected it. The critics abhorred the prospect of hundreds of trucks carrying tons of garbage every day, the smells and the noise of the traffic, as well as the possible dangers from the toxic items that accompanied garbage in a modern industrial society. Like the communal divisions in eastern Washington, the disagreement separated those who saw advantages from economic development from critics who decried the destruction of a rural life, in which they saw themselves as workers and stewards of the land. Ideologically, the opponents were not Luddites or even profoundly ecological people who wanted to live as close to a state of nature as possible. They believed in modern agriculture and had actively participated in the transformation of the land to make it more productive, but they rejected changes that brought the harshness of urban industrialization into their midst.

The initial decision of the Ministry of the Environment to build a landfill in the Ein Hashofet area demonstrates the complexity of the garbage issue. As Bezner mounted his campaign against the landfill, he found himself in direct opposition to Uri Marinov, the director general of the ministry. Marinov was not a typical representative of industry, unsympathetic to environmental considerations. Rather, he was a well-known environmentalist who had a background in veterinary medicine and had been one of the founders of the Environmental Protection Service when it was first established in 1973. When that service became a full-fledged ministry in 1988, Marinov became its first director general, the highest civil service employee in the ministry, and was involved in environmental issues both nationally and internationally.

Marinov understood how difficult it was to make progress on the environmental front in Israel. In the government it was considered a low priority, and the public was very reluctant to participate in environmental activity. He put this situation in blunt terms reminiscent of statements from old-time environmental activists: "Until today the environment is not considered a very important issue in Israel. Certainly, things have changed since the 1970s, but with all our wars, peace, immigration, and other national priorities, I would say the most difficult job we have is to 'sell' the issue of the environment to our decision makers."[30]

At the same time, Marinov was an experienced government employee who knew how to manipulate the political system to build some authority and budget for the fledgling Ministry of the Environment. Victories were incremental, however, and the ministry remained one of the most poorly funded in the government. Successful ministers often left that cabinet post to become heads of larger, more amply funded ministries, subjecting the Environmental Ministry to frequent turnover and vacancies. Nevertheless, Marinov pursued several major priorities for the country, and oversaw the plan to build facilities for the ever-increasing garbage Israel was producing.

Marinov had little patience for the opposition that had developed to the proposed Ein Hashofet landfill. He saw the problem of overflowing waste in poorly built landfills throughout the country and believed the new landfill was a major improvement. He was utterly convinced by the experts in hydrogeology that such a landfill would not be dangerous to the water supply and would be a step forward in dealing with the country's environmental situation. He viewed the opposition as "NIMBY *par excellence:* We don't want a sanitary landfill in our backyard. I met with them, and they were telling me that as youngsters they used to run around the hills in shorts and they do not want it to change. I agree; I don't want it to change, either, but what shall we do with the waste? Wherever you propose a sanitary landfill, ten people will object. What can we do? We need to have sanitary landfills. And always not in my backyard."[31]

The issues that energized Bezner and his supporters—quality of life and protection of the pastoral landscape—did not persuade Marinov. For him, the nostalgia for a time gone by only obscured the serious issues of illegal, poorly maintained garbage dumps. "The fact that someone is against something," he argued, "does not necessarily make him pro-environment. If they object to landfills and prefer dumps all over, to me this is anti-environment." He further supported his attack on the opponents by pointing to other sources of pollution in their environment that they readily accepted: "I don't see them protesting against their own factories in the kibbutz that pollute the environment. The landfill would cause less environmental damage than Mishmar HaEmek's dairy barns. Less smell than their chickens."[32]

While Marinov may have exaggerated the benign consequences of the landfill and the existing sources of pollution already on the kibbutz, he did point to the significance of symbols. The smell of garbage is not analogous to the smell of dairy barns or chicken coops; those smells are a by-product of working the land productively and being in close touch with nature. Like the wheat farmers in eastern Washington, opposition to solid wastes in the soil and water did not necessarily encompass opposition to pesticides or even the small-scale factories that are found on every kibbutz. Unlike other forms of pollution from machines or fertilizers, garbage provides no advantages, no additional comfort or efficiency or productivity. Garbage represents the detritus of modern society; it is life's unwanted remains, which only hold the prospect of ugliness, discomfort, and danger. Furthermore, the landfill would principally serve the needs of city dwellers, who produced endless waste without taking responsibility for getting rid of it. Why should rural kibbutz and moshav residents bear the burden of urban residents' lifestyle?

The bitter differences extended beyond memories of earlier days and the symbolic worthlessness of garbage. The value of scientific expertise was also called into question by the debate over the landfill. Marinov, like Giora Yanai and other supporters at Kibbutz Ein Hashofet, was persuaded by the experts that state-of-the-art equipment could prevent the pollution, water contamination, and odors that had earlier characterized dumps and that local residents continued to fear. Yanai described his faith in the scientific and technological experts, just as Marinov had documented the lengths to which they had gone in securing technical assessments: "In the end, I am satisfied in the same way that I believe in medicine. I am not a doctor, and at a certain point, I have to believe the doctors. I might get a second opinion, but that is what happened here. People took ecological tests for ten years. I got professional views that said there would be no damage to the water and the soil, so I accept it. At a certain point, I have to believe the experts. That's it."[33]

Bezner, like most community activists, was much more skeptical about the infallibility of the "experts." To illustrate his point, he told the following story: "In the late 1940s, when Ben Gurion was prime minister, he wanted to build the city of Beersheva. Two experts told him that he could not build a city on the edge of the desert. 'Fine,' said Ben Gurion, 'take away these experts and bring me two others who will advise me to build the city.' And that is what happened. For every expert they show me that says the dump will not create problems, I can bring two experts on the other side."[34]

The struggle over expertise is a major issue between many community activists and their opponents. The activists are laypeople, often at a disadvantage because of their lack of technical sophistication and their intimidation when scientific terms and formulas are thrown at them. But the grassroots activists bring their own experience, a profound personal investment in the area, and a growing conviction that the experts are merely hired hands brought in to provide the conclusions that the government or industry wants. Leaders of community groups learn that they must educate themselves quickly and contact experts who can provide them with the ammunition to fight back. To this end, national groups often provide the essential specialized knowledge.

This is precisely how Bezner proceeded. His own kibbutz of Mishmar HaEmek spent thousands of dollars on engineering consultants. He received legal assistance from the Union for Environmental Defense, a public-law interest group, initially funded by Econet and organized by Alon Tal, dedicated to working with community groups on behalf of the environment. Bezner joined with those in Beersheva who were fighting a similar plan for the southern half of Israel, and met researchers from Israel's major universities who were devising alternatives to the plan of the Ministry of the Environment.

The controversy remains unresolved. Uri Marinov lost his position at the Ministry of the Environment when the Labor government of Yitzhak Rabin defeated the Likud in 1992. But new faces did not necessarily bring an end to the plan to site a landfill in the Ein Hashofet area, where the financial leaders have once again affirmed the importance of proceeding for the economic well-being of the kibbutz. Legal battles are underway that will serve to delay the project even further, but no one is certain of the final outcome. Bezner is hopeful that a plan proposed at a major university meeting on the subject will win further support. That plan involves transporting the garbage to a mine deep in the Negev desert, where there are no residential settlements and no sources of water, while the country develops a more sophisticated system of separating, reusing, and recycling its wastes.

Perhaps even more than in eastern Washington State, the ongoing controversy involving the Ministry of the Environment and Kibbutz Mishmar HaEmek, pitting men like Uri Marinov against Reuven

Bezner, has evolved into an environmental battle with the starkest divisions. Each side fervently believes that it has its community's best interest at heart. Each feels that its position contributes to resolving a major national problem. Both sides have the personal credibility, based partially on their heritage as pioneers in building the young state of Israel, to claim that they are now on the frontier in moving the country into the next stage of its development. In the midst of such seemingly legitimate claims and counterclaims can we point to all or any of the antagonists as people of courage? Should Uri Marinov be awarded that distinction for firmly focusing on his nation's garbage-disposal difficulties and for seeking a resolution? Should Reuven Bezner at Mishmar HaEmek be labeled a man of resolve and bravery for his willingness to fight a potential environmental problem, disrupting his life by devoting his full energy to his cause? Is this a situation where the problem is so severe, the resolution so difficult, that each side is right in its contention? In a politically motivated change Marinov has been removed from his central position. Bezner remains determined. The personal conflict between the antagonists has now ceased. But the drama over the placement of garbage facilities has yet to be resolved worldwide.

Building a New World

When the Velvet Revolution occurred in Czechoslovakia in 1989, environmentalists were jubilant. They had participated actively in Charter 77 and other dissident movements, and had persuaded the public that the Communist government had been responsible for gross environmental violations and degradation of the quality of life. They knew the public overwhelmingly agreed with their analysis that environmental concerns and human rights were the critical issues facing Czechoslovakian society: "At the beginning of 1990, given the question 'What is, in your opinion, the most important problem to be tackled by the government?' five out of six citizens—83 percent exactly—of the Czech Republic answered, 'finding a solution to the environmental crisis.' They considered all other problems less urgent, including limited choice of goods in the shops, lack of housing, inadequate supply of medicaments or the situation of health care in general."[35]

Yet the activists knew that even in the joyous moment of victory, there were a raft of difficulties facing them. They were painfully aware that the landscape was littered with dying forests, excessive pollution, contaminated water and food, inadequate sewage treatment, and un-recorded amounts of toxic and solid waste. In addition, the country was embarking on a difficult transition period with imminent changes in the economy, culture, and education, and it was becoming increasingly clear that there had been relatively little planning among the dissidents for a post-Communist society. In fact, they had deliberately papered over strong differences to keep the anti-Communist coalition together in the heady days when everything seemed possible.

The dissidents quickly emerged as political and environmental leaders in both the Czech Republic and in Slovakia. They knew that damage to the ecosystems of the country had begun early in the century, but that deterioration had intensified significantly when the Communists took control. The strategy under that regime made military production, heavy industry, and mining top priorities for Czechoslovakia. The Communists had convinced themselves that Bohemia (western Czechoslovakia on the German border) would ultimately be the land of military confrontation with the West, so they had determined to extract and use the resources there as quickly as possible. Everyone interested in the problem knew that huge areas had been strip-mined and left a scarred and devastated landscape. By the 1970s and 1980s, there was growing recognition of an ecological crisis, and the government responded by increasing resources to nature-protection societies and by sponsoring the development of scientific inquiry in this area. Many of the postrevolutionary leaders of the 1990s had joined the state-run environmental organizations during this earlier period. It had been a formative experience for them, but they soon realized that the government's efforts were too little and too late.

One of the most pressing issues throughout Czechoslovakia was the problem of waste. A 1991 survey showed that of 2,020 operating landfills, only 6 percent were in accord with legal requirements. Another 8,000–15,000 landfills no longer in operation presented serious environmental risks, since many were leaking contaminants into the ground or water. Still in operation were 220 antiquated incinerators that incorporated no chemical treatment of the toxic ash they produced.[36] According to the best estimates of the newly formed Ministry of the Environment, Czechoslovakia produced more than 600 million tons of waste each year, of which 83 percent came from mining and exploitation (extractive industries). Most of the mining wastes were simply left on the ruined soil. The land was not restored, and when it became uninhabitable, workers were moved and given salary increments to compensate for the disadvantageous living conditions.

As they confronted the issues of the post-Communist world, many environmentalists saw opportunity as well as threat. The nation had not yet become a consumer society, producing the extraordinary amounts of packaging and material goods that had resulted in ever-increasing amounts of waste in the West. Here in postrevolutionary Czechoslovakia was an opportunity to raise public consciousness, foster new values, and balance collective and individual rights after forty years of dictatorship. Pavel Šremer, the first Slovakian deputy minister in the Federal Ministry of the Environment, articulated the primary goal of many activists: "It may be a cliché, but in my opinion the most important thing is to change the way people think. Many people think the solutions to our problems are technocratic, but I don't agree. We need a major change in thinking and in lifestyle."[37]

A comprehensive strategy for improving landfills and pollution would be much easier to implement if ideas about the quality of life shifted from an intense emphasis on cars and other material goods to a focus on creating a sustainable environment. But the changes did not come easily. As the much-hated Communist government disappeared, so did the guarantees of social security, jobs, and affordable housing that citizens had come to rely on. The long-awaited freedom and individual rights had a downside for many citizens, who had not been prepared for the dislocation that accompanied the transition to a market economy. Privatization brought a sense of growing opportunity, but for environmental activists, there seemed to be too little emphasis on the common good. The public turned away from ecological concerns, and environmental leaders were unable to speak convincingly of energy conservation and meaningful alternatives to materialism. Their organizing efforts lacked public support and interest in the face of many competing demands.

Juraj Zamkovsky was a student in Bratislava, Slovakia, when he joined the Slovak Union of Landscape and Nature Protectors (SZOPK) in 1987. Like many young Slovakian students, he had been influenced by the publication of *Bratislava Nahlas,* and became increasingly active in the environmental movement and in the Slovakian dissident organization People Against Violence (VPN).[38] As a student in Bratislava, he became particularly interested in a waste dump in Budmerice, a small village in Slovakia, where his family lived. Although all the residents could smell the dump behind the chemical factory, which was the town's leading industry, before 1989 no one was allowed any information about the contents. Zamkovsky once persuaded the guards that he was a student doing research, and managed to penetrate the barriers to see more than seventy acres of unprotected toxic wastes from pesticides and fertilizer production, which fouled the air and endangered the local residents. And Budmerice was not alone in facing serious conditions; Slovakia was filled with munitions factories and other heavy industries related to defense. Only after the Velvet Revolution did citizens fully understand that many of these industries were spewing untold amounts of pollutants into the air and water, and that some towns were suffering extraordinarily high rates of cancer.[39]

When VPN became politically influential throughout Slovakia in late 1989, Zamkovsky decided he would form a local branch in Budmerice. He was determined to focus citizen attention on environmental issues, particularly toxic wastes, and to avoid the emphasis on retribution against former Communists that threatened to consume people's attention.[40] Zamkovsky left the university and moved to the village, bringing speakers, musicians, and other cultural events to attract local support. He became a very popular figure, was elected to the village council, and became head of the environmental program. Zamkovsky's whole plan was to create a culture of solidarity among town residents to empower them to share in decision making for the good of the community generally, and to build a constituency for important environmental improvements specifically.

As a member of the village council, Zamkovsky prepared a program for the toxic-waste dump that currently threatened the air and water supply. Factory leaders, on the other hand, continued to believe they could convince the villagers to support the status quo if they brought in a technical team that would submit thousands of pages of writing and offer expert testimony that the dump was up to standards. The factory, with its five thousand employees and its monopoly on producing certain pesticides, was central to Budmerice's economy, and it had always functioned with no regard for environmental damage. Juraj Zamkovsky studied the technical materials and obtained valuable advice from Gary Coleman of the National Toxics Campaign in the United States. With this assistance, Zamkovsky was ultimately successful in proving that the factory had never implemented its own operating plan for cleanup and safe disposal of waste. He and his supporters held public hearings in which they showed slides of the toxic-waste dump to illustrate the magnitude of the problem, which residents had smelled but never seen. The activists organized a petition demanding a complex analysis of the environmental impact of the dump, and virtually everyone in the village signed it. In addition, they were able to demonstrate that the toxic wastes had contaminated the water and that 30 percent of the local population was actually drinking deadly water. Finally, the factory officials were forced to agree to pay for a serious environmental-impact study, to be conducted without political interference. That study produced recommendations for a new operating plan as well as the construction of a water pipeline to bring acceptable drinking water to the houses near the dump. These hard-won victories seemed to convince the people that change was possible. The postrevolutionary society was developing in just the way Zamkovsky and his colleagues had hoped. They had successfully defined the problems in ways the public understood. They had built a core group of young residents to work with Zamkovsky. They had kept their public support as Zamkovsky courageously confronted the authorities and demanded change.

But Zamkovsky was restless and not fully satisfied. After several months of excellent progress, he felt isolated from VPN leaders in Bratislava. In a time of extraordinary change, he wanted to know about new laws that were being enacted and to plan new strategies for organizing his village. Toward these ends, he moved to Bratislava, hoping still to spend two days a week in Budmerice. He thought that some of the new young leaders who had been elected to the village council would be able to maintain the momentum of change: "I tried to organize a group of young people to work on environmental issues. I started to teach them English in order to develop a partnership with a community in another country. I wanted our young people to go and see different ways of doing things, because they were caged in this village. I thought this would make them active. But it was terrible because I did not have enough time. They came to the English lessons so they wouldn't disappoint me, but they felt that I didn't have time for them or for the village."[41]

Just as Zamkovsky left Budmerice for Bratislava, serious economic problems surfaced. Government subsidies were cut off, resulting in higher prices and less job security. Not unexpectedly, many villagers blamed the VPN for their troubles and began to distrust the new village government, just as they had lost faith in the Communists in years gone by. All the old problems seemed to remain or even worsen. Unfortunately, the newly elected young idealists on the village council had no training for political responsibility. They did not understand the relationship between local and district government, nor had they any idea how to secure funds for the village. Despite great victories in forcing a serious environmental impact study of the factory, the residents saw none of the toxic wastes disappear. The activists were unsuccessful in maintaining a culture of solidarity, nor could they build lasting alternative networks of power.

As the mood of optimism faded, Juraj Zamkovsky became a maligned figure, and he believed that it was dangerous for him to return to the village. Nationalists advocating separation from the Czech Republic became increasingly influential politically. The media focused on scandals in the lives of politicians, reinforcing the idea that no public officials could be trusted to work in the public interest. Zamkovsky lamented his earlier decision to move back to Bratislava: "Leaving was a terrible mistake. I didn't complete what I started. Now the situation is that most people really hate us. The former Communists are spreading terrible rumors about us. Today we are thought of as the people who sold the village to the factory, that we didn't stop the waste disposal. They think that we were dishonest and took money to get the water pipeline built. None of this is true." Zamkovsky knew that his was not the only disappointment. As the environmental leaders moved from dissidence to governmental positions, they often lost their connections to their constituents. Zamkovsky spelled out the serious consequences: "One of the reasons that the environmental movement [throughout the country] was strong before the revolution was that it had very strong personalities. After the revolution, these personalities quickly became political figures and had no more time to work with the grassroots. The loss of leaders almost destroyed the movement. We lost our most active group, and the people at the bottom no longer felt supported."[42]

In her book *The Haunted Land,* Tina Rosenberg also found the Slovakians quick to lose interest in social and political reform once they realized that the days of cheap food and guaranteed employment were over. Slovakians, always suspicious of the Czechs, the more dominant and cosmopolitan part of the federation, had little tradition of dissidence. Despite the initial popularity of the VPN and the surge of pride that had accompanied *Bratislava Nahlas,* nationalist politics soon came to dominate the political landscape. Rosenberg cites one sociological survey of eight hundred small-town Slovakian mayors in 1993 that asked the subjects to rank the relative prestige of social groups in the society. It was not surprising that the historically reviled Gypsies were near the bottom of the list. Much more telling was the fact that this berated minority was closely followed by dissidents.[43]

Although Juraj Zamkovsky had only short-lived success in Budmerice, he did not give up his mission. He was pleased to spend three months working with the National Toxics Campaign in the United States, where he refined his own skills and formed international connections that are vital for building a vibrant NGO grassroots community. He and his colleagues in the Czech Republic have had to rethink their options in a political context that emphasizes a free-market economy. The activists know all too well how little regard there is for the growing environmental problems, such as the importation of waste from Germany, the lack of adequate separation of toxic and solid waste, the mounting residues from chemical and agriculture enter-

prises, and the absence of an infrastructure for recycling. The environmental advocates have supported the development of legislation, educational programs, and international partnerships, which they hope
will provide the resources and expertise to move their program forward. Zamkovsky, like many of the revolutionary environmental leaders, is searching for a model that uses limited resources in a socially
responsible manner. He and his colleagues want to work with progressive churches, schools, and local governments to build a consensus for
a true green development program: "Now we are trying to rebuild support for the grassroots. We don't want more leaders, because leaders
leave and the situation will be the same. We want to show that we can
work at the local level without money or larger support. The people
think that financial problems are the major ones, but this is not true at
all, because finances are always going to have less value because of
poor management, no organization, no plans of what to do with the
money, even if the government should provide funding."[44]

Building grassroots support in Slovakia or the Czech Republic requires the dedication of Juraj Zamkovsky and the dozens of other environmental leaders who have spent their lives waiting for the opportunity to create a new society. But they are fighting an uphill battle.
Despite the obvious damage that has resulted from waste dumps like
the one in Budmerice, or the mine wastes that have devastated Bohemia, there is not yet a critical mass of people who define themselves
as stewards of the land or as political actors able to organize a sustained campaign for environmental improvement. Until activists are
able to present the problem in a manner that has local and public appeal, the pressures of economics and the appeals of consumer goods
will be hard to overcome.

Neighbors in Battle

Nobody likes garbage, and nobody wants it in his or her homeland. In
recent years, this orphan of modern industrial society has rent deep divisions between local activists intent on preserving the land as they
knew it and a strong coalition of industrial and government officials

seeking to contain costs and find reasonable solutions to vexing problems. Yet the division is deeper than that between local and regional outlooks. The two sides hold antithetical views on the meaning of land and differ on how much trust to place in technological solutions to environmental degradation. Whereas regulators and industry officials emphasize the national need and state-of-the-art equipment, activists talk of stewardship of the land and implementation of a strong program to reduce waste at the source and to separate garbage much more carefully for recycling and reuse.

All the activists—whether in Benge, Washington; Mishmar Ha-Emek, Israel; or Budmerice, Slovakia—had some initial success in building a culture of solidarity with others who shared their strong affinity for the land and their dream of an environment that preserved the cleanliness and the purity of their rural or small-town settings. But this solidarity among neighbors and like-minded friends came at a high price. Situated right among them were other folks who were equally adamant about building the landfill or garbage dump or continuing the productivity of the local factory. These conflicts did not resemble the usual tensions between workers and management, or even between local residents and distant bureaucrats or profit-minded corporate executives. Instead, these quarrels often had the character of a terrible family rift or a civil war. Greg Beckley's bitter comment that he would no longer spend money at the stores of certain local merchants underscores a resentment and divisiveness more devastating than any other conflict in the recent memory of eastern Washington residents. In a similar vein, Ein Hashofet founders had lived at Mishmar HaEmek and there had learned the skills necessary to found a new kibbutz in the 1930s. These pioneers considered themselves to be members of sister kibbutzim, working side by side to cultivate the land and build the Zionist dream, and they never imagined that their children would be on opposite sides of such a divide. Budmerice residents may have been less idealistic, but their growing anger at Zamkovsky and his fellow environmentalists ripped through the small town, creating hostility and exacerbating distrust just as the residents faced formidable changes in every aspect of their lives.

The anger and tension generated by these conflicts put great pressure on the activists. Leaders had to articulate problems more clearly than ever so that they could appeal to the undecided members of the community. They had to contain their outspoken opposition if they were to have any chance of convincing officials that the public would not support damage to the local land. The core groups had to maintain the energy to continue the battle on the local issues, while forming coalitions with national and international groups addressing similar problems. They had to retain a small-town, personal definition of their problems, but could not settle for a simplistic understanding of issues that were at once wide-ranging, technical, and highly political. They needed access to experts who would assist them in developing their arguments and protect them against charges of naiveté and lack of expertise. None of this came easily to volunteers, whose full-time jobs and family responsibilities had to be juggled with their commitment to safeguarding their communities against the intrusion of unwanted garbage and toxic wastes. Yet their solidarity with those who supported them and their unwavering belief in the justice of their position sustained them across the years of difficult struggle to preserve their lands and way of life.

5

Protecting the Precious Natural Resources

Most grassroots activists are motivated by an immediate threat to their neighborhoods. Concerned Neighbors organized when the Stringfellow Acid Pits overflowed, sending thousands of gallons of toxic water coursing through their community. The Downwinders of Eastern Washington came together when they realized that they shared medical problems and risks that were acquired during the years they lived near the Hanford Nuclear Reservation. Similarly, the families of Haifa and the mothers of Prague responded to the growing incidence of asthma and respiratory problems caused by unbridled pollution in their cities. We have seen again and again that early action often resulted from a strong jolt to individual and collective consciousness. As people came to believe that their families and neighborhoods were threatened by external forces, they determined to undertake action that could change or remedy the assault on local health and safety.

This personal motivation was the essential catalyst that moved many to initiate action. As these local residents became increasingly involved in trying to solve their community's problems, they often developed a much more comprehensive assessment of the environmental hazards they faced. Their initial focus on eliminating a toxic-waste dump or preventing the construction of a landfill frequently led activists to acquire a larger understanding of the related problems of waste disposal, radiation exposure, and pollution. But despite this more comprehensive perspective on regional and national environmental problems, their central focus remained firmly fixed on defending the health and safety of their communities. They were particularly effective in forcing government and corporate officials to consider risks to local populations, and to modify policy decisions that had previously been based solely on considerations like national security and economic policy.

Grassroots activists also included other environmentalists whose main focus was on preserving whole ecosystems that often extended beyond the boundaries of their neighborhood. These environmentalists shared many characteristics with activists who were primarily responding to immediate community-based environmental problems. In the United States, for example, many environmentalists have devoted themselves to saving regional forests from clear-cutting or from the construction of new logging roads. These activists, like their counterparts working on specific community hazards, also define their role as citizens who are protecting the quality of life for their families and their communities. The defenders of the forest often concentrated their energies on the local watershed in their region, and immersed themselves in the conflicts that came up in regional hearings rather than in Washington. They engaged their neighbors as actively as possible by appealing to practical as well as abstract and spiritual arguments about the value of maintaining the natural landscape and the complex variety of plants and animals that depend on unspoiled forests. They became knowledgeable about the legal conflicts surrounding endangered species and wilderness protection, and augmented their philosophical commitment with practical arguments.[1] They also built a strong sense of solidarity with like-minded activists and tried to win the public-opinion battle. With hopes of building an alternative network of power, they contacted journalists, scientists, and sympathetic government representatives.

In Israel, as in the United States, there are activists who want to preserve their natural heritage. While there are no ancient forests in Israel, activists have mobilized to save undeveloped areas in their small country from the demands of its growing population and ever-expanding housing projects. In the mid-1990s, they opposed the construction of a major new highway intended to bisect the country from north to south, and moved to protect undeveloped lands along the proposed route. They rejected the argument of the project's supporters that public policy must accommodate the growing number of cars that clog the existing highways; instead, they urged construction of mass-transit alternatives that would be less damaging to the landscape. Although they were not successful in defeating the highway project, the environmentalists did call attention to the larger problem of overdevelopment and the need for maintaining indigenous wilderness, be it desert or swamp. A parallel situation existed in the Czech Republic, where activists, who had a long history in nature-protection societies, were outraged by the ongoing destruction of small villages and the surrounding forests as strip mining and the construction of power plants devastated whole areas of the country. They combined their concern about pollution-related declining life expectancy with a profound passion for the preservation of the land.

But these environmentalists also differed in significant ways from Lisa Crawford, Hatim Kana'aneh, Reuven Bezner, Ja'ra Johnova, and others whom we discussed in earlier chapters. Activists who were dedicated to the preservation of undeveloped land and natural resources understood the significance of the threats to individuals, neighborhoods, or even larger populations, but they rejected a purely anthropocentric environmentalism. They urged their friends and colleagues to foster an increasing respect for the planet, which would manifest itself in part by a movement to retain some land in its most natural form. These activists worried about the survival of ancient forests, not only because their children might not have sufficient lumber, but also because the forests are at the heart of complex, irreplaceable ecosystems. They sought to protect wilderness, whether forest, desert, or prairie, so that unfettered open land could remain a permanent part of the landscape.

While this more abstract form of environmentalism had some legitimacy in the public mind because it was closely linked to earlier conservation and nature-preservation movements, its emphasis on preserving natural resources also represented a more radical departure from conventional ideas that had influenced many contemporary environmental movements. Activists intent on saving natural treasures for their own sake insisted that the future well-being of all living things rests on a vision that limits humans' right to exploit the earth. Instead, these proponents of nature insisted that we must reexamine our own needs as part of a larger context that takes into consideration the health and perpetuation of all plants and animals.[2]

The battle over who owns nature and natural resources can be profoundly divisive. In the United States, western settlers and developers have always assumed that owners could extract resources from their land, whether lumber, minerals, or water, without regard to the long-term impact on birds, fish, or even the people who lived downstream. The idea that the preservation of the environment enhances our quality of life has gained some credence in recent years, as can be seen in the Earth Day celebrations, the publications of environmental groups, and even in some protective legislation (e.g., the National Wilderness Act). Yet convincing the public, legislators, and corporate officials of the significance of preserving natural ecosystems in the face of demands for economic development and job security has remained an uphill battle.

This chapter examines groups in each country that want to extend the neighborly impulse for healthy communities. These activists are committed to the popular motto "Think globally, act locally." They remain keenly aware that local decisions have consequences throughout the planet, and thus are dedicated to saving their lands from rapacious industrialization and development that is depleting natural resources at an accelerating rate. However, these environmentalists do not dream of living in some preindustrial Garden of Eden. Rather, they are local residents searching for methods guaranteeing the sustainable use of natural resources. Some activists are mindful of the needs of workers who fear that the cessation of mining, logging, or construction will interfere with their livelihoods; however, others have formed adversarial relations with those who blame the environmentalists for declining extractive industries. Ecologically minded activists argue that long-term sustainability can coexist with a healthy economy, but they insist that any formula must incorporate a new emphasis on the significance of undisturbed areas. Their use of growing scientific evidence documenting the importance of protecting ecosystems often creates conflicts with those outside the movement who define them as tree lovers threatening jobs, exports, and corporate profits. The activists' only hope of resolution depends on building support for a compromise that acknowledges new views of nature and its significance in human existence. Their willingness to engage in a long-term struggle represents a particular form of courageous behavior. They have to be prepared for years of confrontation with those who oppose all efforts to put natural resources and open spaces off limits. Their time, effort, and emotional investment is often considerable, disrupting many other activities and requiring a profound belief in the urgency of the cause.

Defending the Forests

Northern California is renowned for its giant redwoods and ancient sequoias, trees that have lived for hundreds and even thousands of years, and these vast conifer forests up and down the West Coast have now become the battleground for environmentalists in California and throughout the Northwest. Extensive logging has decimated millions of acres of virgin forest that used to cover the land. The remaining ancient forests are a patchwork of national parks, national forests, state lands, and privately held acreage, often owned by former railroad companies that have found greater profits in the trees bordering the train tracks than in the failing railroad industry. The effort to save the most magnificent of these trees is almost a century old, and harks back to the work of John Muir and his contemporaries. These early conserva-

tionists were determined to establish the first national parks to protect the sequoias and create recreational areas where Americans could
enjoy these imposing monuments of nature. Up and down the coast of
northern California, contemporary environmentalists have fought to
protect its rich natural heritage, frantically working to reduce the
clear-cutting that has ravaged most of the private lands; in recent
years extensive logging operations have threatened public lands as
well. Activists have been trying to save the remaining ancient forests
and to limit clear-cutting in all mature forests, since this method of
logging destroys whole ecosystems and threatens watersheds, wildlife,
and the fishing industry.[3]

In the early years of the twentieth century, most logging activity
was done on private lands, and the United States Forest Service was
mainly concerned with maintaining trails and protecting public forests
from fires and other forms of natural destruction. After World War II
the population of the West rose dramatically, creating a much higher
demand for construction lumber. The Forest Service became much
more focused on assuring a continuing supply of wood, and began to
assign portions of public lands for the timber industry to cut.[4] To assist
in the ongoing production of wood, the Forest Service emphasized
maximum yield, and built logging roads and provided essential infra-
structural support for the timber industry. Often the logging of public
lands was ultimately only profitable to private industry because the
roads into the thick forests and up the mountainsides were built at
public expense, at no cost to the companies.

Protecting the future supply of lumber and the watershed were the
primary objectives of the Forest Service, but increasingly its officials
were pressed into considering other uses. By 1960 the Forest Service
was mandated by law to oversee multiple use of the forests, including
wood production, water, forage, recreation, and protection of fish and
wildlife.[5] As environmentalists became concerned with the extent of
logging and the rapid reduction of forest land, they began to challenge
Forest Service decisions. The Forest Service personnel continued to
see themselves as the only knowledgeable professional managers, and
often resented the environmentalists' pressure to limit clear-cutting
and to incorporate environmental objectives into policy decisions about

the use of public lands. Until very recently schools of forestry trained their graduates to see forests almost exclusively in terms of wood production, with little attention to ecological or aesthetic uses.[6] Most schools that trained foresters emphasized scientific management, which focused on balancing cut and growth to produce long-term sustained yields. To maximize yield without destroying future productivity, professional foresters concentrated on improving pest control, eliminating competing vegetation, and using better seed and fertilizers for replanting trees. But their major emphasis was on dividing forests into units with trees of uniform age to create "even-age" plots. These plots could then be clear-cut with large machinery, thereby reducing labor costs for the industry. These managers focused on commercial production, a concept that was totally at odds with environmentalists' concerns about biodiversity.[7] The differing views of what constitutes a healthy forest often led to tension between the environmentalists and the Forest Service professionals, the two groups most passionately concerned with the future of the forests. Only in the last few decades have some professionals broadened their research and their understanding of a healthy forest. The New Forestry, as it has come to be called, emphasizes ecology and conservation biology as much as the economics and silviculture that dominated professional programs for many decades.[8] Although new kinds of training and research have begun to make their way into the curricula of schools of forestry, change in the Forest Service has been slower in coming. Implementing new ideas means promoting some of the newly trained people into the upper reaches of Forest Service management and changing research and program priorities.[9]

By the time Tim McKay arrived in Arcata, California, as a student at Humboldt State College in 1967, the great timber boom was already beginning its decline. There were fewer jobs for loggers than there had been ten years earlier in the northern California town, and a new, more environmentally sensitive population was growing around the rapidly expanding university. McKay himself had always had an appreciation for the outdoors, but he did not define himself as an environmentalist. He had been active in high school in the young Republicans and had campaigned for Barry Goldwater in 1964, echoing the values of his parents. But as a college student McKay became involved in anti–Vietnam War activity and worked as a volunteer for Senator Eugene McCarthy in the 1968 presidential election. His early understanding of forest issues began to develop when he left college to take a six-month job with the Forest Service, where he worked with a team of surveyors to subdivide forests into plots and mark off areas for future clear-cutting. He recognized that many of his coworkers on the survey teams were resigned to the destruction of the forests. Sometimes at lunch they would toss litter on the ground, saying, "What's the difference? This is just going to be clear-cut anyway."

Despite an interest in natural history and forest ecology, McKay did not fully understand the complex issues involved in sustainable forestry. While working for the Forest Service, he observed how much its bureaucrats enjoyed planning and implementing big projects, such as cutting roads into a mountainside. When his surveying work took him into deep wilderness, McKay recognized that a series of roads and clear-cuts were going to change the forest ecosystem in that area forever. His increasing intimacy with the issues made him uncomfortable with the existing policies and philosophy that dominated Forest Service decisions.

In 1974 McKay and a group of friends formed a branch of Friends of the Earth, and he began working for the expansion of Redwoods National Park. The park had been established in 1968, but active logging continued on the headwaters at the edge of the park. Many environmentalists strongly opposed the cutting of these thousand-year-old trees. They argued that the park itself would not remain viable, because its streams were constantly threatened by the sedimentation from nearby logging. Wild creatures would not be able to travel safely if their natural habitat was interrupted by exposed clear-cuts. McKay joined others who actively worked to expand the boundaries of the park and to save as much of the area as possible. Both the Forest Service and the timber industry opposed any expansion of the park, and they convinced workers that the timber industry represented the best interests of the local economy.[10] The controversy intensified; cars sported bumper stickers reading "Don't park my job," while others promoted the virtues of the park system. The local population was deeply divided on the issue. Ultimately a compromise was fashioned by several congressmen: it allowed the federal government to acquire lands that would connect existing parcels of redwoods that mostly belonged to the state, creating a larger, more unified protected tract. In return for the removal of this acreage from any logging use, employees were given special benefits from a government protection program, and the timber industry received thousands of acres of other prime land.

While working with the Friends of the Earth chapter in Arcata, McKay heard about a job opening at the North Coast Environmental Center, a small activist organization that had been created in 1971 out of Earth Day activities. Initially, the center had two paid positions that were federally funded by the CETA program, but as the Redwoods Park issue heated up, opponents argued that CETA money should not be used to fund an organization that was trying to ruin the local economy by limiting the number of logging jobs. The other employee had to leave when CETA money ceased, and for a while McKay remained the only paid worker.

As of this writing, eighteen years later, McKay is still director of the small environmental center, engaged in multifaceted work to save the Headlands Forest and promote regional environmental preservation. He engages ceaselessly in education, legal battles, and political work[11] and has become so immersed in environmental action that for him it represents a deep philosophical and political commitment to a way of life and to the long-term health of the region.[12] McKay has had the satisfaction of helping to develop plans for landscape ecology, biological diversity, and watershed management that actually made their way into proposed legislation. He rejects single solutions that attempt to solve one problem while ignoring the complexity of surrounding ecosystems: "Talking about watersheds is a much more holistic way of conceiving of the environment rather than using a fragmented approach to protecting stands of full-grown trees. The holistic vision is what our movement is about. Preserving old-growth forests is as much a watershed issue, with dwindling runs of fish that were the mainstay of many cultural groups in our area, as it is an issue about spotted owls, which tends to loom largest in the minds of the legislators."[13]

At the same time, McKay's deep devotion to preserving the region has had personal costs. The problems he faces are never ending, and remedying them often requires an investment of time and energy that strains family relationships:

> It is kind of a workaholic commitment with crises that you have to respond to and that cut into any personal time. My former wife was involved when we founded Friends of the Earth, so it was something we did together. But it became an issue that I would or could not divorce myself in a disciplined way from the work environment, and I wasn't there at 6:00. Towards the end, it was pretty clear that she was jealous of the work and the environmental center. She would say, You can't save the world. I never necessarily thought that I could, but if there's an opportunity to do something that seems like it ought to be done, I should do it. She felt I was too committed. I believed that both of us were blessed to have this opportunity to do this righteous work.[14]

Tim McKay's commitment to his cause reflects the approach of many other activists. While his is a paid staff position and most others are filled by volunteers, the investment of the self is almost comparable. His was never a high-paying job with limited hours or involvement with circumscribed community projects. These projects required an open-ended commitment. When his wife accused him of trying to "save the world," she was criticizing him for not having any boundaries between his job and the rest of his life. He did not know how to balance his environmental allegiances with a fuller concern for other relationships. Tim McKay could not accept her critique. Rather, he defined his efforts as a "blessed" chance to do "righteous work." Such a sacred opportunity could not be restricted within the confines of an eight-hour day. For McKay and many others fighting the devastation of the forests or the evils of chemical or nuclear contamination, the costs of defeat were simply too great and the rewards of victory too gratifying.

McKay's eloquent defense of the sacredness of his work belies the fact that he faced many frustrations. Despite his disclaimers, he was troubled by the ever-increasing pace of work and the erosion of his personal time. Corporations promoting logging had much more substantial resources to fight political and legal battles. Furthermore, as his experience grew and his views deepened, he also found it difficult to accommodate the naive passion of new activists who were drawn to the cause of saving the forests.[15]

> No matter how passionate you are for an issue, the longer you are involved with it, you are going to become more expert, and have a depth of understanding and appreciation for the range of what is going on. The newly initiated and passionate often don't understand. They think that passion alone is the key to doing the right things. So it is kind of frustrating sometimes to deal with these people. The grassroots zealots are most suspicious of the people at the top of the environmental organizations in Washington, D.C. They always think they are going to make some sort of deal based on expedience rather than the right thing. But it is not always clear that they know what the right thing is.[16]

Striking a balance between the purists who want to defend every tree and the timber industry that wants to expand its cutting into increasingly dangerous places is a burden to McKay. McKay's search for balance is emblematic of the problems facing those who seek to create a sustainable environment. They are keenly aware of the ongoing, rapid deterioration of natural resources and of the need to protect irreplaceable forests and wilderness. But at the same time, they recognize competing demands to exploit those resources for economic gain. They fear that extremists on both sides will torpedo any chance to save crucial lands where biodiversity can flourish.

In the early 1990s, Susie Van Kirk was Tim McKay's devoted colleague. For years, she volunteered forty or more hours a week defending the forest against the ravages of clear-cutting and the streams against degradation by the removal of gravel and the inflow of sediment. Van Kirk had been a graduate student in biology, but she ceased her studies when her children were young and her husband was studying for an advanced degree. They moved to Arcata in 1969, when her husband obtained a position at Humboldt State College, and they remained there permanently. As a young shy mother, Van Kirk stayed home with her three small children, which gave her the opportunity to read broadly and to form independent opinions about local, regional, and environmental issues. She undertook her first political action in the 1970s: protesting the construction of a controversial freeway, a project that had mobilized many members of her community. Later, she went to meetings of the local branches of the Sierra Club and the Audubon Society, and became chair of the conservation committee, a position that gave her access to the continual reports being filed by the timber industry and the Forest Service. Slowly, over a period of years, she began to intervene actively to prevent excessive cutting in the national forests.[17] Whenever she believed that the Forest Service had evaded the law requiring Environmental Impact Statements or Environmental Assessments, Van Kirk filed an appeal and sometimes litigated decisions. The work was grueling at times, but she never flagged in her commitment: "If you don't participate in every step, if you don't comment on the drafts extensively, if you don't raise all the issues, if things don't go as you feel they should and you want to take legal action or even appeal action, you have to stay on top, and you have to meet the deadlines. . . . And if you are dealing with four districts and six rivers in the region, then there is a lot of work."[18]

Van Kirk's statement pinpoints how conscientious the devoted environmentalist must be. It is not a matter of only signing a petition, or of writing a check, or even of joining a demonstration. Contesting a legal action, a court order, or an injunction necessitates understanding procedures, following detailed instructions, and minding specific deadlines. The "good-hearted" citizen must be transformed into the activist obsessed with technical detail.

Over the course of many years of advocacy, Van Kirk experienced both victory and defeat. In some cases, extensive cutting continued while her appeals were delayed and ignored, until it was too late and the irreversible damage was done. Yet in another instance, the Sierra Club Legal Defense Fund filed a suit to save a roadless area adjacent to a wild and scenic river in the Shasta Forest. Four years later, Van Kirk reported, the trees were still intact, although the possibility of reconsideration was always present. A quiet, reserved woman, Van Kirk did not appear to be a likely candidate to confront powerful figures in the county. But her willingness to be present at every hearing and to be involved in the daily detail of decision making gave her a sense of authority and entitlement to act on her beliefs. But this confidence was diluted by the tension and mixed emotions that characterize adversarial proceedings: "The Forest Service is government, and they are managing public lands, so I feel like I have a lot of say. But when you have the purchaser there, and he had his road crew already in there, and you are arguing over whether to leave any trees along this creek or not—it's just hard. There is a lot of emotion, and people get mad; people say really rude things to people."[19]

Maintaining the integrity of Van Kirk's position was often difficult, especially when the timber-industry executives tried to take the high road by claiming to preserve jobs and strengthen the economy. It took real courage to speak up, often as the lone environmentalist, at hearings dominated by logging companies. Susie Van Kirk felt she had to step forward.

> What's more important? The timber proprietor says, "I've these guys that have got to feed their families, and they already have their equipment up here," and I am saying, "Well, what I'm really concerned about, if you take all these trees on the slope, you are going to have some mass waste in your stream channel." They argue that the trees are all dead, that they have to take them all in order to plant new trees. But what you really have is a major difference in worldview, standing there talking about these trees. And the Forest Service, of course, supports the timber industry.[20]

This difference in worldview animated all of Susie Van Kirk's conversation. She saw the forest as a complex, living natural world, but had to make her case each time against those who saw the trees as nothing more than raw materials for industry.[21] Although she was sometimes tired and discouraged, she never gave up: "Sometimes I don't know if it's worth it, but I don't know what the alternative is. I can't see walking away from it. I have a real low tolerance for things that I think are unjust and unfair. And when I see what goes on, I know it's not just unfair, it's wrong, and I feel like I have to make the effort, even if I fail. Somebody has to speak for the resources and the trees, and often I am the only person there to do it."[22]

Like Tim McKay, Susie Van Kirk's deep and abiding commitment to her sense of justice profoundly disrupted any conventional personal life. Her husband had little to do with her work, and they appeared to live quite separate lives. "We just each do our own thing. When he was teaching, he was really busy. His other thing is fishing. So he goes off, he's gone all day, all summer long fishing since he's retired."

Susie Van Kirk, like Tim McKay, was moved by a strong sense of justice and a need to do something to improve an intolerable situation. Van Kirk and McKay have no illusions about saving the world, nor do they assume a holier-than-thou position. They cannot speak for all environmentalists who are concerned about the forests and the complex ecosystems within them. Radical Earth Firsters who focused on civil disobedience by spiking trees or disabling equipment never believed that the education and legal challenges used by activists like McKay and Van Kirk were adequate to match the massive corporate and governmental powers determined to cut the ancient trees.[23] Officials in the Washington offices of major environmental organizations often felt that grassroots activists like Van Kirk were too single-minded about the rivers and forests that fall in their watershed. But McKay and Van Kirk and thousands like them are deeply engaged in their communities. They believe profoundly that they are part of a larger society where social relations and political commitments matter. They may not belong to civic groups like the Rotary Club or Parent Teacher Association, where Robert Putnam saw a serious decline in participation.[24] Nor are McKay and Van Kirk single-issue activists who only want to preserve the trees in their own backyard. Given their worldview and their belief in maintaining the untouched natural landscape, they will stay involved in the long-term struggle for environmental and social justice. They feel a personal responsibility for the health of the community around them. For example, Susie Van Kirk also serves dinner at the local shelter three nights a week. She considers it an obligation to create a friendly atmosphere for local men who are down and out.

This explanation for her involvement at the shelter is as direct as her explanation for her role at the environmental hearings: "Someone has to speak for the trees." She, like Penny Newman or Lynn Golumbic, is a culture mender, a citizen who directly confronts a serious issue and seeks to repair it.

Changing Environmental Values

Eilon Schwartz is a doctoral student in environmental studies at Hebrew University in Jerusalem and director of the Abraham Joshua Heschel Center for Nature Studies. He is deeply concerned about the narrow view of environmental issues exhibited by most Israelis:

> The development in Israel is extraordinary. It is going at such a rapid rate that nobody can keep track of it and nobody can get a handle on it. Population growth, the peace process, and the growing expectations about a rising standard of living are all causing this boom. Roads are being built, people are buying two cars, couples are commuting in different directions. There is very poor planning and still no serious consideration of environmental impact.
>
> More troubling than that is that the only environmental consideration is in terms of human health. There is no place whatsoever for public debate about the value of open spaces psychologically, aesthetically, culturally, not to mention the more far-reaching questions of the damage you do to the land and animals and plants. There is no place for the ethical dimension in the discussion, and it is very troubling.[25]

Schwartz's concerns represent the views of the most sophisticated activists. Beyond the pollution of air and water, beyond the disposal of solid and toxic waste, Schwartz wants his fellow Israelis to have respect for the land, to grant plants and animals a place in the creation and future of the country. But these ideas run contrary to other deeply rooted goals. Avner de-Shalit, a political scientist at Hebrew University specializing in environmental politics and philosophy, has written several articles exploring the historical reasons that Zionism has largely precluded the kind of ethical discussion that Eilon Schwartz is seeking to introduce.[26] Early Zionist history, de-Shalit argues, was based on a romantic attitude toward nature and the glorification of rural life. Young settlers in the early twentieth century rejected their history in the Diaspora. In Eastern Europe, the government had often denied Jews the right to own and work the land, and Jews in Russia and Poland had spent their lives longing for Zion and a place to call home. These young idealistic immigrants saw themselves as returning to the national and cultural roots of their ancestors, where they would cultivate the land, eschew the cities, and purify the national soul. When the realities of summer heat, desert, and swamp discouraged the young romantics, they intensified their efforts to conquer the land and "make the desert bloom."

The idea of working and changing the land bred great love for Eretz Yisrael (the land of Israel) among the early Zionists. The immigrants developed a romantic attachment to their new homeland, in part by conquering the unfamiliar and hostile terrain. Planting flowers and trees civilized the land by making it look more like the familiar terrain of Europe, but these experiences did not build emotional ties to the untouched wilderness.[27]

As Zionism developed, it soon replaced "romantic ruralism" with an ideology of development. By the 1930s the Jewish community in Palestine had to respond to the needs of large numbers of immigrants who were arriving as refugees from Nazi-occupied Europe. Rapid population growth[28] caused a shift in emphasis from romantic attachment to the land to industrialization and urbanization. Economic development would provide housing and jobs for the newcomers, and it also served an ideological goal of building the country in fulfillment of the Zionist dream. De-Shalit argues that this construction of Zionist ideology had direct implications for attitudes toward the environment. He analyzes three major projects—afforestation, draining swamps, and construction—undertaken by the government in order to provide work for immigrants, develop the country, and fulfill the Zionist ideology of "civilizing" the country. The Zionist leadership presented these projects as national efforts to build the country, and all three had profound effects on changing the environment. Afforestation provided quick and easy employment for immigrants, but at the same time it helped to sustain the myth of returning the land to the way it appeared in the Bible. In fact, afforestation often meant changing the Middle Eastern terrain to eliminate the natural desert environment and to create a land that resembled Europe more than the Middle East. Similarly, draining the Hula swamp north of the Sea of Galilee was intended to eliminate malaria, liberate the soil for agriculture, and make the land accessible to new populations. As it turned out, de-Shalit concludes, malaria had been defeated before the project, the land was agriculturally worthless, and the transformation destroyed many indigenous animals and plants. But despite growing awareness that the program had failed, the myth of the benefits of draining swamps was so prevalent that for many years afterward no criticism of the policy was possible. Only recently, a half century after the initial draining, the Jewish National Fund undertook to reflood about one-third of the area in an effort to undo the damage and rehabilitate the land.

Like the afforestation and swamp-draining projects, construction took on a patriotic, nationalistic tone.[29] Clearly, new immigrants required housing and places to work. But the leaders tried to give a greater meaning to the idea of building cities and towns to replace the sparsely settled barren land. Much of the ideology of conquering and settling the wilderness was incorporated into songs that young children learned in school and in their youth groups. Avner de-Shalit and Moti Talias quote from one song, popular throughout the 1950s and 1960s, extolling the virtues of construction and the modern society it would produce: "We shall build you, our beloved country, and make you beautiful; we shall cover you with a robe of concrete."[30]

Although in the last decade unbridled love of construction and territorial change have given way to some concern for the environment, the consequences of this early history remain deeply entrenched in the debates that characterize the country. Since the 1980s, as we have seen, a nascent environmental movement has campaigned for pollution controls, more adequate waste disposal, preservation of agricultural land,

and protection of the water supply. Despite growing success on these fronts, some of the most progressive activists despair that discussions about environmental issues remain firmly planted in a totally anthropocentric worldview. There is little regard for the biocentric argument that the wild and untouched are valuable, and that trees and plants and animals have rights to exist that override their value to human beings.[31]

Most Israeli environmentalists understand the need to protect limited natural resources, but continue to cast their arguments in terms of human health because it is the most efficacious way to build support for their issues. Uri Marinov, the first director general of the Ministry of the Environment, defended his staff for their reliance on compromise and the adoption of politically acceptable arguments. He believed that the mobilization of society around the issues of development in the early decades of statehood was so profound that few people ever stopped to ask questions about environmental impact. When Marinov and others in the Environmental Ministry sought to change behavior by seeking regulation and control over new construction projects, they "realized that most head-on conflicts with proponents of development would only be of nuisance value and would have very little effect on the decision-making process within the country."[32] Given his reading of the national mood, Marinov and other officials defending the environment made a point of never appearing to be working against economic development. They wanted both the public and others in the bureaucracy to think of them as cooperative, serious professionals who would be partners in planning and development decisions. Accordingly, they could have some ameliorative influence by requiring an environmental assessment before any decisions to build, but they could never introduce a conservation ethic into the Ministry of Housing or into the Lands Authority, which distributed and sold public land. Without such long-term conservation considerations, Marinov admitted, no one was able to prevent "the massive and unnecessary destruction of fragile and rare ecosystems and beautiful landscapes."[33]

Eilon Schwartz grew up in the United States and emigrated to Israel for ideological reasons. He first lived in Kibbutz Kiturah, a cooperative community in the Arava desert, where several dozen young

American families created a small communal society, engaged primarily in agricultural work, and lived close to the land. After several years, Schwartz and his wife and children decided to move to the city, where he could pursue his graduate studies and attempt to make some impact on environmental values in the country. In 1994, Schwartz and his colleague Jeremy Benstein opened the Abraham Joshua Heschel Center for Nature Study.[34] The purpose of the center was to go beyond the work of the existing legal defense and grassroots groups. They wanted to develop a Jewish approach to the natural environment that would give their ecological concerns deep spiritual connections.[35]

The goals of the center are far-reaching. While celebrating the increase in media attention to environmental issues and the growing grassroots interest, Eilon Schwartz decries the level on which the policy is discussed: "It is a very utilitarian kind of way of looking at the planet and the land and the earth and life in general. . . . In the public debate there is no place whatsoever for the value of open spaces other than as public-health issues. Even if you were to speak of psychological, aesthetic, or cultural issues, not to mention the more far-reaching questions of what damage you do to land and animals and plants, there is no place for this discussion. So that's the bad news. It's pretty bad." It is here that the Center finds its role, establishing programs that extend the dialogue about the ways in which Israelis relate to their land: "I guess if we have a niche, it is the niche of trying to deal with some of these questions that are a little bit more amorphous, trying to change the debate to contain within it a discussion of the ways in which we relate to the earth and the planet."[36]

Because Schwartz and Benstein believe that the environmental crisis is basically a spiritual crisis, they see their mission as bringing a values-oriented approach to environmental education. They are critical of what they call "positivistic science education," which assumes that the facts speak for themselves. They are always looking to stretch the arguments for preserving open space beyond the immediate benefit to the people around them. They want Israelis and all others to recognize the sacred qualities of the land and to think about its existence in future generations.

To pursue these goals, the Heschel Center runs seminars for Israeli residents and for visitors from abroad who have come for "an Israel experience." These experiential seminars take people into the desert and provide them with texts that allow them to raise philosophical questions about the meaning of place and homeland. A second major project has been to prepare an environmental curriculum for the schools. The first component of that curriculum was piloted in 1995 with fifth and sixth graders in twelve schools. Schwartz and Benstein trained teachers and observed responses in the classroom on a regular basis. They were encouraged by the early feedback. Their units were not designed to study pollution or garbage per se, although the Center recognizes that these are serious problems. Rather, they focused on topics entitled "Wonder," "Home," "Connections to Place," and "Values."

Schwartz recognizes that the Center has taken on a task far beyond the scope of its three current workers. But for our purposes the significance of their work lies not in the projects themselves, but rather in their attempt to broaden the questions addressed by environmentalists and lovers of the land of Israel. In the two years of its existence, established organizations like the Society for the Protection of Nature have contracted with the Heschel Center for leadership-training seminars, and teachers, students, and naturalists have responded well to the initial workshops and field experiences offered by the Center. But Schwartz is concerned that these study trips not be perceived as an outdoor vacation, where the beautiful scenery becomes merely a backdrop to a good time. A successful workshop should make participants uncomfortable by asking them to consider difficult questions that might clash with mainstream conceptions of the good life.

There are some hints of success in broadening the discourse about environmental values. The Ministry of Environment bulletin recently published an article by Yoav Sagi, the head of the moderate Society for the Protection of Nature, in which he raised the problem of overdevelopment very directly: "Do we want Israel's nature and landscape-based traditions to disappear under concrete and cement, to be later revisited only in books, picture albums, or museums? Is it our fate to live in a vast city-state and to experience the irony of fulfilling our need for open spaces by traveling to other lands?"[37]

Despite this recognition in an official publication, Eilon Schwartz and his colleagues have their work cut out for them. They have to develop a whole new consciousness that will often be defined as romantic and utopian, if not antiprogress and dangerous, by those who have tied their fortunes to an ever-expanding population and economy.

Nature Is Hard to Find and Even Harder to Protect

In 1994, Josef Vavroušek delivered an environmental-law seminar in Buenos Aires, Argentina, entitled "Searching for Human Values Compatible with the Sustainable Ways of Living." Vavroušek, the late director of the Faculty of Social Science at Charles University in Prague, had been the first federal minister of the environment after the Velvet Revolution of 1989. One of the most respected environmentalists in the Czech Republic, Vavroušek passionately believed that technocratic solutions would never resolve the profound issues facing his country. Education and a change of attitude toward nature were crucial if Czechs and Slovakians were to achieve sustainable use of natural resources.

In his Argentinean address, Vavroušek examined the high costs of Western-style development as it has unfolded in Western Europe and North America. While acknowledging the attractions of a consumer culture and a high standard of living, he focused on the long-term costs of using resources so intensively: "All these mentioned processes [of development] contribute to the rapid deterioration of nature and human environment on global, regional, and local scales. Air pollution leads to acid rain, ozone layer depletion, and climate changes. Forests lose their vitality, trees are cut down, soil is desertificated due to erosion, growing salinity, diminishing water content, and humus loss. Humans have negative—and irreversible—impact on natural resources, the gene pool, and Earth's life-supporting systems."[38]

Vavroušek went on to itemize major changes that he believed were crucial to creating a healthier global environment. His first category of change was entitled "Relation of Man to Nature," in which he emphasized the need for a revolutionary shift from a "predatory, exploitative relation to nature" to a much more complex relation that emphasized "respect for life in all its forms and for nature as a whole." These were the themes he had developed in his years as an environmental leader in Prague, first in the anti-Communist underground and later as a respected and charismatic leader in Czech environmental circles and in the Civic Forum.

Despite Josef Vavroušek's commanding presence and his articulate formulation of the need to break from old ideas and build a new relationship to nature, the position he espoused made little headway in Czech society. He died prematurely in 1995 in a tragic accident, leaving his country in the midst of a consuming drive to promote internationally attractive free markets, economic growth, and a wide array of imported consumer goods. His efforts in the first post-Communist government to establish environmental priorities were quickly modified by his successor, Frantisek Benda. In the government of Václav Klaus, Benda headed a weak ministry with a small budget and poor enforcement mechanisms. The move to implement changes that might ameliorate the most pressing pollution and waste-disposal problems proceeded slowly. Benda made no effort to incorporate the environmental organizations' views on pending legislation or policies, nor did he attempt to win their support.[39] The long-term struggle to live more easily with nature was no longer a priority in the Ministry of the Environment. This task was left to other environmental colleagues like Pavel Šremer and Bedrich Moldan. These activists had joined Vavroušek in major governmental positions in the early postrevolutionary years. They had hoped to set their fellow countrymen on a radical, new environmental course, but left the government after Václav Klaus was elected, and continued their activities in nongovernmental organizations.

Although the tension between respect for nature and the push for progress in the form of industrialization and economic development paralleled that found in the United States and Europe, societies that developed under a Marxist-Leninist ideology experienced a particularly strong emphasis on material growth and human labor and virtually no consideration for the value of nature. One environmentalist seeking to build a common understanding of the problem explained the ideological underpinnings that had proved so hostile to conservation and respect for nature in Czechoslovakia, as in most Communist states:

> Labour was the only human activity worthy of recognition, and production was the foundation of all human activity, to which obstacles and limitations had to be removed. When nature was in the way of production, it was tamed and subdued. Rivers were straightened, transferred, or chained. Hills were levelled, valleys filled in, forests cut and replanted somewhere else. Even towns and churches were moved when needed. Nothing escaped the force of human labour, which adjusted and transferred everything. When a party official said, "It is a production task," discussion had to stop and ecologists had to remain quiet.[40]

Some of this ideology echoes similar refrains in the United States and Israel. Love of nature rarely competed successfully with the call for progress and the imperatives of economic development. But Czechoslovakia's concentration of power in one authoritarian party that directed all institutions in the society made it even more difficult to introduce new ideas. At the same time, the Communist government allowed for the development of a countertrend. Determined to keep criticism of its aging industrial plants to a minimum, the government allowed the state-sponsored nature organizations to indulge in a love of nature, which seemed relatively harmless and far removed from government policy. Thus, organizations like Brontosaurus and SZOPK in Slovakia sponsored nature education, weekend camps in the countryside, and other activities.[41] A small dedicated group of ecologists, like Vavroušek and Šremer, understood well the inherent danger of regarding nature simply as a set of resources to be exploited and obstacles to be overcome, but they had little opportunity to express their views openly as a loyal opposition. Most of the public had no exposure to discussion of these issues, and little understanding of the sources of environmental degradation. As conditions worsened and air and water pollution became major health issues in the 1980s, public sentiment briefly ranked environmental issues as a high priority. But even in those heady days, when environmental activists were part of the revolutionary leadership, few thought that nature-preservation activities could seriously compete for scarce resources.

There were several inhibiting factors that prevented visionary environmentalists from spreading their views among the broader public. For more than a decade, dedicated activists were accustomed to meeting in small private circles of dissidents, exchanging information about the environment, discussing their opposition to the regime, and, finally in the late 1980s, exerting public pressure as the government weakened and the spirit of perestroika permeated society. But the necessity of maintaining secrecy and trust among dissidents remained a high priority, and this prevented activists either from promoting a program of biodiversity or from developing a structure for public education—the lobbying and public relations activities that are crucial to enhancing popular awareness and changing public views.

Foreign observers were often taken aback by the inability of the activists to communicate effectively outside their dissident subculture. Susan Cleveland was a young American working in Czechoslovakia in the early days of post-Communism. Like many idealistic Americans, she had come to Czechoslovakia in the early 1990s to teach English. Later she took a position with the Partnership for Eastern Europe, which was supported by the German Marshall Fund and other American foundations eager to help in the transition to democracy. As the program officer for both the Czech Republic and Slovakia, she oversaw grants to small grassroots NGO programs that focused on implementing local environmental improvements. Her biggest challenge was encouraging groups to think about public participation and about educating to raise awareness. She observed that the most experienced and dedicated environmentalists formed a closed circle, talking largely to a small group of their peers who understood their language and assumptions. Cleveland believed that most of the larger public had little knowledge about the relationship between automobiles and pollution or little understanding that energy conservation might improve the foul air they were breathing every day. Until some of these basic ideas were communicated to the general public in an understandable and accessible form, there would be little reason to expect people to resist the sudden influx of imported cars and wastefully packaged consumer goods. Meanwhile, the unenlightened populace ignored pleas for more public transportation and continued to use disposable items and to generate unnecessary solid waste.[42]

In this case, the tight bonds of solidarity built among the environmental activists had some negative consequences. Most of the activists had been dissidents under the Communists and had built their movement in a period when public trust was very low. Although the culture of solidarity among these environmentalists helped them survive in a hostile atmosphere, it did not emphasize public relations and strategies for raising consciousness. Some, like Juraj Zamkovsky in Slovakia, learned how difficult it could be to sustain public support. Others backed off and attempted to develop projects that small groups could undertake without requiring too much community engagement.

The chasm between sophisticated environmentalists and the larger public was exacerbated by the 1992 election of Václav Klaus as prime minister. Klaus, the minister of finance in the first government led by President Václav Havel, was architect of the economic-reform program implemented almost immediately after the transition government was established. Klaus had been a key figure in the Civic Forum, the leading movement against the Communists in Prague and the dominant group in the initial governing coalition. When the Civic Forum split in 1991, he became the head of the more conservative Civic Democratic Party, intent on moving ahead with privatization and the development of a free-market economy. He won strong support in the elections, promising a program that would encourage privatization, anti-inflation, foreign investment, and other measures to transform the centralized, administered, failing economy into a vibrant, consumer-based market. For him, these priorities took precedence over most environmental considerations, which would involve the state in the kinds of social regulation that he sought to end. In an interview in the United States in 1992, he articulated his complete disdain for regulation and government intervention: "We are not interested in the . . . socialist dreams of leftist liberal economists on this side of the ocean, in various universities here. We have to fight such ideas in Czechoslovakia. . . . We need neither third ways nor market socialist dreams, no perestroyka kind of thinking. We want to enter an ideological turnpike and proceed as fast as possible toward a market economy."[43]

Klaus's speech marked a distinct break from the philosophy espoused by Vavroušek and by Czechoslovakia's first president, the heroic Václav Havel. Havel represented the highest aspirations of the Czech people; as a writer, he took many occasions to voice the importance of respect for the planet and the urgency of the immediate environmental conditions. He decried previous philosophies that placed humans over all other living things: "In my opinion there are many reasons why the environment in our country is in such a catastrophic state. One of the reasons is the fact that the previous establishment was founded on a sort of proud ideology which proclaimed that Man was the final, though mortal, master of the Earth. . . . Man deduced his right to treat Nature as he will, to treat the Earth as he will. Because he was the master, the most perfect and cleverest. This ideology is enormously dangerous. Because, in the end, it puts Man above Nature and separates him from it."[44]

Havel argued for "humility of Man before the Universe, before Nature, the respect for the Earth, to grass, to trees, to everything living."[45] He recognized that his approach to environmental issues was abstract, and did not begin with a call for new scrubbers or filters on polluting plants. In the early days he had joined Vavroušek and others in urging citizens to rethink their place on the planet, but that idealism eventually gave way to Klaus's more practical and accessible demand for investment and economic growth. As the old security of full employment, guaranteed pensions, and free health care and education gave way to an emphasis on individual achievement, many focused almost exclusively on the demands of the transition to capitalism, and quickly forgot the messages of Havel and the environmental leaders.

The long history of disregard for nature, the closed circle of environmentalists, and the passionate focus on the free market by the government leadership all combined to reduce the priority of environmental issues. These historical factors undermined the salience of more visionary concerns about changing human understanding of the centrality of nature. But even in a more open-minded atmosphere, it would have been difficult to concentrate resources on nature protection unless it was clearly linked to solving human health problems.

Every assessment since 1989 has pointed to the severity of the environmental problems in the Czech Republic and Slovakia and the negative impact on human health. Even the most dedicated and informed activists felt compelled to turn their attention from a more far-reaching goal of protecting natural resources and undeveloped land to focus on immediately threatening issues. Concerns such as forest protection, which are associated in other countries with aesthetics as well as with long-term protection of natural ecosystems, have taken on a different meaning in the devastated region of northern Bohemia. Once an area of dense forests that covered hundreds of thousands of acres in Germany, the Czech Republic, and Poland, the "Black Triangle" now suffers from the worst pollution in Europe. More than 25 percent of the trees have suffered severe damage or death, a consequence of strip-mining and pollution from unprotected power plants that spew heavy black smoke over the entire area. The destruction has been so great that whole towns, some dating back to the Middle Ages, had to be moved when they became uninhabitable. Tree-planting projects are now necessary to cover mountain slopes that are otherwise subject to erosion and serious flooding, but most saplings cannot survive in the contaminated soil. In this context, environmentalists have to find an ideology that sustains their commitment to a deep and abiding relationship with nature, yet also addresses urgent problems of human health and regional survival.

In theory, the language advocated by Vavroušek and Havel continues to inform national environmental policy. A statement issued by the Ministry of the Environment, "The Principles of the Czech Environment Protection Policy," incorporates the vocabulary that would lead to integrating a healthy respect for nature into plans for economic development and improving human health.[46] In practice, many observers fear that time is short and that little progress was made in the first five years after the revolution. Air-quality specialists from all over the industrialized world have gathered to view the shocking elimination of gases, which intermittently have interacted to produce symptoms like numbness or joint pains in residents of local towns. Many experts have assessed these emissions as an international disaster. In reviewing all of Eastern Europe's environmental accomplishments at the end of 1994, one discouraged World Bank consultant told

a *New York Times* reporter, "Achievements? They are few, rather fragile and very dispersed."[47]

In the face of these problems, grassroots groups have developed
small, local projects to keep the possibility of progress alive. The Partnership for Eastern Europe continues to fund local groups that engage
the public in participating and making decisions to implement improvements and raise awareness. In November 1995, for example, it
awarded grants to thirteen groups, whose programs ranged from organizing community involvement to prevent the cutting of trees along
roads and protecting growth around ponds to opposing the construction of a waste dump and organizing the creation of an alternative
plan. The leaders continue to speak of longer-term ecological health,
but it may require some years of modest improvements and a stable
economy before protection of natural resources and a plan for biodiversity become a broader concern.

Expanding the Horizons

Citizen activist groups often organized in response to a local problem that threatened the health and well-being of the community.
Motivated by the discovery of contamination or pollution, local organizers were often intent on developing strategies to compel the government and industry to solve the problem. The commitment and drive of
these grassroots activists often derives from the immediacy of their
concerns. The personal relevance of a local environmental threat
serves to heighten activists' sense that they are entitled to speak out
and make demands, for they can never be accused of interfering in
someone else's business.

In contrast, environmentalists intent on protecting unspoiled
wilderness, natural landscapes, and rich biological diversity necessarily find themselves outside their immediate neighborhoods, moving
beyond local issues and local boundaries. They want to broaden the
terms of the environmental debate and to defend plants and animals
that may have no direct relationship to humans. Whether they speak

for the trees, as Susie Van Kirk did in many meetings of the Forest Service, or defend animal rights or argue for a rethinking of the human exploitation of the world's resources for economic development, these environmental activists are arguing for a worldview that is less anthropocentric. They advocate a limitation on the liberal emphasis on individual rights that has thus far dominated Western thought and progress. Most of the activists understand that they are involved in an uphill battle, for they are promoting values that undermine deeply held ideas about economic development, corporate profit, and consumer culture. Opponents often caricature environmentalists who campaign for biodiversity as caring more about spotted owls than about decent working families.

The more devastated an area, the more difficult it is to introduce ideas that place human concern in the larger context of saving the planet. Yet these environmental advocates have not been without some victories. The concept of sustainable development has become part of every environmental vocabulary. Understanding of the term "sustainable" still varies greatly: from sustainable yields of a valuable product to sustained ecological diversity. Yet even the most constricted use of the term suggests that future needs must be part of present-day planning. Not all of the world's finite resources can be available for the present generation. This interpretation of the problem represents increased awareness. The struggle will not end soon, and while activists despair over the rapid loss of habitat and the demise of hundreds of plant and animal species, they continue to press for a healthier world. As their numbers grow and their coalitions broaden, their views will be heard by larger numbers of people and by decision makers throughout the world.

6

The Courage of Ordinary People

Many scholars who study acts of courage focus primarily on military and police situations or on other heroic events that occur in the effort to save the lives of others. Such actions are dramatic, requiring, for instance, the split-second decision to charge a machine-gun nest raining lethal fire on one's comrades, or to rush into a burning boiler room to rescue injured sailors before rising waters engulf them.[1] But for grassroots activists, courage takes another form. The situations they face are rarely life threatening; rather, their battles demand a longer-term investment of time and energy. Nonetheless, courage is a major component of their actions. They must be ready to withstand withering criticism of their credibility, competence, and integrity. They must face attacks that may sully their reputations, isolate them from one-time friends and neighbors, and even cause rifts within their own families. Under extreme circumstances, grassroots activists face physical threats, police harassment, and imprisonment.

Knowing these risks, ordinary people in our study exhibited determination and courage when they proclaimed the dangers of serious environmental situations and committed themselves to building a sustained collective campaign to demand accountability and remediation. Thus, while their decisions did not reflect the single act of heroism associated with military bravery, these activists had to muster the stamina to spend years intensively involved in their cause, resulting in stress and the disruption of the rhythm of their lives. Friends and colleagues often experienced burnout, providing a constant reminder of the difficulties of the long-term crusade to ensure a safe environment.

This is precisely what occurred to Cheryl Washburn and Cathy Hinds, two women who were fighting the effects of a hazardous-waste site in Maine. Over time Cathy Hinds continued the struggle, but Cheryl Washburn began to withdraw from total involvement. She explained her inability to sustain intense activity:

It takes a certain person to be able to keep at it all the time. Cathy is one of those people. She's strong, and in some ways strong willed. For me, it came down to wanting to live a normal life. I didn't want to be faced with this thing every day, or I'd be a basket case. I didn't want to go to all the meetings, to keep butting my head against a wall. As Cathy slowly started doing more, I slowly backed off. Cathy has a way with words—she knows how to put things, and I was glad to let her take over. I'm proud of what we did—and I'm proud of her for keeping it up.[2]

The philosopher Douglas N. Walton argues that courageous behavior is rare in contemporary industrial society:

Perhaps another reason that courage today seems an absurd or outdated virtue is the growing lack of cohesiveness in social structures and group purposes. In vast modern industrial societies, the individual feels anonymous and often loses identity with the community as a group. This phenomenon in North America has often been remarked upon. Twenty-six bystanders watched as Kitty Genovese was brutally murdered on the street. Not one even calling the police. The current expression is "nobody wants to get involved." A kind of moral anomie is described by Camus in *L'Etranger*—an individual fails to feel even the smallest sympathy or emotion at the death of another. The attitude seems to be a moral aimlessness, a lack of purpose beyond one's own egoistic interests. To one in this frame of mind, courage—taking personal risks to try and save another or to help the group or community in time of trouble—seems simply an irrational risk—no gain at all.[3]

Using a new approach that focuses on sustained and collective courage, we have encountered scores of instances where citizens have banded together to help their communities. In contrast to Walton's assertion, grassroots activists have displayed impressive strength and resilience in caring for others and in their willingness to put themselves at risk to assist their community. They have exhibited endurance and intelligence, and fortitude in overcoming their fear, qualities that reflect Socrates' definition of courage: "Socrates seems to agree that courage involves the mastery of fear and other passions by something like resolve of mind or will, though he also insists that there is more to courage than that, that endurance must be guided by intelligence or wisdom to be the human virtue of courage."[4]

Why were the grassroots environmental activists able to engage in such behavior when so many of their fellow citizens apparently have not responded with comparable courage? Our research points to several distinctive dimensions. First, a courageous response to a community's problems does not occur in a vacuum. It is not based on a spontaneous decision. Rather, courageous citizens call on a reservoir of social capital that they have developed over many years and have been ready to invest in the community when a crisis arose. Those we studied cared about their neighbors and saw their own fate as intertwined with that of others. After careful reflection, they believed fully in the rightness of their cause. With this conviction, as Socrates would attest, they could not be moved. Activists were ready to become "culture menders."[5] Second, they had a strong commitment to the efficacy of united action. The activists believed that they could make a difference.

They felt that the authorities would be responsive to their petition if it were based on a strong demonstration of public support. The environmental crusaders rejected cynicism and refused to accept a future without hope. Third, courageous behavior depended on the activists' ability and willingness to accumulate the evidence and expertise that would allow them to press their case. They had to counter with confidence and competence the technological experts and policy makers who belittled their concerns. To achieve this goal they had to secure strategically placed allies. These could be members of other environmental groups, legislative leaders, public-interest attorneys, and cooperative workers in the polluting industries who could supply firsthand information. Fourth, these purveyors of courage had to overcome fear and intimidation. The activists knew that the reduction of serious environmental problems would not occur without years of struggle. The opposing government bureaucrats and corporate managers and their supporters would all extract a price for challenging the status quo. The crusaders' determination to persist in the face of such obstacles attests to their belief in the democratic process and to their profound commitment to act for the common good. This faith in the justice of their cause and in their personal competence overcame the intensity of their fear of retaliation. Without their courage, without their willingness to endure on behalf of their beliefs, without their determination to help their communities, serious environmental problems would lie buried beneath the surface, with the potential to do great damage to unknowing and unprotected victims.

The Reservoir of Social Capital

Grassroots activists were deeply involved in the affairs of the community. They were not alienated or passive citizens unwilling and unable to show concern for others. Their sense of self was fully engaged in what happened to their families, neighborhoods, regions, and countries. They may have become environmental activists later in life, but they had been prepared by a previously developed and strongly held value system. These values included a sense of caring for others, a feeling of responsibility for their safety, and a slowly evolving but nonetheless strong commitment to act when others were in danger. The activists were conveyers of what Robert Putnam and others have labeled social capital. People such as Lynn Golumbic in Israel, Ja'ra Johnova in Czechoslovakia, Penny Newman in the United States, and many others may have exercised civic responsibility in more conventional ways until an environmental crisis propelled them into the public arena. But their community-based system of values had been developed and implemented earlier in PTAs, Green Circles, and other organizations, and had been released as they prepared to step forward into a leadership role. With their principles intact, they built grassroots organizations and thus joined a militant vanguard in defending communities from victimization by government and corporate bureaucracies. These women and others like them were vital menders of their torn, disrupted, or endangered cultures.

Each of the women cited above had borne children and had sought to raise them in the safest and healthiest areas. Penny Newman had spent countless hours volunteering to help improve the school system in Glen Avon, California. Ja'ra Johnova had taken the dangerous step of signing the Charter 77 document petitioning the Czechoslovakian government to respect human rights, and for years was part of a dissident group in Prague. Lynn Golumbic, who had moved to Israel from the United States so that she and her young family could participate in the effort to build a democratic Jewish state, joined AACI (Association of Americans and Canadians in Israel), which focused on a wide range of social issues. For all of them, assuming a leadership role to confront environmental emergencies represented a major commitment and much greater public exposure. Yet this new action was grounded in past experiences and beliefs. Helping the community in a time of crisis was in clear continuity with their strongly held values. Although their new roles ruptured old schedules and made new demands, these roles were built on a foundation that could weather the intensive demands of community leadership.[6]

This reservoir of social capital, this principled connection to others, is a core component of courageous behavior. The risks of speaking out about a problem and assuming leadership could be costly, as Tom Bailie learned. Bailie, the farmer in eastern Washington State whose land abutted the Hanford Nuclear Reservation, epitomizes the grass-roots activist whose past experiences prepared him to announce the existence of a crisis, even if such action was undertaken at his own peril. Bailie had deep roots in the area; he grew up on his parents' farm, raised a family, and ran for political office. He understood that speaking out against the Hanford nuclear facility entailed substantial risks. He would be a marked man from then on—someone who had punctured the cultural fiction, the commonly held faith that nothing was wrong, that everything was under control. Nevertheless, he urged his neighbors and other area residents to face the seriousness of their situation. He told stories of deformed animals and of an epidemic of cancer, illness, and death. Bailie urged all who would listen to question the very source of their sense of economic security. He encouraged them to challenge the government and corporations that provided their livelihood. This was not a scenario that was likely to make Bailie a local hero, and for years he was an object of ridicule and scorn. His was a dangerous position, but it was one that he was determined to hold, no matter what the personal cost.

As mentioned earlier, Tom Bailie had suffered from severe physical illness during his childhood. Polio had hospitalized him for months; his own father, despairing of his son's survival from the dread disease, had actually prayed for his merciful death while standing at Tom's sickbed. This intense suffering during his early years, his repeated encounters with deformed animals on his parents' farm, and his personal experience with the monitoring of school children by the scientists from Hanford led Bailie to feel that "something was wrong." And he was right. As an adult, he became deeply distressed when his neighbors became seriously ill or died from cancer. The "cancer map" generated by a nearby couple, which plotted the number of people who had suffered from the disease, became his ever-present reminder and a central piece of evidence influencing his thoughts and emotions. It provided meaning to his decision to continue telling his stories, for many had died, and many others were debilitated. Bailie felt a special sense of mission to organize those who later called themselves Downwinders.

His actions were not taken precipitately; they had gestated over many years, and derived from more than a sense of personal victimization. As a long-term member of the community who was active in local affairs, Bailie had a strong sense of personal responsibility to seek justice for all the victims of government and corporate negligence in the Hanford region: "What I have to do goes beyond my marriage and my other family relationships. I'm sorry. I don't know what I have to do to complete this, but I'll be glad when it's done. We still have to find out what the nuclear gang has done to those of us that live here, and how it has affected our lives and affected our health. We've just scratched the surface."[7]

On the Efficacy of Grassroots Action

Crusaders like Tom Bailie, Penny Newman, Lynn Golumbic, and Ja'ra Johnova assumed the personal responsibility to confront serious environmental problems that affected their communities. Their involvement began when they became convinced that remedial action would not be undertaken voluntarily by the perpetrators. Despite the intransigence of the polluters, these grassroots activists believed that gathering information, focusing attention, and organizing to combat social problems could make a difference in every society, whether democratic or authoritarian. Their belief in the potential of organizing ordinary people drove them forward even in Czechoslovakia, where the government had a history of repressive reactions against protesters. These strongly held cultural assumptions about their entitlement to speak out on public affairs and about the efficacy of united actions were crucial ingredients in the activists' willingness to be stigmatized as the bearers of bad news, and reinforced their readiness to put themselves at risk to resolve major social issues. According to Walton's definition, they were among that rare breed of citizens in modern industrial society who define their own interests according to the well-being of others. Yet they were not altruists. They were realists who believed that personal or familial safety could not be achieved by hiding from a crisis. Only by facing it directly and deciding what each individual could do to resolve it could the community members move forward to overcome frightening hazards in their midst. While they sought distant goals, they believed fully that they could achieve them.[8]

Mary Sinclair embodied this belief when she raised her concerns about the safety of a nuclear power plant being built in her community of Midland, Michigan. While she was "pro-nuclear," she had a sufficiently good background in science to understand the problems that plagued the civilian nuclear industry. She believed strongly in the right and responsibility of citizens to speak out on central issues. However, she didn't anticipate the hostile reaction she provoked. As Anne Witte Garland tells it,

> [Mary] started writing letters to the editor of the *Midland Daily News,* in which she suggested "in the mildest terms" that there were problems to be discussed. The letters were published, but weren't received in the spirit she intended. She was surprised by the response. "I had simply taken what I thought was a routine action by a citizen," she says, "one I had seen as an obligation, since normally, if you live in a community and understand that something is wrong, you try to do something about it. The hostile reaction shocked me. People didn't like anything that constituted the least challenge to what Dow, Consumers Power, and the AEC were saying. They were a big power bloc; I knew that. I just hadn't realized *how* big."[9]

Like Mary Sinclair, Harold and Dorothy Clinesmith in eastern Washington state, Reuven Bezner in northern Israel, and Juraj Zamkovsky in Bratislava, Slovakia, were all firm believers in the potential good that could result from determined efforts on their part. As members of farming communities, Bezner and the Clinesmiths had a deep relationship to the land. They had lived on it and worked it for many decades, and felt responsible to protect it from outsiders intent on ruining its fertile and productive qualities. Moreover, they realized that to be successful they had to develop activists' skills. They had to learn much more about the threats of garbage, the limits of the technology of landfills, the economics of waste disposal, and the alternatives to burying solid and toxic wastes near their homes. Sentimental appeals based on childhood memories or the area's traditions were insufficient. For their protests to be taken seriously, they had to match the expertise and knowledge of corporate and government witnesses. Reuven Bezner wryly joked about becoming a "doctor" of garbage as he gathered information on waste disposal from every region in Israel. Harold Clinesmith built a local organization and later worked with like-minded environmentalists both locally and throughout the country, who assisted and encouraged him as he developed strategies to oppose a new toxic-waste facility. While only in his twenties, Juraj Zamkovsky was motivated by the success of the Velvet Revolution in his native Czechoslovakia and the growing importance of People Against Violence to bring vital environmental knowledge to his village of Budmerice in Slovakia. Zamkovsky, like many others, misjudged the volatile political realities and ultimately had to face failure and disappointment in his project. Yet his analysis of the causes enabled him to move on to play a major role in the Slovakian environmental movement.

In all of these cases, the activists drew upon a reservoir of social capital and invoked their right to act and their belief that they could achieve their environmental goals. This potent mixture drove them forward to gather even more confirming data to support their claims. Their next step in building a sustained form of courageous behavior was to obtain the evidence, for without it, despite their best intentions, they would be defeated.

With Facts on Their Side

The activists' faith in their mission and belief in their skills were essential ingredients in mounting a long-term campaign. In virtually every case they also had to accumulate evidence that would support their opinion that an environmental hazard directly threatened their community. They needed to convince the undecided among their neighbors that their passion was supported by credible and documented evidence. Similarly, the crusaders had to reveal to their adversaries that local residents could not be intimidated by the experts' claims to superior knowledge or greater economic resources. Gathering data was essential if they were to prove that they were a force to be reckoned with.

For Tom Bailie, the unfolding of layer after layer of once-classified information slowly undermined the arguments of his detractors and confirmed his suspicion that the Hanford Nuclear Reservation was releasing dangerous emissions onto the local population. The same government and corporations that were charged with protecting the safety of the region's citizens turned out to be culpable for knowingly releasing radiation onto civilian populations in the area. Despite their public-relations claims to the contrary, these bureaucratic organizations had shown blatant disregard for the safety of nearby communities. The testimony of Tom Bailie, Lois Camps, Judith Jurgi, and the cancer-death maps of Leon and Juanita Andrewjeski were now supported by government documents and other hard data that had been obtained as a result of a decision by several organizations to file a Freedom of Information Act (FOIA) inquiry. The Freedom of Information Act, which had been enacted in 1966, was crucial to furthering the activists' cause. To make full use of the FOIA, Bailie and the other activists had to rely on the technical assistance of allies in the press and in HEAL, the local public-interest group. Once they had government data confirming their claims of radiation exposure, their allegations could no longer be dismissed as the statements of paranoid personalities. Those who had risked their reputations by questioning the secrecy of the national security state or by challenging the economic viability of the defense-based economy now had the facts on their side. Family members might still be embarrassed and humiliated by the public controversy surrounding the crusaders, but they were also sobered by the evidence, which gave weight to the deadly consequences of the problem.

Not all societies have a Freedom of Information Act, and activists frequently had to use indirect methods to secure the necessary data. In Slovakia, before the fall of the Communists, a group of dedicated environmentalists knew that they had to compile the documentation that would reveal the desperate state of the environment if they were to raise public awareness and open a dialogue with government officials. The activists believed that years of silence had to end and that the time was ripe to challenge the Communists. After decades of repression, the possibility of change was now in the air. Although "socialism with a human face" had been crushed in 1968 by Soviet tanks, by the late 1980s even Soviet leaders talked of reforms that sounded like the model they had destroyed twenty years earlier. The circulation of new ideas suggested to the activists that the time was right for a bold but carefully planned action that would expose the immensity of the environmental damage. With retaliation, harassment, and even imprisonment possible outcomes, the environmentalists knew that their effort had to be grounded in incontrovertible evidence. The best source of data was the government itself, and the activists spent months surreptitiously gathering information from officials who did not suspect that their contributions would be collated, matched, and eventually integrated into a report; taken together, the accumulated evidence painted a dismal portrait of government environmental policy.

The publication of *Bratislava Nahlas* provided documented assertions about the abysmal failure of the Communists to protect the country from air, water, and land contamination. The writers of the report, drawn from all professional fields, sought to avoid the label of political "dissidents." Rather, they claimed legitimacy as recorders of hard data that pointed to dangerous environmental conditions. The publication of the evidence substantiated their accusations and yet heightened the vulnerability of the activists. Would the government now confiscate the report, harass and arrest them, or subject them to violence? Was assassination a possibility? The *Bratislava Nahlas* group was prepared for the inevitable retaliation, having lived with its threat for years.

Overcoming Fear

Jan Budaj and Maria Filkova in Slovakia, Tom Bailie and Penny Newman in the United States, and Lynn Golumbic, Reuven Bezner, and Dr. Hatim Kana'aneh in Israel all epitomize the complex dimensions of courageous behavior within the grassroots environmental movement. They embody the challenge of exposing a major social problem and assuming a leadership role to resolve it. How did they and other activists withstand the fear of retaliation? What are the emotional, social, and cultural foundations of courageous behavior that support and sustain the decision to become a citizen crusader despite omnipresent threats? Where did they find the resolve to blow the whistle on community problems often shrouded in secrecy and vehemently denied by powerful and potentially vindictive interests?[10]

Activists were enabled to move against powerful interests by four major factors. First, they transformed their anger into a positive determination to take action. Second, they were not fatalists; they believed that their situation could be changed and were willing to invest time and energy to bring those changes about. Third, they depended on the trust and comradeship that developed in their local groups to sustain their motivation and commitment in the face of frustrations and setbacks. Finally, these grassroots activists overcame the inevitable fear of retaliation by defining the environmental problems they confronted as more severe, more troubling, and more threatening than their fears of rejection and isolation.

Anger often served as a major initial motivator and eventually became a central emotional resource. Activists exhibited strength by vehemently rejecting their victimization. They were enraged by officials who spoke of concern and protection for the public while failing to act to remedy serious environmental risk. According to Garland:

> Anger is often at the center of [activists'] transformations from private actors in restricted universes to public leaders in universes encompassing all the important issues of the day. The anger comes, of course, from a variety of sources. And it crosses the putative barriers of age and racial differences; differences in education, background, and lifestyle; and differences in religious and political belief.

Gale Cincotta, who declined to allow her Chicago neighborhood to be exploited by real estate developers, claims that what motivated her most urgently was her anger. "When you look carefully at what's going on around you, you have to get angry. I got mad, and that gave me courage."[11]

All the activists refused to accept their current situations as simply a matter of fate. For Penny Newman and her neighbors, the plume of dangerous chemicals moved underground like an unstoppable and unbearable plague toward their homes. For Dr. Hatim Kana'aneh, sewage-induced disease in his village in northern Israel remained a constant reminder of his people's vulnerability. Despite his excellent medical training, he had been unable to prevent suffering and grief throughout the area inhabited by Arabs. For both Newman and Kana'aneh, their day-to-day exposure to continuing problems put their own anxieties and fears in perspective. Nevertheless, as leaders they were on the front line, and they became lightning rods for derision from their critics. Their motives were constantly questioned. Doesn't she really crave the limelight? Did he really care about his community? Weren't they undermining the region's economic health, or making far too many demands on the government?

Trust proved essential in sustaining commitment and solidarity among the activists. The accusations, the demeaning comments, even the threats of physical attack or arrest and imprisonment in Czechoslovakia, were all made bearable by the culture of solidarity that existed in the activists' group. Neighbors and colleagues had come to have a shared vision of the community's problems. They had confronted the disasters head-on. The most committed felt it was their responsibility to see the struggle through to the best conclusion possible. Pavel Šremer, a longtime dissident and one of the core group in the *Bratislava Nahlas* movement, emphasized how mutual trust sustained them through difficult times. Each Bratislava participant had an assigned set of tasks, and the others had faith that it would be completed. To stop their work, to be paralyzed by the fear of what the government could do to them, would grant their adversaries an unacceptable victory. Faith in their cause and support for each other were strong incentives during their months of intensive, secret activity.

The emotion of anger and the culture of solidarity were crucial components enabling most group members to overcome the fear of pressing for change, but certain organizational developments were equally necessary. Even in the most informally organized neighborhood groups, leaders emerged to play central roles in maintaining an effective effort. Women like Penny Newman of Concerned Neighbors in Glen Avon, California, or Lisa Crawford of Fernald Residents for Environmental Health and Safety (FRESH) did not start out as leaders. The very act of organizing presented a challenge that enabled them to develop their skills as public speakers, learn the necessary technical information, and build consensus for their strategies in the community. They experienced the anxiety of wondering whether they could do the job. Were they competent to testify before a congressional committee or lobby a state legislator? Would public officials humiliate and embarrass them or their friends? They did not overcome these fears alone. In the early days, their husbands urged them forward, and congressional aides mentored them in preparing to testify and helped them obtain government reports. Other environmental activists tutored them in organizing strategies, and perhaps most important, their peers displayed great faith in their abilities. These peers were willing to work hard out of the limelight to make small successes possible: some created lists of prospective members; others made endless phone calls; still others studied and mastered myriad technical reports.

Leaders like Penny Newman and Lisa Crawford became the spokeswomen who articulated the group's views in public. They presented a strong and competent face to the media. They could tell dramatic tales of threats to their children's health and describe their inability to prevent illness or correct the course of a disease. Their disturbing histories reflected the fears and anxieties of their friends and neighbors, but their leadership did not end with fear. They were eloquent in their descriptions of organizing and reaching out to join hands with others in their communities. Theirs were stories of women pushing aside feelings of vulnerability to forge links and create allies in the struggle to combat powerful adversaries. For a community group to survive the turmoil of lengthy engagement, a leader like Penny Newman or Lisa Crawford had to develop and maintain the energy and commitment to bring about significant change. In turn, Penny Newman, Lisa Crawford, and hundreds of others like them found their lives transformed as they became recognized community leaders.

Activists faced fear of failure, fear of criticism and ridicule, fear of attack and assault, and fear of imprisonment and exile, but these fears did not stop them, for they believed that the costs of inaction were even higher. Their most difficult obstacles were not the anxieties of reprisal. Rather, they had to face the difficulties of burnout, of dissolution when an initial victory was in hand and yet the long-term problems seemed so difficult to resolve. A successful court case did not end pollution or provide adequate solutions for toxic wastes; preserving one stand of ancient forest might not have any bearing on land ten miles away. Activists had to reject the understandable pressure to say, That's enough. In different ways, with distinctive cultural and personal measures, they had to balance the scales. They had decided to act. They had faced down their most profound fears and their deepest despairs. They did not succumb to the prevalent strategy adopted by many in modern society. They did not retreat into privatism—shutting their doors and windows to focus on individual needs and comforts. By continuing to tie their own well-being to that of the larger community, they sustained and reinforced the motivations of others around them. For example, several members of the Stringfellow core group explained how much they depended on their leader, Penny Newman. One friend described their relationship and its significance in sustaining her motivation over a long period of time. "Penny will depend on me to do a lot of the mundane tasks. Sometimes, it seems like, oh no, she's asking me to do another thing, when I already have five things to do. Then she'll send me a bouquet of flowers or drop a little note of appreciation. And that makes it easier, makes you feel like you just can't give up."[12]

Despite the ongoing problems and frustrations in all three societies—the United States, Israel, and Czechoslovakia—the leadership, the bonds of solidarity, and the groups' persistent challenge to uninterested or negligent authorities enabled the communities to achieve some significant victories. While much environmental remediation remains to be done, the crusaders have succeeded in forcing the government and corporations to respond to their continuing pressure. At times the successes were quite dramatic. Both Concerned Neighbors

in California and FRESH in Ohio won major legal victories and ex-
tracted government commitments to contain and remedy significant
environmental damage. The United States Department of Energy admitted years of illegal radiation exposure and turned its attention and
some of its resources to cleaning up the most contaminated sites. The
Electric Power Company in Haifa, Israel, agreed to provide data on
air pollution and to reduce daily emissions. The government of Israel
withdrew its agreement to cooperate with the United States to build a
tower in the Negev desert, despite its earlier commitment. The Communist government of Czechoslovakia, in power for forty years, although backed by its own ruthless secret police and the threat of Soviet tanks, fell to the popular forces of students, workers, and
intellectuals whose ranks included many environmentalists. Such victories were important in and of themselves, but they also served to
sustain motivation among activists. Convinced that their efforts were
not futile, they rededicated themselves to continuing their long-term
struggle for a safe environment.

In the Name of the Children

For Penny Newman or Lisa Crawford in the United States, for Lynn
Golumbic in Israel, and for the Prague Mothers, their children were a
direct inspiration to act and served as a central emotional impetus for
courageous behavior. Ja'ra Johnova said it most directly when she
stated that if she didn't act now, how could she in the future look her
as-yet-unborn child in the eye? Children, then, even the unborn, serve
as potential evaluators of action or inaction in the face of life-changing
events. The fears of confronting state authority and demanding attention to debilitating problems of air pollution were swept away by the
yet-unspoken questions from a child's voice: What have you done to
make my life better? What steps have you taken to protect me from the
threats of ill health? Parents, we are usually told, are the role models
for their children. They embody appropriate behavior both in the pri-
vacy of the home and in the public arena. Yet we seldom emphasize

that influence also runs the other way. Children can directly affect the actions and involvement of their parents. Most frequently, we notice that parents "settle down" when they have children, taking fewer risks as they assume responsibility for their young. Paradoxically, in the case of the citizen crusaders, the opposite was true. Their children ended the inertia, anxiety, and fear that served to enforce conformity and acquiescence to the norms of the community. As parents identified the needs of their defenseless children, they often overcame earlier patterns of behavior and took great risks to speak out courageously in the political arena.

Another student of toxic communities, Michael Edelstein, has emphasized the special role of women in organizing their communities:

> Women tend to predominate in leadership positions of groups concerned with toxic exposure. This phenomenon may be due to a number of factors. In the communities that tend to suffer most from toxic contamination—blue-collar, lower middle-class, or poor areas—women tend to stay home and care for the children. They have established social networks available for quick action, and they are more likely to recognize patterns of ill health in the neighborhood. Men in the affected communities often work for polluting industries. They may see themselves as having failed in their role as protector of the home, or they may view as unmasculine the public admission of fears and concerns over health and safety. Finally, unlike men, women may be a little more distanced from the dominant social paradigm of economic growth and, therefore, less willing to rationalize risks as necessary for economic well-being.[13]

There were, of course, men who were deeply involved in protecting the well-being of children. Dr. Hatim Kana'aneh came back to Israel in 1970 after years of study in the United States. He returned because of his dedication to provide health care in his Arab village of Arrabe as well as other underserved Arab villages in the northern Galilee. This resolve to stay and lead the crusade for good health ended after a tragic and bloody confrontation in 1976 between villagers and Israeli troops. Six young Arabs died on Land Day, as it came to be called, when they protested the government's confiscation of village lands. Dr. Kana'aneh despaired over relations between Israeli Arabs and their government, and he and his immediate family moved to Hawaii, where earlier he had studied and had met his wife. He took a position as a physician there, yet after two years the family returned to Arrabe. They were drawn home to the safety, support, and nurturance that, they believed, could best be found among kin and neighbors in their village. Dr. Kana'aneh quickly resolved that certain forms of environmental illness now had to be addressed. He did not want his children or others to grow up in villages where raw sewage ran freely down the hillsides. As a result, he assumed a far more active and public role in protecting the health of all of the Arab children in his area by organizing the Galilee Society to achieve those ends.

As we have seen with Dr. Kana'aneh and many others, environmental threats often motivate parents to undertake public activity, to call attention to a problem, to put the spotlight on the inequities in the social order, and to demand remediation. Those who exposed themselves to potential difficulties often acted precisely because they were heeding the unspoken voice of their young offspring.

The courage of ordinary people was built on social ties, belief in united action, anger, determination, prior experience, and responsibility to children. All of these components of courage served to create a broader vision among activists. They were able to look beyond the present moment, beyond the current economic, political, and social realities, to envision a future where community responsibility and public accountability would thrive.[14] Children became a metaphor in articulating their concern for future generations. Children were the most important reason for continuing to struggle, even if the resolution of deep-seated problems seemed unlikely to happen soon. Replanting a forest was an act of faith in the future, just as years-long efforts to deal with waste disposal represented a commitment to save the land from ultimate contamination. The grassroots environmental activists were determined to keep these hopes alive for their children, grandchildren, and the generations to come. They spoke in many languages for those who could not yet speak for themselves.

Methodological Appendix:

Tracking the Environmental Crusaders

During the last several years, we have learned much about the environment and about those who have vowed to protect it. We have heard activists speak of the dangers that they, their children, and their neighbors confront as they reside in communities contaminated by toxic waste and air, water, and soil pollution. We have sat with others angered and disappointed by government and corporate decisions that threaten nearby forest ridges or virgin land and clean water. We have also heard the voices of their critics, who doubt the sincerity, seriousness, and accuracy of the complaints by environmental activists. While some of these detractors acknowledge the existence of environmental challenges, they emphasize the primacy of economic development, national security, or the containment of costs in creating public policy. As we have learned firsthand, controversy always swirls around the protesters.

Our main purpose in this study has been to understand the activists' backgrounds, motivations, goals and methods, strategic alliances, and contribution to the maintenance of a vibrant democratic society. Toward this end we conducted more than 140 interviews in three countries between 1991 and 1996. In the United States, where we interviewed eighty-six people, we focused on small, locally based groups organized around nuclear-bomb factories; activists protesting radiation exposure, hazardous-waste contamination, or the building of incinerators and garbage-disposal facilities in their communities; and grassroots crusaders determined to halt clear-cutting of nearby old-growth forests that are rapidly disappearing. In addition to intensive interviews with leaders and core-group members of these grassroots

environmental efforts, we also spoke with local journalists and officials, and leaders of public-interest groups. Whenever possible, we attended public meetings where controversies were aired. Interviews
and firsthand observations were supplemented by thousands of pages
of documents, ranging from monthly newsletters, organizational reports, and siting maps to articles by investigative journalists.

The American subjects of our study were located in five states—
Washington, California, Idaho, Oregon, and Ohio. A large group of activists resided in the communities surrounding the Hanford Nuclear
Reservation in eastern Washington and the Fernald, Ohio, nuclear-
bomb factory. We interviewed leaders and core-group members in both
communities who were deeply concerned with the radiation exposure
that had occurred over a period of decades. To obtain a more textured
understanding of those cases, we also interviewed public-interest-
group staff, union leaders, and government officials, all of whom had
had ongoing interactions with community activists.

In the areas surrounding the Hanford Nuclear Reservation we interviewed eleven people, including five Downwinders who believed
that they had been exposed to radiation years earlier and subsequently suffered from serious health problems. There were three men
and two women, all in their mid to late forties, only one of whom had
completed a bachelor's degree. One of them was a Native American
whose reservation abutted the nuclear reservation. The others, journalists and members of the Hanford Education Action League (HEAL),
a public-interest organization, were in their thirties and forties, and
virtually all had a college degree or more. We also attended a Rotary
Club meeting in Yakima, Washington, where Tom Bailie, a leading
Downwinder, had been invited to speak. This was a very important
moment. In contrast to the hostile reaction Bailie had experienced in
the years of his "storytelling," the Rotarians greeted his remarks with
interest and concern. They were impressed by an ABC documentary
that featured Bailie. The climate of opinion was clearly shifting as
word of the dangers became more widespread and the Hanford facilities were awarded multimillion dollars in federal cleanup contracts.

The seventeen people interviewed at Fernald, Ohio, included twelve
members of the Fernald Residents for Environmental Safety and

Health (FRESH), nine of whom were women and three their husbands. This was largely a working- and lower-middle-class group. Only two of the younger women had a college education. Of the twelve FRESH members, three were in their thirties, including the leader, who at thirty-five was the youngest in the group. The remainder were in their fifties and sixties. In addition to the FRESH activists, we interviewed five other men, two union representatives, one manager from Westinghouse, one representative of the Department of Energy, and one longtime employee of the Fernald plant itself. Beyond individual interviews, we attended a public meeting where plant representatives addressed community concerns about cleanup plans. The FRESH members were very skeptical about the plans and challenged many of the speakers' claims. A spirited discussion ensued, and we observed the solidarity among FRESH members, who cheered each other on.

In Glen Avon, California, we studied Concerned Neighbors, a grassroots group living just below the Stringfellow Acid Pits, a major Superfund site that had flooded their community with toxic waters. Like their counterparts in Washington and Ohio, these residents were transformed from uninvolved citizens to active participants demanding government and corporate accountability to protect them and their families from further health risk. In addition to interviewing seven members of the core group, we visited the site with the local EPA director, met with a spokesperson for the principal industries that were being sued by Concerned Neighbors, and attended a locally televised public panel in which both sides participated. The legislative aide to the local congressman was very involved and offered her own perspective on the personalities and the issues. All but one of the Concerned Neighbors we interviewed were women, equally divided between those with high school and those with college education, with a preponderance in their forties and early fifties. They had been members of the group for at least a decade, beginning their involvement when many were in their thirties and early forties, with school-age children.

To expand our study to yet another major controversy, this one involving the future placement of a hazardous-waste and garbage facility, we traveled to the wheat-growing region of eastern Washington. This area has minimal annual rainfall but rich topsoil, ideal conditions for wheat growing. Most of the wheat farmers there have long considered themselves conservative Republicans. Some are fourth-generation tillers of the land who never imagined that they would protest anything until the news arrived that a private waste-disposal company planned to build a toxic-waste dump in the midst of their farms. We met with several dozen of the farmers at a picnic for their group and interviewed twelve of the activists, including several of the leaders. Our respondent group was equally divided between men and women, but all the leaders were men. There were an equal number of high school and college graduates. About half were between the ages of 55 and 65, and the others ranged from 25 to 42. Our presence at the picnic was celebrated as evidence of interest from people beyond their local area, and we were awarded the door prize—a quilt lovingly made of fabric cut from old, discarded jeans.

The issues the wheat farmers confronted were not isolated or specific only to them. We spent many hours with eleven residents of Kellogg, Idaho, who were struggling with the aftermath of decades of silver mining that had left the entire town contaminated by the toxic residue. As we drove into the town, the verdant landscape of the nearby mountains disappeared and the land appeared burned, as if no vegetation could grow in the vicinity of the now-closed mines. In addition, throughout the state of Washington we spoke to activists opposing construction of medical and other incinerators because they believed these facilities would threaten the health and safety of their neighborhoods. Often the groups were very small, engaging the passions of just a handful of people, who could call on their neighbors if a vote or other immediate event were scheduled. Although we have not presented specific portraits of these communities in the book, their experiences informed our understanding of grassroots activism.

The clear-cutting of old-growth forests throughout the western states also evoked strong responses from local residents. As demand for lumber increased dramatically in recent decades and family-owned timber operations came into the hands of large corporations, confrontation between local activists and logging interests grew to new heights. Small grassroots groups, sometimes organized as local chapters of the national environmental groups, like the Sierra Club, National Wildlife

Federation, or the Audubon Society, often disagreed vociferously with their national headquarters, which, they believed, were compromising away valuable lands in order to maintain good relationships with members of Congress and Forest Service representatives. The grassroots crusaders devoted themselves to saving plots of land designated for clear-cutting. We interviewed five of these activists in Washington State and ten up and down the northern coast of California who described their appearances at local hearings, their participation in regional alliances, and their undying commitment to maintain sustainable forestry without destroying ecological habitats. Virtually all of those involved in the preservation of the forests were college educated, middle-class, white, and overwhelmingly in their forties. Among our interviewees, there were twice as many women as men.

At times, we drove deep into the woods to meet with activists. The late Judi Bari, a well-known Earth Firster, had already been the victim of a car bombing by those who opposed her politics, so she lived well out of public view. She agreed to meet us in her home and told us in detail about her efforts to preserve the forests. Others organized small environmental centers in their houses or in low-rent buildings in small mountain towns. We visited these locations and saw their attempts to build quasi–community centers where activists could meet and create solidarity around urgent forest issues.

In addition to conducting intensive interviews and visiting the sites in question, we maintained contact with our principal informants through letters, phone calls, and follow-up interviews. As we completed drafts of individual chapters, we sent the relevant parts to the major activists under discussion, seeking verification of the facts and any additional up-to-date information they could provide. This method of continuing contact was also a form of reciprocity for their hospitality and willingness to participate in the study. They had welcomed us in part because of our previous research on whistleblowers, which assured them of our long-standing interest in citizens' efforts to demand government and corporate accountability. In most encounters we presented the activists with a copy of our book *The Whistleblowers: Exposing Corruption in Government and Industry,* which provided a direct indication of the nature of our interests and the type of volume we would likely produce out of the current investigation. We were appreciative and impressed by their openness, particularly since many were engaged in long-standing litigation. Only one interviewee refused to allow us to keep the tape of our conversation, because her lawyer advised her against it.

This research process of seeking engaged environmental activists, interviewing them, revisiting the principals, and maintaining contact to monitor events over a period of several years was replicated in Israel and the former Czechoslovakia. In both countries, most activists spoke English. In a few instances, we were accompanied by excellent translators.

Israel has eight organizations devoted largely or exclusively to exposing environmental threats, organizing citizen reactions, presenting legal challenges, and establishing contacts with other national or international ecological efforts. In addition, there are seventeen affiliated organizations whose primary purpose is other than environmental activism but that occasionally work on such issues. Some of these affiliated organizations, such as the Association of Americans and Canadians in Israel (AACI), have a standing committee focused on the environment. Beyond the main environmental organizations and the affiliates are five to ten small groups, which at any given moment may organize around a local issue.[1] In total, we interviewed thirty-three Israelis who were involved in the environmental movement. Most were participants in one of four grassroots groups then confronting pollution or other damage in their communities or were working with one of the four umbrella organizations that actively supported grassroots efforts.[2] We also conducted interviews with three scientists who had a long-standing commitment to environmental protection, two employees of the Ministry of the Environment, and several individuals who were dedicated environmentalists, often volunteering on projects they considered significant.

Although all the interviewees were Israeli citizens, it is notable that ten had emigrated from the United States. All of them were fully integrated into Israeli society. A few had arrived within the last decade, but many had been living in Israel for more than a quarter century. Yet their awareness of the environmental movement in the

United States and their frequent trips back enabled them to make a major contribution to raising awareness about Israel's ecological problems. Virtually all of the thirty-three were university educated. While the largest number of respondents were men (twenty-two), women (eleven) had significant leadership positions in grassroots groups as well as in the umbrella organizations. It is notable that the members of the recently created and innovative public-interest law group, the Union for Environmental Defense, were in their thirties, but most of the others were older. A few were in their forties, but the largest number were over fifty.

Upon our arrival, we were fortunate to receive the assistance of Dr. Alon Tal and his newly organized Union for Environmental Defense (UED). Located in Tel Aviv and committed to using the legal system to advance environmentalists' goals, the UED had contacts with community-based groups throughout the country. Dr. Tal oriented us with regard to the most current controversies and actors and provided us with an introduction to several key activists. Our subsequent interviews took place in the city of Haifa, where a citizen-based group was fighting the air pollution produced by the heavy concentration of petrochemical and other industries, in a small town near Jerusalem where residents were organizing to reduce the pollution from the local cement factory, and in two kibbutzim whose members were at loggerheads over the construction of a regional landfill to be located between them, with the potential for great economic gain but with the possibility of devastating environmental impact.

Other interviews were conducted with the small but vibrant community of environmental activists who had fought for conservation and nature preservation from the earliest days of Israel's settlement. These old timers recounted a history of environmental practices in the 1930s, 1940s, and 1950s. They described their efforts to raise awareness of growing environmental problems in a society that was otherwise preoccupied with issues of military security, economic development, and immigrant absorption. The environmentalists pointed to the deterioration of the water supply, the contamination of land with intensive fertilizers and pesticides, and the growing danger of over-development, which threatened to eliminate the ecosystems of the deserts and hills of this small country, in order to accommodate the demands of a rapidly growing population and a prospering economy.

In addition, we were eager to include environmentalists from the Israeli Arab community. We were fortunate to have introductions to several, including Dr. Hatim Kana'aneh, a founding member of the Galilee Society for Health Research and Services, a citizen-based environmental group particularly concerned with the deleterious health effects of inadequate sewage-disposal facilities, industrialization and overdevelopment of their rural setting, as well as other health and environmental issues. We met Dr. Kana'aneh first in Tel Aviv in 1992 and later in his office in northern Israel. A few years later, in 1996, we continued our contact by visiting him in his village of Arrabe. Dr. Kana'aneh and his colleagues saw their efforts as part of a larger struggle for social justice for the Arab minority in Israel. Voluntary organizations like the Galilee Society were relatively new in the Israeli Arab community. Interviewing its leaders offered a different dimension to our understanding of Israel's environmental problems and progress.

In the spring of 1992 we traveled from Israel to Czechoslovakia, where we knew that environmentalists had played an important part in the Velvet Revolution against the Communists in 1989. We were greatly assisted by the report of two American environmental lawyers, David B. Hunter and Margaret Bowman, who had recently spent nine months in the country under the auspices of the German Marshall Fund. Their report detailed all the environmental groups, with the names, addresses, phone and FAX numbers of all the crucial contact people. According to the Hunter and Bowman report, there were, at the commencement of our study in 1992, approximately fifteen environmental NGOs in Prague, ranging from very small friendship-based groups to the state-funded Czech Union of Nature Protectors, with "several regional offices and hundreds of local clubs scattered throughout the country." In addition, there were a series of small environmental centers throughout the Czech Republic. In Slovakia, Hunter and Bowman identified five separate environmental NGOs. The Slovak Union of Landscape and Nature Protectors (SZOPK), the main nature society founded under the Communist government, had numerous local clubs and regional offices throughout Slovakia. Projects in these groups included organizing demonstrations, publishing a newsletter, or nature magazine, and urging energy conservation and restoration of rural and historic buildings.[3] For our research the report was like manna from heaven. We contacted the key people who were involved in environmental issues, people comparable to their counterparts in the United States and Israel, and were able to enlist their cooperation. In these early post-Communist years, the activists were eager to share what they had accomplished in the hope of establishing relationships and learning more about similar groups in the West. They were pleased to be part of a study where their situation would be analyzed comparatively.

We interviewed a total of twenty-five people, who represented five grassroots groups, four centered in Prague and one in Bratislava. Several other interviewees were major figures in the environmental movement, past or present employees of the Federal or Czech Ministry of the Environment. In addition, we spoke with five Americans who were living in Czechoslovakia and working closely with environmental groups, either through the Peace Corps, the Ministry of the Environment, or the German Marshall Fund. Slightly more than half of the respondents were men. As in Israel, the women held significant leadership positions in the grassroots groups, and all the respondents in the Czechoslovakian portion of the study were university graduates. Compared to those in Israel, the small activist group was decidedly younger. Approximately half the group were in their twenties and thirties. Almost all the others were in their forties. Those who were in their late forties had resisted during the Soviet invasion in 1968, and the seeds of their dissidence had been planted during that time of national upheaval.

We began by interviewing several members of the newly formed Federal Ministry of the Environment. These civil servants had been dissidents in both the Czech Republic and Slovakia and had only recently taken positions in the new government. For some, it was a huge leap from their role as dissidents and outcasts, who could only work as coal stokers or janitors, to leadership positions in a new ministry. Although they may have felt uncomfortable in their formal offices, they proved to be exceptional informants as they described the dramatic efforts of environmentalists in both the Czech Republic and Slovakia to mobilize citizens, often under the nose of Communist officials. They were well acquainted with all the major grassroots groups and directed us to some of the crucial participants, who reinforced the information we already had.

On their suggestion, we traveled to Bratislava, the capital city of Slovakia, which had little history of activism and dissidence under the Communists. There we interviewed a group of activists who clearly were an exception to the conformist ethos. These men and women recounted their efforts in the late 1980s to transform the program of the official Communist nature club into a clandestine effort to accumulate censored and hidden environmental data. They were pleased to tell how they succeeded in publishing and distributing their report, exposing major hazards for the first time to the local population. Our interviews went on late into the night at the offices of the local environmental group where several of the participants obviously enjoyed reminiscing about the recent heroic past.

This effort to expose environmental hazards occurred even more frequently in Prague, where small numbers of dissidents had been active since the 1977 publication of Charter 77, which challenged the government's record on human rights. In the course of the 1980s this protest expanded to include numbers of small but determined environmental groups. When we arrived in 1992, and even more so when we returned in 1994, we found many of these groups struggling to define their role in a post-Communist society. The much-hated evil of Communist oppression had been defeated, but pollution and other environmental hazards had not diminished. The introduction of consumer capitalism, the election of a conservative free-market government, and the division of Czechoslovakia into two separate nations in 1993 all exacerbated the challenges.

As we contemplated the writing and analysis for the study, we decided to draw upon the lives of the major activists to ground our discussion. The task was made easier by the statements of participants in the grassroots groups, who invariably pointed to one or two of their leaders as embodying the spirit and substance of the united group effort. The lives of the leaders revealed, in the starkest terms, the transformation that had occurred as communities organized to confront or prevent major environmental destruction. While we know that there are scores of other activists in the three countries who could have served as central figures in our narrative, we are convinced that the issues presented and the activists discussed represent a substantial reflection of the most serious environmental issues and the responses by residents in the United States, Israel, The Czech Republic, and Slovakia.

Notes

Notes to the Introduction

1. Kai Erikson, *A New Species of Trouble* (New York: W. W. Norton, 1994), 149.
2. Ibid., 150.
3. Rick Fantasia, *Cultures of Solidarity* (Berkeley and Los Angeles: University of California Press, 1988). Ann Swidler, "Culture in Action: Symbols and Strategies," *American Sociological Review* 51 (April 1986): 273–86. William Gamson, "Social Psychology of Collective Action," in *Frontiers in Social Movement Theory,* ed. Aldon D. Morris and Carol McClung Mueller (New Haven: Yale University Press, 1992), 53–76.
4. There are many scholarly efforts to combine social psychological and resource-mobilization approaches to the study of social movements. See, for example, Doug McAdam, John D. McCarthy, and Mayer N. Zald, "Social Movements," in *The Handbook of Sociology,* ed. Neil Smelser (Newbury Park, Calif.: Sage Publications, 1988); Eric L. Hirsch, "The Creation of Political Solidarity in Social Movement Organizations," *Sociological Quarterly* 27, no. 3 (1986): 373–87; Jean L. Cohen, "Strategy or Identity: New Theoretical Paradigms and Contemporary Social Movements," *Social Research* 52 (Winter 1985): 663–716; Myra Marx Ferree and Frederick D. Miller, "Mobilization and Meaning: Toward an Integration of Social Psychological and Resource Perspectives on Social Movements," *Sociological Inquiry* 55, no. 1 (1985), 38–61; Bert Klandermans, "Mobilization and Participation: Social-Psychological Expansions of Resource Mobilization Theory," *American Sociological Review* 49 (October 1984): 583–600; and John D. McCarthy and Mayer N. Zald, "Resource Mobilization and Social Movements: A Partial Theory," *American Journal of Sociology* 82, no. 6 (1977), 1212–41.
5. Lois M. Gibbs, *Dying from Dioxin* (Boston: South End Press, 1995), 144–45.
6. Harry C. Boyte, *Commonwealth: A Return to Citizen Politics* (New York: Free Press, 1989), esp. chap. 1.
7. Rachel Carson, *The Silent Spring* (Boston: Houghton Mifflin, 1962).
8. Robert C. Mitchell, Angela G. Mertig, and Riley E. Dunlap, "Twenty Years of Environmental Mobilization: Trends Among National Environmental Organizations," in *American Environmentalism: The U.S. Environmental Movement, 1970–1990,* ed. Riley E. Dunlap and Angela G. Mertig (Philadelphia: Taylor & Francis, 1992), 11–26; see also Mark Dowie, *Losing Ground: American Environmentalism at the Close of the Twentieth Century* (Cambridge, Mass.: MIT Press, 1995), esp. chap. 8.
9. Mitchell, Mertig, and Dunlap, "Twenty Years of Environmental Mobilization," 18.
10. Since the 1980s, the literature on grassroots environmental movements in

the United States has burgeoned. Some of the earliest works came out of the Love Canal struggle. Lois Gibbs, *Love Canal: My Story* (Albany: State University of New York Press, 1982), was a personal memoir on one of the early successful campaigns by local residents. Adeline Gordon Levine, *Love Canal: Science, Politics, and People* (Boston, Mass.: Lexington Books, 1982), was a monograph on that subject. Love Canal was also studied by two other sociologists. See Martha Fowlkes and Patricia Y. Miller, "Chemicals and Community at Love Canal," in *The Social and Cultural Construction of Risk,* ed. Brandon B. Johnson and Vincent T. Covello (New York: Reidel, 1987). Since that time numerous important studies on grassroots activism have appeared, including Michael R. Edelstein, *Contaminated Communities: The Social and Psychological Impacts of Residential Toxic Exposure* (Boulder, Colo.: Westview, 1988); Phil Brown and Edwin J. Mikkelsen, *No Safe Place: Toxic Waste Crisis and Childhood Leukemia in Woburn, Massachusetts* (Berkeley and Los Angeles: University of California Press, 1990); Nicholas Freudenberg, *Not in Our Backyards: Community Action for Health and the Environment* (New York: Monthly Review Press, 1984). Robert D. Bullard, *Dumping in Dixie: Race, Class, and Environmental Quality* (Boulder, Colo.: Westview, 1990), idem, *Confronting Environmental Racism: Voices from the Grassroots* (Boston: South End Press, 1993), and idem, ed., *Unequal Protection: Environmental Justice and Communities of Color* (San Francisco: Sierra Club Books, 1994), are particularly significant on the environmental-justice movement, as is Andrew Szasz, *Ecopopulism: Toxic Waste and the Movement for Environmental Justice* (Minneapolis: University of Minnesota Press, 1994). Robert Gottlieb, *Forcing the Spring: The Transformation of the American Environmental Movement* (Washington, D.C.: Island Press, 1993), and Dunlap and Mertig, eds., *American Environmentalism,* give a good overview of the recent history, as does Dowie, *Losing Ground*; see also Donald Snow, ed., *Voices from the Environmental Movement: Perspectives for a New Era* (Washington, D.C.: Island Press, 1992). An important recent book is Paul Lichterman, *The Search for Political Community: American Activists Reinventing Commitment* (New York: Cambridge University Press, 1996). Jonathan Harr's best-seller, *A Civil Action* (New York: Random House, 1995), is an excellent account of the costs of litigation in Woburn, Massachusetts. Joni Seager, *Earth Follies* (New York: Routledge, 1993), addresses feminist ecology.

11. Nicholas Freudenberg and Carol Steinsaper, "Not in Our Backyards: The Grassroots Environmental Movement," in *American Environmentalism,* ed. Dunlap and Mertig, 27–37.

12. In recent decades there has been an increased methodological emphasis on cross-national studies. Despite this trend, the overwhelming majority of studies on social movements continue to focus on single-country research. John Crist and John McCarthy, "If I Had a Hammer: The Changing Methodological Repertoire of Collective Behavior and Social Movement Research," *Mobilization* 1, no. 1 (1996): 87–102.

13. Ministry of the Environment, *Israel Environment Bulletin* 15, no. 4 (1992).

14. Although the signing of the Oslo accord between Israel and the Palestinian Authority has not officially changed the status of Israeli Arabs, who remain citizens of Israel, the transformed political situation did bring Arabs and Jews interested in the environment into closer working relationships with each other.

15. Duncan Fisher, "The Emergence of the Environmental Movement in Eastern Europe and Its Role in the Revolutions of 1989," in *Environmental Action in Europe,* ed. Barbara Jancar-Webster (Armonk, N.Y.: M. E. Sharpe, 1993), 90.

16. Ibid., 93.

17. Barbara Jancar-Webster, "Eastern Europe and the Former Soviet Union," in *Environmental Politics in the International Arena,* ed. Sheldon Kamieniecki (Albany: State University of New York Press, 1993), 199–221.

18. David B. Hunter and Margaret B. Bowman, *An Overview of the Environmental Community in the Czech and Slovak Federal Republic* (Washington, D.C.: Center for Environmental Law, 1991).

Notes to Chapter 1

1. Carmen Sirianni and Lewis Friedland, "Civic Innovation and American Democracy," *Change* (January–February 1997): 14–23.

2. Robert D. Putnam, "Bowling Alone: America's Declining Social Capital," *Journal of Democracy* (January 1993): 65–78. See also his later essay, "The Strange Disappearance of Civic America," *American Prospect* (winter 1996): 34–48. For a critique of Putnam's thesis, see Alejandro Porter and Patricia Landolt, "The Downside of Social Capital," *American Project* (May–June 1996): 18–22. Nicholas Lemann, "Kicking in Groups," *Atlantic Monthly,* April 1996, 22–26.

3. Putnam, "Bowling Alone," 77.

4. Michael Brown, *Laying Waste* (New York: Pantheon Books, 1979); Adeline Gordon Levine, *Love Canal: Science, Politics, and People* (Boston, Mass.: Lexington Books, 1982); Jonathan Harr, *A Civil Action* (New York: Random House, 1995); Phil Brown and Edwin J. Mikkelsen, *No Safe Place: Toxic Waste Crisis and Childhood Leukemia in Woburn, Massachusetts* (Berkeley and Los Angeles: University of California Press, 1990).

5. Greg Mitchell, *Truth . . . and Consequences* (New York: Dembner Books, 1977), 87–127; Fred A. Wilcox, *Waiting for an Army to Die* (New York: Vintage Books, 1983); Ralph Blumenthal, "Agent Orange: How the Fund Will Work," *New York Times,* May 9, 1984.

6. Several scholars have contested Putnam's numbers. Some have found modest increases. See Sidney Verba, Kay Schlazman, and Henry Brady, *Voice and Equality: Civic Voluntarism in American Politics* (Cambridge, Mass.: Harvard University Press, 1995).

7. Among the burgeoning literature, see Bron Taylor, Heidi Hadsell, Lois Lorentzen, and Rik Scarce, "Grass-Roots Resistance: The Emergence of Popular Environmental Movements in Less Affluent Countries," in *Environmental Politics in the International Arena,* ed. Sheldon Kamieniecki (Albany: State University of New York Press, 1993), 69–89. In the same volume, see also Barbara Jancar-Webster, "Eastern Europe and the Former Soviet Union," 199–221.

8. Alberto Melucci, *Nomads of the Present: Social Movements and Individual Needs in Contemporary Society* (Philadelphia: Temple University Press, 1989), in his discussion of new social movement theory, points out that many of these present-day movements consist of "invisible" networks of small groups of ordinary citizens. In 1994, the Citizens Clearing House for Hazardous Waste reported that they had been in contact with eight thousand local groups working on some aspect of the hazardous-waste issue. Many of these groups are short-lived, so there is constant turnover. See Bob Edwards, "With Liberty and Environmental Justice for All: The Emergence and Challenge of Grassroots Environmentalism in the United

States," in *Ecological Resistance Movements,* ed. Bron Raymond Taylor (Albany: State University of New York Press, 1995), 39. For a critique of the applicability of new social movement theory to United States activism, see Edward J. Walsh, "New Dimensions of Social Movements: The High-Level Waste-Siting Controversy," *Sociological Forum* 3, no. 4 (1988): 586–605.

9. Anne Witte Garland, *Women Activists* (New York: Feminist Press, 1988); Michael R. Edelstein, *Contaminated Communities: The Social and Psychological Impacts of Residential Toxic Exposure* (Boulder, Colo.: Westview Press, 1988).

10. Stephen L. Fisher, ed., *Fighting Back in Appalachia: Traditions of Resistance and Change* (Philadelphia: Temple University Press, 1993), 317–24, describes neopopulist theory and its critics. For an excellent discussion of the complexity of commitment to the environmental cause, see Paul Lichterman, *The Search for Political Community: American Activists Reinventing Commitment* (Cambridge: Cambridge University Press, 1996).

11. Zelda F. Gamson, "Higher Education and Rebuilding Civic Life," *Change* (January/February 1997): 10–13, points out that the learning that takes place in these groups is "problem-centered and mission-oriented," involving participants in multidisciplinary and multiorganizational efforts.

12. Interview with Lisa Crawford, February 28, 1992.

13. Ibid. On grassroots mobilization, see Michele Andrisin Wittig and B. Ann Bettencourt, eds., *Social Psychological Perspectives on Grassroots Organizing,* a special issue of *Journal of Social Issues* 52, no. 1 (1996). For an analysis of the forces mediating for and against the growth of grassroots activism, see the article by Marc Pilisilk, JoAnn McAllister, and Jack Rothman, "Coming Together for Action: The Challenges of Contemporary Grassroots Community Organizing," in ibid., 15–37. For an analysis of the complexity of recruitment to social movement involvement, see Edward J. Walsh and Rex H. Warland, "Social Movement Involvement in the Wake of a Nuclear Accident: Activists and Free Riders in the TMI Area," *American Sociological Review* 48 (December 1983): 764–80. For the significance of "spontaneity" in recruitment and action, see Lewis M. Killian, "Organization, Rationality, and Spontaneity in the Civil Rights Movement," *American Sociological Review* 49 (December 1984): 770–83.

14. For a discussion of this process, see Harry Boyte and Sara Evans, *Free Spaces: The Sources of Democratic Change in America* (New York: Harper & Row, 1986); see also Harry Boyte, *The Backyard Revolution: Understanding the New Citizen Movement* (Philadelphia: Temple University Press, 1980).

15. Doug McAdam, Sidney Tarrow, and Charles Tilly, "To Map Contentious Politics," *Mobilization* 1, no. 1 (1996): 17–34; Doug McAdam, "Micromobilization Contexts and Recruitment to Activism," *International Social Movement Research* 1 (1988): 125–54.

16. Interview with Lisa Crawford, February 28, 1992.

17. Lisa Crawford, "Battling the Nuclear Bomb Establishment: The Emergence of FRESH" (paper delivered at a conference entitled "Education at the Grassroots: Women and the Struggle for a Safe Environment," Smith College, Northampton, Mass., April 9, 1995).

18. This development from disenchantment to organized protest is analyzed in Bert Klandermans, "The Social Construction of Protest and Multiorganizational Fields," in *Frontiers in Social Movement Theory,* ed. Aldon D. Morris and Carol McClung Mueller (New Haven: Yale University Press, 1992), 77–103.

19. Christina Cocek, "A Lantern in the Window: Notes from a New and Hopeful

Activist," *Everyone's Backyard* 14, no. 1 (1996): 4–6. Changing definitions of reality and of meaning associated, for example, with those who are adversaries are analyzed in a more general discussion by Sidney Tarrow, "Mentalities, Political Cultures, and Collective Action Frames: Constructing Meanings Through Action," in *Frontiers in Social Movement Theory,* ed. Morris and Mueller, 174–202.

20. "Mount Dioxin Leaves Neighbors Sickened," *Republican American* (Waterbury, Conn.), March 11, 1996, 2a.

21. Quoted in Lois M. Gibbs, *Dying from Dioxin* (Boston: South End Press, 1995), 252–53.

22. Florence T. Robinson, "Whose Costs and Whose Benefits: The Tribulations of 'Thrown Away' Communities" (paper delivered at a conference entitled "Education at the Grassroots: Women and the Struggle for a Safe Environment," Smith College, Northampton, Mass., April 9, 1995).

23. Ibid.

24. The full text can be found in Gibbs, *Dying from Dioxin,* 309–11.

25. See Brown and Mikkelsen, *No Safe Place;* Robert D. Bullard, *Dumping in Dixie: Race, Class, and Environmental Quality* (Boulder, Colo.: Westview, 1990); idem, ed., *Unequal Protection: Environmental Justice and Communities of Color* (San Francisco: Sierra Club Books, 1994); Stella M. Capek, "The 'Environmental Justice' Frame: A Conceptual Discussion and an Application," *Social Problems* 40, no. 1 (1993): 5–24; Celene Krauss, "Women and Toxic Waste Protests: Race, Class, and Gender as Resources of Resistance," *Qualitative Sociology* 16, no. 3 (1993): 247–62.

26. Penny Newman, personal correspondence, July 22, 1996. For an astute and compassionate analysis of what happens to communities that experience environmental disasters caused by the actions of business or government, see the works of Kai Erikson, *Everything in Its Path* (New York: Simon & Schuster, 1976) and *A New Species of Trouble* (New York: W. W. Norton, 1994).

27. For a presentation of this process by a researcher using participant observation methods, see Lichterman, *The Search for Political Community.* For a discussion of the link between social conflict and social movements, see Alain Touraine, "An Introduction to the Study of Social Movements," *Social Research* 52, no. 4 (1985): 749–87.

28. Rick Fantasia, *Cultures of Solidarity* (Berkeley and Los Angeles: University of California Press, 1988), describes the oppositional cultures that form among workers as they attempt to resist the hegemony of management's definitions of the workplace. See esp. chap. 6.

29. Interview with Devorah Ben Shaul, April 12, 1992.

30. By 1993, the Ministry of the Environment had initiated a National River Administration to coordinate efforts to restore Israel's rivers. In their own language, they were searching "for a cure which would transform the country's rivers from channels of death into sources of life." Ministry of the Environment, *Israel Environment Bulletin* 18, no. 4 (1995): 2.

31. The English-language newspaper was read by a small minority of Israelis, but it was very important to government officials, who knew that it was a major source of communication with interested parties abroad.

32. Interview with Heyedrich Mendelssohn, April 8, 1992.

33. Interview with Devorah Ben Shaul, April 12, 1992.

34. Ibid.

35. Interview with Ivo Silmav'y, May 7, 1992.

36. Ibid.

37. Many observers have noted the importance of outside leadership and resources in helping the former Soviet countries make the transition to democracy.
See, for example, Sharon L. Wolchik, "The Czech Republic and Slovakia," in *The
Legacies of Communism in Eastern Europe,* ed. Zoltan Barany and Ivan Volgyes
(Baltimore: Johns Hopkins University Press, 1995), 176. In Slovakia, the government began increasingly to fear outside support for the development of an independent civic sector of NGOs, and sought legislation in 1996 to curb outside support for
environmental and other groups. Environmentalists, recognizing the danger of losing international support, mounted a campaign to defeat the proposed legislation.
Juraj Zamkovsky and Juraj Mesik, "Slovak Republic: The Civil Society in Jeop-
ardy," unpublished memorandum, April 1996.

Notes to Chapter 2

1. Richard Rhodes, in his major study *The Making of the Atomic Bomb* (New
York: Simon & Schuster, 1986), wrote that the "national security state that the
United States has evolved toward since 1945 is significantly a denial of the American democratic vision: suspicious of diversity, secret, martial, exclusive, monolithic,
paranoid" (785).

2. For a discussion on grassroots mobilization and the end of the Cold War, see
David S. Meyer and Sam Marullo, "Grassroots Mobilization and International Politics," in *Research in Social Movements, Conflicts, and Change: The Transformation
of European Communist Societies,* ed. Louis Kriesberg and David R. Segals (Greenwich, Conn.: JAI Press, 1992), 99–140.

3. Keith Schneider, "Now the U.S. Asks What Its Radiation Did in the Cold
War," *New York Times,* July 29, 1990, News of the Week in Review section.

4. The development of Hanford Nuclear Reservation is described in Paul Loeb's
Nuclear Culture (Philadelphia: New Society Publishers, 1986); Jim Thomas,
"Atomic Deception: Oh What a Tangled Web!" *Perspective* (Spokane, Wash., HEAL),
nos. 10–11 (summer/fall 1992): 4–7, 17ff.; Rhodes, *The Making of the Atomic Bomb.*

5. Interview with Tom Bailie, July 31, 1991.

6. Ibid.

7. Interview with Judith Jurgi, August 9, 1991.

8. Louise Kaplan, "The History of HEAL," *Perspective* (Spokane, Wash., HEAL),
nos. 10–11 (summer/fall 1992): 8–9.

9. Myron Peretz Glazer and Penina Migdal Glazer, *The Whistleblowers: Exposing
Corruption in Government and Industry* (New York: Basic Books, 1989), 171–77.

10. Interview with Karen Dorn Steele, July 25, 1991; Kaplan, "The History of
HEAL," 9.

11. Jim Thomas, "New Details of Green Run's Sorcery," *Perspective* (Spokane,
Wash., HEAL), nos. 10–11 (summer/fall 1992): 21, 26ff.

12. Karen Dorn Steele, "Hanford's Bitter Legacy," *Bulletin of the Atomic Scien-
tist,* January/February 1988, 17–23; Keith Schneider, "U.S. Sees a Danger in 1940s
Radiation in the Northwest," *New York Times,* July 12, 1990; idem, "Now the U.S.
Asks What Its Radiation Did in the Cold War."

13. Several major health studies were set in motion after this information was
released. The Hanford Environmental Dose Reconstruction Project was authorized

by the Department of Energy to estimate how much radiation a person living near Hanford might have received from 1944 to the present. The work was overseen by a technical steering panel of scientists and public representatives, including HEAL and other public groups. The second major study, mandated by the United States Congress, is the Hanford Thyroid Disease Study, conducted by the prestigious Fred Hutchinson Cancer Research Center under contract to the Center for Disease Control. Its purpose is to establish if there has been increased thyroid cancer, as has been expected. (Washington Nuclear Waste Advisory Council, "Who to Talk to About Hanford: A Resource Guide," May 1991.)

14. Interview with Don Carter, August 9, 1991. Despite this emotional reaction, few environmental activists have absorbed a radical political critique of American society. Richard P. Gale, "The Environmental Movement and the Left: Antagonists or Allies?" *Sociological Inquiry* 53 (spring 1983): 179–99.

15. For discussion of the role of anger, see Alberto Melucci, *Nomads of the Present: Social Movements and Individual Needs in Contemporary Society* (Philadelphia: Temple University Press, 1989), 210–11; Carol Stearns and Peter N. Stearns, *Anger* (Chicago: University of Chicago Press, 1986), 225–39; Anne Witte Garland, *Women Activists* (New York: Feminist Press, 1988), xv–xviii. On trust, see Bernard Barber, *The Logic and Limits of Trust* (New Brunswick, N.J.: Rutgers University Press, 1983), and Francis Fukuyama, *Trust: The Social Virtues and the Creation of Prosperity* (New York: Free Press, 1995).

16. For discussion of social movement solidarity, see Verta Taylor and Nancy Whittier, "Collective Identity in Social Movement Communities," in *Frontiers in Social Movement Theory*, ed. Aldon D. Morris and Carol McClung Mueller (New Haven: Yale University Press, 1992).

17. Interview with Lois Camps, July 29, 1991.

18. Interview with Russell Jim, August 1, 1991. Kai Erikson, *A New Species of Trouble* (New York: W. W. Norton, 1994), chap. 1, has an excellent discussion on the devastating impact of displacing the Ojibwa from their ancestral lands and way of life.

19. Karen Dorn Steele, "Nuclear Watchdog Group Thrives on Controversy," *Spokesman-Review* (Spokane, Wash.), January 24, 1988; Kaplan, "The History of HEAL."

20. Lois Camps, personal correspondence, October 20, 1991.

21. *New York Times,* November 7, 1988, A1.

22. Keith Schneider, "Military Has New Strategic Goal in Cleanup of Vast Toxic Waste," *New York Times,* August 5, 1991, A1.

23. Government Accountability Project, "Bridging the Gap," winter 1994; U.S. Department of Energy, *Closing the Circle on the Splitting of the Atom: The Environmental Legacy of Nuclear Weapons Production in the United States and What the Department of Energy Is Doing About It* (Washington, D.C., 1995), vii.

24. Ian Lustick, *Arabs in the Jewish State* (Austin: University of Texas Press, 1980).

25. Ministry of the Environment, *The Environment in Israel: National Report to the United Nations Conference on Environment and Development* (Jerusalem, 1992).

26. Interview with Lev Fishelson, April 12, 1992.

27. Ministry of the Environment, *The Environment in Israel,* 139, 149.

28. Interview with Yoav Sagi, April 8, 1992.

29. Interview with Alon Tal, March 17, 1992.

30. Interview with Shirley Benyamin, April 27, 1992.

31. Interview with Alon Tal, March 17, 1992; New Israel Fund, "NIF Report," fall 1991, 1ff.

32. Interview with Uri Marinov, April 1, 1992.

33. *New York Times,* November 27, 1992. The project was planned to cover six square miles, which would include forty-seven antennas, 180 feet high, and sixteen transmitters, plus a high-voltage cable that would extend to the Dead Sea. For a full description, see Avner de-Shalit and Moti Talias, "Green or Blue and White? Environmental Controversies in Israel," *Environmental Politics* 3, no. 2 (1994): 274–78.

34. Interview with Yoav Sagi, April 8, 1992. De-Shalit and Talias, "Green or Blue and White?" 277–78, point out the arguments made by local residents about unknown effects of electromagnetic radiation on human health, and the demise of popular tourist attractions ultimately had more impact than did concern about the birds.

35. Interview with Yoav Sagi, April 8, 1992.

36. Baruch Kimmerling and Joel S. Migdal, *Palestinians* (New York: Free Press, 1993), 159–84.

37. Interview with Hatim Kana'aneh, December 30, 1992.

38. Ibid.

39. Lustick, *Arabs in the Jewish State,* 129–30.

40. Nira Reiss, *The Health Care of the Arabs in Israel* (Boulder, Colo.: Westview Press, 1991), 157–65.

41. Interview with Hatim Kana'aneh, December 30, 1992.

42. In most European countries and in Israel, voluntary organizations are referred to as NGOs, or nongovernmental organizations.

43. Dr. Hatim Kana'aneh stepped down as director in June 1995. He was succeeded by Dr. Basel Ghattas, an environmental engineer trained at the Technion in Haifa. Interview with Hatim Kana'aneh, January 4, 1996.

44. Interviews with Hatim Kana'aneh, December 30, 1992, and January 4, 1996; see also the *Jerusalem Post,* December 4, 1992.

45. Vladimir V. Kusin, *From Dubček to Charter 77* (New York: St. Martin's Press, 1978).

46. Interview with Josef Vavroušek, June 12, 1994.

47. Pavel Šremer, personal correspondence, August 31, 1995.

48. Patrick G. Marshall, "The Greening of Eastern Europe," *Congressional Quarterly* 1, no. 26 (1991): 849–72.

49. Paul Šremer, personal correspondence, August 31, 1995.

50. Václav Havel, *The Power of the Powerless* (Armonk, N.Y.: M. E. Sharpe, 1985).

51. Carol Skalnik Leff, *National Conflict in Czechoslovakia* (Princeton: Princeton University Press, 1988), 263–65; Rudolf Tokes, ed., *Opposition in Eastern Europe* (Baltimore: Johns Hopkins University Press, 1979), 52–53.

52. Interview with Pavel Šremer, May 15, 1992.

53. Interview with Jan Budaj, May 11, 1992.

54. *Bratislava Nahlas* (SZOPK, 1987).

55. Interview with Juraj Zamkovsky, May 10, 1992.

56. Interview with Maria Filkova, May 11, 1992.

57. Interview with Jan Budaj, May 11, 1992. Such a belief in "creating a new value system" applies more generally in resistance to oppressive regimes. See He-

lena Flam, "Anxiety and the Successful Oppositional Construction of Societal Reality: The Case of Kor," *Mobilization* 1, no. 1 (1996): 103–21.

58. For an analysis of the growth of dissidence in repressive regimes, see Anthony Oberschall and Hyojoung Kim, "Identity and Action," *Mobilization* 1, no. 1 (1996): 81–83.

59. Tina Rosenberg, *The Haunted Land* (New York: Random House, 1995), 3–125, describes the complex and sometimes destructive efforts to uproot all those named as collaborators in the secret-police files.

60. Christo Stojanov, "The Post-Socialist Transformation," in *Research in Social Movements,* ed. Kriesberg and Segals, 211–36.

61. Some long-standing activists continue to struggle for environmental improvement. Since 1993, Dr. Mikulas Huba has chaired the Society for Sustainable Living in Slovakia, which maintains strong contacts with its Czech counterpart and groups throughout the world. Pavel Šremer, personal correspondence, August 31, 1995.

62. There is an extensive literature on resource mobilization by social movement activists. See, for example, Doug McAdam, John D. McCarthy, and Mayer N. Zald, "Social Movements," in *The Handbook of Sociology,* ed. Neil Smelser (Newbury Park, Calif.: Sage Publications, 1988); Enrique Laraña, Hank Johnston, and Joseph R. Gusfield, eds., *New Social Movements: From Ideology to Identity* (Philadelphia: Temple University Press, 1994).

Notes to Chapter 3

1. Evelyn Nakano Glenn, "Social Constructions of Mothering: A Thematic Overview," in *Mothering: Ideology, Experience, and Agency,* ed. Evelyn Nakano Glenn, Grace Chang, and Linda Rennie Forcey (New York: Routledge, 1994), 22–24.

2. Linda Rennie Forcey, "Feminist Perspectives on Mothering and Peace," in *ibid.*; Seth Koven and Sonya Michel, "Introduction: 'Mother Worlds,' " in *Mothers of a New World,* ed. Seth Koven and Sonya Michel (New York: Routledge, 1993), 1–42; Ann Snitow, "A Gender Diary," in *Rocking the Ship of State,* ed. Adrienne Harris and Ynestra King (Boulder, Colo.: Westview 1989), 48–52; Sara Ruddick, "Mothers and Men's Wars," in ibid., 75–92. For an empirically based analysis of the similarities and differences between women and men on a significant emotional response, see Robert Wuthnow, *Learning to Care* (New York: Oxford University Press, 1995).

3. Amy Swerdlow, "Pure Milk, Not Poison," in *Rocking the Ship of State,* ed. Harris and King, 226.

4. Forcey, "Feminist Perspectives," 372. For an analysis that emphasizes the central role of women throughout the developing world, see Bron Taylor, Heidi Hadsell, Lois Lorentzen, and Rik Scarce, "Grass-Roots Resistance: The Emergence of Popular Environmental Movements in Less Affluent Countries," in *Environmental Politics in the International Arena,* ed. Sheldon Kamieniecki (Albany: State University of New York Press, 1993), 69–89.

5. Interview, January 17, 1992.

6. Ibid.

7. Resource-mobilization theorists have defined in great detail the ways in

which social movements must accumulate certain resources to promote their causes. In these new, informal groups resources have to be integrated with close friendships, intimate ties, and informal organizational strategies. See, for example, Doug McAdam, John D. McCarthy, and Mayer N. Zald, "Social Movements," in *The Handbook of Sociology*, ed. Neil Smelser (Newbury Park, Calif.: Sage Publications, 1988); Enrique Laraña, Hank Johnston, and Joseph R. Gusfield, eds., *New Social Movements: From Ideology to Identity* (Philadelphia: Temple University Press, 1994); W. A. Gamson, B. Fireman, and S. Rytina, *Encounters with Unjust Authority* (Homewood, Ill.: Dorsey Press, 1982). For a critique of resource mobilization, see Alberto Melucci, *Nomads of the Present: Social Movements and Individual Needs in Contemporary Society* (Philadelphia: Temple University Press, 1989), 21–23.

8. In her study of Women Strike for Peace in the 1960s, Amy Swerdlow points out that "the key women of WSP maintained that they had left their homes only to save the children and that when the political emergencies, such as the nuclear threat and the Vietnam War, were resolved they would return to full-time home-making. Yet most of the women of WSP never did go home, because when the Vietnam War was over they no longer perceived the home as the center of their lives or responsibilities." *Women Strike for Peace* (Chicago: University of Chicago Press 1993), 239.

9. Ann Swidler, "Culture in Action: Symbols and Strategies," *American Sociological Review* 51 (April 1986): 273–86, shows how important culture is in supplying a set of strategies of action. In unsettled periods, when old strategies no longer work, new ideologies came into play to compete with older, more accepted ideas and actions.

10. Carmen Sirianni and Lewis Friedland, "Civic Innovation and American Democracy," *Change* (January–February 1997): 14–23.

11. See the Methodological Appendix for details on the numbers of women we interviewed. The significance of women has been noted by many. See, for example, Nicholas Freudenberg and Carol Steinsaper, "Not in Our Backyards: The Grassroots Environmental Movement," in *American Environmentalism: The U.S. Environmental Movement, 1970–1990*, ed. Riley E. Dunlap and Angela G. Mertig (Philadelphia: Taylor & Francis, 1992), 29–30. In their study *No Safe Place: Toxic Waste Crisis and Childhood Leukemia in Woburn, Massachusetts* (Berkeley and Los Angeles: University of California Press, 1990), 45, Phil Brown and Edwin J. Mikkelsen point out that the leaders in most toxic-waste-site organizations are working-class or lower-middle-class women at home with their children. Thus, they both have time and are likely to know about neighbors' health problems.

12. Interview with Penny Newman, January 14, 1992.

13. Ibid. The breach of trust was a fundamental factor in the rise of many community resistance groups. For an astute analysis, see Bernard Barber, *The Logic and Limits of Trust* (New Brunswick, N.J.: Rutgers University Press, 1983), and Francis Fukuyama, *Trust* (New York: Free Press, 1995).

14. Interview with Sally Mehra, January 13, 1992.

15. Tilly alerts us that the development of such indigenous social movements is most likely to occur in opposition to state authorities that claim to represent local citizenry. Charles Tilly, "Social Movements, Old and New," in *Research in Social Movements: Conflicts and Change*, ed. Louis Kriesberg and Bronislaw Misztal (Greenwich, Conn.: JAI Press, 1988), 1–18.

16. Penny Newman, "Making the State of California and Major Corporations Pay for Environmental Pollution" (paper delivered at a conference entitled "Educa-

tion at the Grassroots: Women and the Struggle for a Safe Environment," Smith College, Northampton, Mass., April 9, 1995).

17. Neighborhood groups provide crucial ties and support for the formation of protest and resistance efforts. For a discussion of "affinity groups," see William Gamson, "Social Psychology of Collective Action," in *Frontiers in Social Movement Theory,* ed. Aldon D. Morris and Carol McClung Mueller (New Haven: Yale University Press, 1992), 53–76.

18. Swerdlow, "Pure Milk," 227.

19. Penny Newman, "Making the State of California and Major Corporations Pay for Environmental Pollution."

20. Ibid.

21. For an analysis of the development of social movement strategies and tactics, see Mayer N. Zald, "The Trajectory of Social Movements in America," in *Research in Social Movements,* ed. Kriesberg and Misztal. Charles Tilly's analysis of social movement actions against adversaries reveals how nonviolent and nonconfrontational Concerned Neighbors and other grassroots environmental groups were. "Social Movements, Old and New," in ibid.

22. Interview with Linda Spinney, January 15, 1992.

23. Interview with Leannah Bradley, aide to Congressman Brown, January 16, 1992.

24. Unpublished letter from Penny Newman to David Jones, EPA Region IX, January 17, 1991.

25. Interview with Penny Newman, January 14, 1992.

26. Interview with Sally Mehra, January 13, 1992.

27. *Riverside Press Enterprise,* September 16, 1993.

28. Penny Newman, personal correspondence, July 22, 1996.

29. Kai Erikson, *A New Species of Trouble* (New York: W. W. Norton, 1994), 34–35.

30. Interview with Sally Mehra, January 13, 1992.

31. Interview with Paul Strain, January 15, 1992.

32. Interview with Lynn Golumbic, March 23, 1992.

33. Lynn Golumbic, personal correspondence with authors, July 9, 1996.

34. Interview with Lynn Golumbic, March 23, 1992.

35. See Ron Eyerman and Andrew Jamison, *Social Movements: A Cognitive Approach* (University Park: Pennsylvania State University Press, 1991), 138–40.

36. Interview with Lynn Golumbic, March 23, 1992.

37. In 1985, sulfur dioxide (SO_2) concentrations in the air averaged 104 micrograms per cubic meter. By 1995, major improvements, including the burning of low-sulfur fuels, had lowered that number to 11. Janine Zacharia, "Smoke Gets in Your Eyes," *Jerusalem Report,* August 8, 1996, 22.

38. Anthony Oberschall and Hyojoung Kim, "Identity and Action," *Mobilization* 1, no. 1 (1996): 63–85.

39. Lynn Golumbic, personal correspondence with authors, July 9, 1996.

40. "Taking on Haifa's Polluters," *Jerusalem Post,* April 1, 1991.

41. Sirianni and Friedland, "Civic Innovation and American Democracy."

42. There are many studies that show that working women in Western countries continue to do more housework and child care than their husbands, even when they work full-time. In Israel, as in Europe and the United States, the overarching belief has been that a mother, above all, is responsible for her family. The "double day" of a job and home management become very time consuming. See Judith Lor-

206   N o t e s

ber, *Paradoxes of Gender* (New Haven: Yale University Press, 1994), 188–89; Swerdlow, "Pure Milk," 227; Marilyn J. Boxer and Jean H. Quataert, eds., *Connecting Spheres: Women in the Western World, 1500 to the Present* (New York: Oxford University Press, 1987), esp. 199–201.

43. The possibilities for dissent in different social systems are discussed in Zald, "The Trajectory of Social Movements in America," 19–41.

44. From 1971 to 1989, only 1,864 citizens signed Charter 77, and of those, half signed on in 1989, when the government was weak and the danger seemed less ominous. Tina Rosenberg, *The Haunted Land* (New York: Random House, 1995), 29.

45. Interview with Ja'ra Johnova, May 7, 1992.

46. Interview with Anna Hradilkova, May 4, 1992.

47. Ibid. Rosenberg, *The Haunted Land,* 30–31, points out that in Poland one of every two adults was a member of Solidarity, the principal opposition group. In Czechoslovakia, in contrast, the average citizen had his or her basic needs met and was "willing to forgo living in truth as Havel put it."

48. Interview with Anna Hradilkova, May 4, 1992. Such a redefinition of meaning in oppressive regimes occurred in other countries as well. For a discussion of resistance in Poland, see Helena Flam, "Anxiety and the Successful Oppositional Construction of Societal Reality: The Case of Kor," *Mobilization* 1, no. 1 (1996): 103–21.

49. Rosenberg, *The Haunted Land,* 33–34.

50. Interview with Ja'ra Johnova, May 7, 1992.

51. The problems confronting the Prague Mothers affected environmentalists in all the countries of the former Soviet Bloc. Although they had been deeply involved in opposing the Communist regimes, the environmental activists soon understood that problems would not be resolved quickly. Barbara Jancar-Webster, "Eastern Europe and the Former Soviet Union," in *Environmental Politics in the International Arena,* ed. Sheldon Kamieniecki (Albany: State University of New York Press, 1993), 199–221.

52. Interview with Ja'ra Johnova, May 7, 1992.

53. Maria del Carmen Feijoo, "The Challenge of Constructing Civilian Peace: Women and Democracy in Argentina," in *The Women's Movement in Latin America,* ed. Jane S. Jaquette (Boston: Unwin Hyman, 1989), 84. Martha Ackelsberg and Mary Lyndon Shanley, "From Resistance to Reconstruction: Madres de Plaza de Mayo, Maternalism, and the Transition to Democracy in Argentina" (paper delivered at the Latin American Studies Association, Los Angeles, September 1992), argue that the resistance to engaging in "normal" party politics has not ended the Madres' political engagement. They continue to challenge the state with their unique form of political discourse and participation. But the experience of the Prague Mothers seems to confirm Feijoo's analysis that a different form of knowledge is required in a transition from police state to democracy.

54. Interview with Anna Hradilkova, June 9, 1994; interview with Ja'ra Johnova, June 11, 1994.

55. Alberto Melucci, *Nomads of the Present: Social Movements and Individual Needs in Contemporary Society* (Philadelphia: Temple University Press, 1989); Enrique Laraña, Hank Johnston, and Joseph R. Gusfield, eds., *New Social Movements: From Ideology to Identity* (Philadelphia: Temple University Press, 1994).

56. Interview with Pete Kelly, March 2, 1992.

Notes to Chapter 4

1. Louis Blumberg and Robert Gottlieb, *War on Waste* (Washington, D.C.: Island Press, 1989), 58–59. For an analysis of the breadth of the garbage problem, see Jennifer Seymour Whitaker, *Salvaging the Land of Plenty: Garbage and the American Dream* (New York: William Morrow, 1994).

2. Andrew Szasz, *Ecopopulism: Toxic Waste and the Movement for Environmental Justice* (Minneapolis: University of Minnesota Press, 1994), 77–83.

3. See, for example, Nicholas Freudenberg and Carol Steinsaper, "Not in Our Backyards: The Grassroots Environmental Movement," in *American Environmentalism: The U.S. Environmental Movement, 1970–1990,* ed. Riley E. Dunlap and Angela G. Mertig (Philadelphia: Taylor & Francis, 1992), 35. "EPA Watch Program of the Government Accountability Project," an unpublished report (April 1991), compiles reports of numerous incidents involving local groups fighting dumps and incinerators; available from GAP, 1612 K Street, N.W., Washington, D.C. 20006.

4. Most of the towns had populations under a thousand. Ritzville was a slightly larger commercial center.

5. Interview with Greg Beckley, July 28, 1991.

6. Ibid.

7. Interview with Dorothy Clinesmith, July 28, 1991.

8. Stephen L. Fisher, ed., *Fighting Back in Appalachia: Traditions of Resistance and Change* (Philadelphia: Temple University Press, 1993), 320, describes the significance of traditional values, especially land, family, self-rule, and patriotism, to activists in Appalachia who tried to preserve their culture and way of life from strip mining.

9. Interview with John Harder, July 29, 1991.

10. Interview with Greg Beckley, July 28, 1991.

11. Interview with Michelle and Tim Smith, July 28, 1991.

12. Interview with John Harder, July 29, 1991.

13. Interview with Gretchen Harder, July 29, 1991.

14. Interview with Greg Beckley, July 28, 1991.

15. Eileen DeArmon, letter to the editor, *Ritzville Adams County Journal,* December 3, 1992, 17.

16. Ibid.

17. "PR Firms Tell Rabanco How They Are Doing and What They Should Do," *Royal Review,* April 22, 1992, 3.

18. Ibid.

19. Harold Clinesmith, conversations and correspondence with authors during 1996 and 1997.

20. "Plan for Incinerator Put on Back Burner," *Seattle Post-Intelligencer,* August 10, 1994, B3.

21. Norm Wietting, "Improved Technology Creates Changes," *Ritzville Adams County Journal,* February 1, 1996.

22. Blumberg and Gottlieb, *War on Waste,* 282.

23. Marina Ortega and John Gayusky, "Dumping in the Desert," *Everyone's Backyard* 12, no. 2 (1994): 7–8.

24. Shoshana Gabbay, *The Environment in Israel* (Jerusalem: Ministry of the Environment, 1994), 66–78.

25. Interview with Reuven Bezner, March 23, 1992.

26. Interview with Giora Yanai, March 20, 1992.

27. Moshavim are settlements where some land is cooperatively owned. Kibbutzim, in contrast, are communities where all property is held in common.

28. Interview with Reuven Bezner, March 23, 1992.

29. Interview with Itsik Shafran, March 30, 1992.

30. Interview with Uri Marinov, April 1, 1992.

31. Ibid.

32. Ibid.

33. Interview with Giora Yanai, March 20, 1992.

34. Interview with Reuven Bezner, January 2, 1996.

35. Ministry of the Environment of the Czech Republic and the Czechoslovak Academy of Sciences, *Environment of the Czech Republic* (Brno: EkoCentrum, 1990), 9. The quotes are based on a poll by the Research Institute of Commerce and the Gallup Poll London, carried out on February 6, 1990.

36. Environmental Institute report on the Czech Republic, April 1996, www.env.cz/rocenka/r934e/a4.htm.

37. Interview with Pavel Šremer, May 15, 1992.

38. VPN was the major dissenter organization in Slovakia, roughly equivalent to Charter 77 in Prague. After the revolution it became a major political organization vying for power with several other parties.

39. Tina Rosenberg, *The Haunted Land* (New York: Random House, 1995), 78–80.

40. Reformers shared Zamkovsky's concerns about the obsession of many officials with the new Lustrace law, which banned the people who had run the old regime from important government posts. The impulse to prevent secret-police collaborators from taking over important policy positions was understandable, but in actuality it led to a witch-hunt atmosphere in which accurate designation was virtually impossible. Rosenberg, *The Haunted Land,* 3–121, describes the complexity of this process in great detail.

41. Interview with Juraj Zamkovsky, May 10, 1992.

42. Ibid.

43. Rosenberg, *The Haunted Land,* 78–79.

44. Interview with Juraj Zamkovsky, May 10, 1992.

Notes to Chapter 5

1. For a similar approach, see the discussion in James M. Jasper and Jane D. Paulsen, "Recruiting Strangers and Friends: Moral Shacks and Social Networks in Animal Rights and Anti-Nuclear Protests," *Social Problems* 42, no. 4 (1995): 493–512.

2. Erling Berge, "Democracy and Human Rights: Conditions for Sustainable Resource Utilization," in *Who Pays the Price? The Sociocultural Context of Environmental Crisis,* ed. Barbara Rose Johnston (Washington, D.C.: Island Press, 1994), 187–93.

3. At one time in California, there were more than two million acres of old-growth redwood, of which about 4 percent survives. It is the preservation of this last acreage that animates the forest activists and sympathetic politicians. See, for

example, the article by Representatives George Brown and Pete Stark, "A Chance to Save Headwaters Grove," *New York Times,* December 8, 1995.

4. In recent years, the demand for wood increased as Japan became a major export site; see "At Loggerheads," a special Pacific Rim quarterly report of the *Seattle Times,* August 19, 1990.

5. Samuel P. Hays, *Beauty, Health, and Permanence* (New York: Cambridge University Press, 1987), 124.

6. Ibid.

7. Ibid., 395–96; see also Sallie Tisdale, "Annals of Place: The Pacific Northwest," *New Yorker,* August 26, 1991, 37–62.

8. Battles within the forest service became very intense when a number of whistleblowers publicly accused the Forest Service of abusing land and mismanaging resources. See, for example, Timothy Egan, "Dissidents Say Forest Service Shifts Its Role," *New York Times,* March 4, 1992, and an article by whistleblower John McCormick, "Can't See the Forest for the Sledge," *New York Times,* January 29, 1992, op-ed.

9. Elliott Norse, *Ancient Forests of the Pacific Northwest* (Washington, D.C.: Island Press, 1990), 282–84.

10. Hays, *Beauty, Health, and Permanence,* 300.

11. Like many other grassroots groups in California, McKay's North Coast Environmental Center puts out a newsletter, *Econews.* Groups like Earth First in Ukiah, California, publish *Ecotopia.* In Mendicino County, activists publish the *Environmentalist.* All are designed to keep local residents apprised of the issues and to broaden support.

12. Such a personal transformation of a self-concept affects many activists. Anthony Oberschall and Hyojoung Kim, "Identity and Action," *Mobilization* 1, no. 1 (1996): 63–85.

13. Interview with Tim McKay, January 21, 1992.

14. Ibid.

15. Jerry A. Stark, "Postmodern Environmentalism: A Critique of Deep Ecology," in *Ecological Resistance Movements,* ed. Bron Raymond Taylor (Albany: State University of New York, 1995), 259–81.

16. Interview with Tim McKay, January 21, 1992.

17. Van Kirk is one of hundreds of grassroots activists who belong to the national environmental organizations but disagree with the compromises of the Washington-based groups and choose, instead, to fight for one forest at a time. For a discussion of the differences between the locals and the nationals, see Mark Dowie, *Losing Ground: American Environmentalism at the Close of the Twentieth Century* (Cambridge, Mass.: MIT Press, 1995), chap. 8.

18. Interview with Susie Van Kirk, January 22, 1992.

19. Ibid.

20. Ibid. For an excellent theoretical discussion of the sources of such differing worldviews, see Harry C. Bredemeir, *Experience Versus Understanding* (London: Janus Publishing, 1997), esp. chap. 1.

21. Christopher D. Stone, *Should Trees Have Standing? Toward Legal Rights for Natural Objects* (Los Altos, Calif.: W. Kaufmann, 1974), discusses the possibilities for the representation of natural objects in court.

22. Interview with Susie Van Kirk, January 22, 1992.

23. George Sessions and Bill Devall, *Deep Ecology* (Salt Lake City, Utah: G. M. Smith, 1985); Murray Bookchin and Dave Foreman, *Defending the Earth* (Boston:

South End Press, 1990); Rik Scarce, *Eco Warriors: Understanding the Radical Environmental Movement* (Chicago: Noble, 1990); Philip Shabecoff, *A Fierce Green Fire: The American Environmental Movement* (New York: Hill & Wang, 1993).

24. See Chapter 1 for a discussion of Robert Putnam's argument.

25. Interview with Eilon Schwartz, January 1, 1996.

26. Avner de-Shalit, "From the Political to the Objective: The Dialectics of Zionism and the Environment," *Environmental Politics* 4, no. 1 (1995): 70–87; Avner de-Shalit and Moti Talias, "Green or Blue and White? Environmental Controversies in Israel," *Environmental Politics* 3, no. 2 (1994): 273–94.

27. De-Shalit, "From the Political," 74–75.

28. For example, the number of inhabitants of Tel Aviv grew from 41,000 in 1931 to 135,000 in 1935. Ibid., 79. After the establishment of the state in 1948, Israel absorbed an even larger mass immigration from the Middle Eastern and North African countries. In the 1950s and 1960s, Israel's population climbed from 600,000 to almost 3,000,000. Uri Marinov, "How Israel Handles the Environment and Development," *Environmental Science and Technology* 27, no. 7 (1993): 1253.

29. Developing new "frames" of meaning is essential for collective action and often derives from action directed toward alleviating social and economic problems. For an astute analysis of the challenges and significance of changing meanings, see Sidney Tarrow, "Mentalities, Political Cultures, and Collective Action Frames: Constructing Meanings Through Action," in *Frontiers in Social Movement Theory,* ed. Aldon D. Morris and Carol McClung Mueller (New Haven: Yale University Press, 1992), 174–202.

30. Quote in de-Shalit and Talias, "Green or Blue and White?" 289–90.

31. There is an emerging concern about the impact of overdevelopment, which can be seen in popular, as well as environmental, sources. See, for example, Rochelle Furstenberg, "Building on Success," *Hadassah Magazine* 78, no. 5 (1997): 14–15.

32. Marinov, "How Israel Handles the Environment and Development," 1270.

33. Uri Marinov and Deborah Sandler, "The Status of Environmental Management in Israel," *Environmental Science and Technology* 27, no. 7 (1993): 1260. When a major battle ensued in the mid-1990s over the building of the Trans-Israel Highway #5, the ministry supported the construction in return for modest environmental improvement. While most "green" organizations fought the highway plan, which threatened some of the only undeveloped land in the center of the country, the ministry continued its earlier policy of supporting the road project, but tried to incorporate environmental planning in the hope of minimizing damage to surrounding landscape. In contrast, the UED (Union for Environmental Defense) continued its opposition even after they lost the court case against the highway in 1995. They remained active in mobilizing citizen protests and in trying to improve legal requirements for environmental assessment. *New Israel Fund Report,* spring 1996, 2.

34. The center was named for Abraham Joshua Heschel, the contemporary Jewish philosopher who emphasized the wonder of the world in much of his teachings.

35. Jeremy Benstein, "Nature vs. Torah," *Judaism* 44, no. 2 (1995): 162.

36. Interview with Eilon Schwartz, January 1, 1996.

37. Yoav Sagi, "Escape from Megalopolis," in *Israel Environment Bulletin,* winter 1997/5757, 5.

38. Unpublished talk to IUCN Ethical Working Group and Commission on Environmental Law Seminar, Buenos Aires, January 20, 1994.

39. Recent evidence suggests that a new deputy minister appointed at the end of 1993 has reached out to some of the environmental NGOs, opening a small possibility of including their vision in government plans. Adam Fagin, "Environment and Transition in the Czech Republic," *Environmental Politics* 3, no. 3 (1994): 490.

40. Vladislav Balaban, "We Lived at the Expense of Future Generations: A Report on Problems of Sustainable Development in the Czech and Slovak Federal Republic," unpublished report, Bratislava, SZOPK, 1991, 13.

41. See Chapter 2.

42. Interview with Susan Cleveland, May 15, 1992; Fagin interprets the difficulties that all NGOs have in influencing public opinion and public policy as an indicator of the "undeveloped state of civil society in the Czech Republic and of the problems associated with dismantling the communist system," "Environment and Transition in the Czech Republic," 490.

43. Václav Klaus, "Transition—An Insider's View," *Problems of Communism,* January–April 1992, 73–75.

44. Václav Havel, "Nature and Man," in *Lights and Shadows: Environment in the Czech Republic,* ed. J. Nemec (issued on the occasion of the international conference "Environment in Europe," Prague, 1991; publication sponsored by Spie Batignolles), 89.

45. Ibid.

46. In publishing its plan, the government placed first on the list the need "to comprehend the steady and stable development of the society as the major criterion of the evaluation of the economic development." Second was the need "to protect human health and comfort"; third, the need "to protect cultural and environmental values"; fourth, the need to minimize "the consumption of non-renewable resources" and "to preserve the ability of renewable resources to regenerate." The fifth goal, near the bottom of the list, spoke of a larger, more biocentric vision, which was "to protect biological diversity which is a value in itself." Czech Open Information Project, "The Principles of the Czech Environment Protection Policy," Internet, www.bsf.cz/project/environ/gov.htm.

47. Marlise Simons, "East Europe Sniffs Freedom's Air, and Gasps," *New York Times,* November 3, 1994, A14.

Notes to Chapter 6

1. See, for example, Douglas N. Walton, *Courage* (Berkeley and Los Angeles: University of California Press, 1986), and S. J. Rachman, *Fear and Courage* (New York: W. H. Freeman, 1990).

2. Quoted in Anne Witte Garland, *Women Activists* (New York: Feminist Press, 1988), 100.

3. Walton, *Courage,* 18.

4. W. Thomas Schmid, "The Socratic Conception of Courage," *History of Philosophy Quarterly* 2 (April 1985): 115.

5. Ibid., 116.

6. For two perceptive accounts of the significance of leadership when communities are endangered, see David L. Kirp, *Learning by Heart* (New Brunswick, N.J.: Rutgers University Press, 1989), and Philip Hallie, *Lest Innocent Blood Be Shed* (New York: Harper & Row, 1979). For an analysis of the significance of culture in a

time of "unsettled lives," see Ann Swidler, "Culture in Action: Symbols and Strategies," *American Sociological Review* 51 (April 1986): 273–86.

7. Interview with Tom Bailie, July 31, 1991.

8. For an excellent account of such determination against the apartheid system, see Diane E. H. Russell, *Lives of Courage: Women for a New South Africa*
(New York: Basic Books, 1989).

9. Garland, *Women Activists,* 79.

10. In oppressive regimes, activists must construct a new meaning, a new ethical code that requires opposition. Helena Flam, "Anxiety and the Successful Oppositional Construction of Societal Reality: The Case of Kor," *Mobilization* 1, no. 1
(1996): 103–21.

11. Garland, *Women Activists,* xvi–xvii.

12. Interview with Sally Mehra, January 13, 1992.

13. Michael R. Edelstein, *Contaminated Communities: The Social and Psychological Impacts of Residential Toxic Exposure* (Boulder, Colo.: Westview Press,
1988), 141.

14. Such a vision does not, however, appear to draw heavily from radical political thought. Richard P. Gale, "The Environmental Movement and the Left: Antagonists or Allies?" *Sociological Inquiry* 53 (spring 1983): 179–99.

Notes to the Methodological Appendix

1. Ministry of the Environment, *Israel Environment Bulletin* 15, no. 4 (1992).

2. The four organizations were the Society for the Protection of Nature, the
Union for Environmental Defense, Econet, and the Galilee Society for Health Research and Service.

3. David B. Hunter and Margaret B. Bowman, *An Overview of the Environmental Community in the Czech and Slovak Federal Republic* (Washington, D.C.: Center for International Environmental Law, 1991).

Index

Abraham Joshua Heschel Center for Nature Studies, 149, 153–54
activists, environmental. *See* grassroots environmental activists
Agent Orange, 3
air pollution, 49, 78–85, 87–88
Alon, Azeria, 38
alternative networks of power
 building, xv–xvi, 8–10, 27, 47, 109, 136–37
 examples of, 49, 65
 invisible, 197n8
 links to civil rights movement, 13
 significance of, 15
Alvarez, Robert, 31
American Civil Liberties Union, xiv
Andrewjeski, Juanita, 174
Andrewjeski, Leon, 174
anger
 as motivator for activists, 32, 176–77
 See also betrayal
Arrabe, Israel, 43–45
Association of Americans and Canadians in Israel (AACI), 78, 81, 85, 169, 188

Bailie, Tom, 28–30, 31, 32, 57, 170–71, 174, 175, 184
Bari, Judi, 187
Beckley, Greg, 105, 107–8, 109, 132
Benda, Frantisek, 156
Benge, Washington, 104
Benstein, Jeremy, 153
Benyamin, Herschel, 17
Benyamin, Shirley, 17, 18

betrayal
 sense of as a catalyst, xv, 4, 6–10, 14–15, 32–33, 42, 69–70, 93–94, 116
 See also anger
Bezner, Reuven, 114–24, 172, 173, 175
Bowman, Margaret, 190
Bradley, Leannah, 75
Bratislava, Czechoslovakia, 49–57
Bratislava Nahlas, 26, 51–56, 59, 127, 130, 175
Brontosaurus, 157
Brown, George, 73, 75
Budaj, Jan, 50, 52, 55, 56, 57, 175
Budmerice waste dump, 127–30
Bulora, Martin, 49–50
Bureau of Indian Affairs, 113
burnout, individual, 37, 109, 166
Bush administration, 41

Cahuilla Reservation, 113
California
 defending redwoods in, 139–40
 Glen Avon, 3, 68–78, 185
 interviews in regarding clear-cutting, 187–88
 Mendicino County activists, 209n11
 state of, 73, 76
California Indians for Cultural and Environmental Protection, 113
Camps, Lois, 33, 34, 174
Carson, Rachel, xviii, 16
Carter, Don, 32
Center for Community Action and Environmental Justice, 76

Center for International Environmental
    Law, xxiv
Centers for Disease Control, 32, 34, 36
Cerrell Associates, 100–101
Charter 77, 21, 49, 86–87, 169, 192,
    206n44
Chernobyl, 18
children, as an inspiration for environ-
    mental activists, 71, 84–85, 86,
    180–82
Children of the Earth, 20
Cincotta, Gale, 176
Citizens Against Toxic Exposure, 11, 12
Citizens Clearinghouse for Hazardous
    Waste, xvi, xx, 59, 68, 75, 113, 197n8
Citizens Hazardous Waste Coalition,
    109
Civic Democratic Party, 159
civic engagement, 2–6
Civic Forum, 91, 156, 159
civic innovators, 1, 66, 96
clear-cutting, 140–41
Cleveland, Susan, 158
Clinesmith, Dorothy, 103–6, 172
Clinesmith, Harold, 103–6, 109, 111, 112,
    172, 173
Cocek, Christina, 10
Coleman, Gary, 128
Communities at Risk, 76
Concerned Neighbors, 70–77, 83, 179–80,
    185, 205n21
courage, of environmental activists, xvi,
    55–56, 67, 90, 165–82
Crawford, Ken, 6
Crawford, Lisa, 6–9, 96, 178, 180
culture menders, 76–77, 97, 149, 167
culture of solidarity, xv–xvi, 15, 32, 55,
    65, 108, 132, 177–80
Czech Institute for Nature Conservation,
    21
Czechoslovakia
    attitudes on environmental issues,
        156–62
    Bratislava, 49–57
    Bratislava Nahlas, 26, 51–56
    environmental activists as political dis-
        sidents, xxii–xxiv, 19–23, 66–67,
        158–59
    environmental conditions, xxii–xxiii,
        20, 48–56

    interviews in, 191–92
    suppression of environmental informa-
        tion and activity, 26
Czech Republic
    attitudes on environmental issues,
        124–25, 130–31, 156–62, 211n46
    environmental conditions, 125, 161
    requirements to achieve sustainable
        use of natural resources, 155–56
    waning of environmental movement,
        xxiv, 21–23, 92, 93, 130–31
Czech Union of Nature Protectors
    (CSOP), xxiv–xxv, 190

democracy
    and grassroots environmental activity,
        xiv–xvii, 1–24, 66, 84, 89, 96–97
    and secrecy, xiii–xiv
Department of Energy, 7, 28, 34, 35, 36,
    95, 180
de-Shalit, Avner, 150, 151
dissidents, political in Czechoslovakia,
    xxii–xxiv, 19–23, 66–67, 158–59
Downwinders, 26, 28, 32–37, 184

Earth First, xviii, 209n11
Earth Firsters, radical, 148
Econet, 17, 40, 123
Ecos Corporation, 104, 109
Edelstein, Michael, 181
education, environmental, 17–18, 75,
    153–54
Ein Hashofet landfill, 115–23
Elazar, General David, 38–39
Electric Power Company (Haifa, Israel),
    180
engagement, civic, 2–6
environmental activists. *See* grassroots
    environmental activists
environmental contamination, difficulty
    of proving in court, 35–36
environmental education, 17–18, 75,
    153–54
environmental injustice, 12–14, 43, 45,
    46–47
Environmental Justice, Principles of, 13
Environmental Protection Agency, 4, 11,
    73–74, 76, 95, 111, 113
Environmental Protection Service, 120
environmental racism, 11–12

environmental threats
  air pollution, 49, 78–85, 87–88, 92
  buildup of, 3
  coverage by media, 31, 59
  sewage disposal, 45–46
  solid waste, xxi, 99–133
  toxic waste, 11–13, 28, 31–32, 35–36,
    69–70, 76, 99, 103–14
  water pollution, xxi, 49
Enza, 80–81
Erikson, Kai, xv, 76
essentialist argument for women in poli-
    tics, 61–62
expertise
  development of, 9–10
  lack of as a barrier, 4, 10
experts, believability of, 122

Federal Ministry of the Environment
    (Slovakia), 126
Fernald Residents for Environmental
    Safety and Health (FRESH), 7–9, 96,
    180, 184–85
Fernald uranium-enrichment plant, 6–9,
    96, 184–85
Filkova, Maria, 54, 57, 175
Fishelson, Lev, 38–39
Florida, Pensacola, 11
Freedom of Information Act, xiii, 36,
    174
Friends of the Earth, 142, 143

Gabcikovo dam, 50, 57
Gal, Febor, 50
Galilee Society for Health Research
    and Services, xxii, 26, 45–47, 58, 182,
    190
Garland, Anne Witte, 172, 176
German Marshall Fund, 57, 158
Gibbs, Lois, xvi, 75, 196n10
Glen Avon, California, 3, 68–78, 185
Glenn, John, 31
Goldwater, Barry, 141
Golumbic, Lynn, 78–85, 169, 171, 175,
    180
Golumbic, Marty, 78–79, 82
Government Accountability Project, ix,
    xiv
government regulatory agencies, connec-
    tions to corporations, 4

grassroots environmental activists
  accumulating evidence, 51–52, 87,
    173–75
  as leaders, xix, 57–60, 67–68, 84–85,
    130, 178–79, 181, 204n11
  and radical politics, 201n14, 212n14
  belief in efficacy of their efforts, 171–73
  burdens on, 72, 94–95, 106–9, 118,
    143–45, 148, 165, 179
  children as inspiration, 71, 84–85, 86,
    180–82
  courage of, xvi, 55–56, 67, 90,
    165–82
  and democracy, xiv–xvii, 1–24, 66, 84,
    89, 96–97
  development of expertise, 9–10, 117,
    168, 172–73
  as dissidents in Czechoslovakia,
    xxii–xxiv, 19–23, 49–56, 66–67,
    158–59
  as ecologists, 133–63
  emotional motivation, xv, 4, 6–10,
    14–15, 32–33, 42, 69–70, 93–94, 116,
    176–77
  and social capital, 168–71
  solidarity of, xv–xvi, 5–6, 15, 32, 55,
    108, 132, 159, 177–80
  transformation of lives, 8, 15, 83, 85,
    94–95, 101–2, 179
  and whistleblowers, x
  and Zionist ideology, 66
  See also grassroots environmental
    groups
grassroots environmental groups
  diversity of members, xix, 4–5
  Israeli, 39–47
  learning experiences, 73, 81, 112–13,
    198n11
  mothers' groups, 61–97
  and national organizations, 145,
    186–87
  and national security, 26–27, 36
  necessity of public support, 101
  number of, xx
  public relations campaign against,
    110–11
  resources needed, 203–204n7
  significance of allies, 34–35, 65
  and social capital, 4–6
  tactics, 12, 14, 27, 47, 89–90

See also grassroots environmental activists
grassroots environmental movement, history of, xvii–xx
Green Circle, 87–88
Green Party, 57
Greenpeace, xviii, 20–21, 22, 59, 108
Green Run, 31–32
Gurion, Ben, 122

Haifa, Israel, 66, 78–85
Hanford Education Action League, 31, 34–35, 37
Hanford Health Information Network, 34
Hanford Nuclear Reservation, 26, 28–32, 35, 105, 174, 184, 200–201n13
Harder, Gretchen, 106, 108–9
Harder, John, 106–8
Hável, Vaclav, 86, 91, 159, 160, 161
Headlands Forest, 143
Hinds, Cathy, 166
Houff, Dr. William Harper, 31
Hradilkova, Anna, 88, 89–90, 91, 92
Huba, Mikulas, 50, 57, 203n61
Hunter, David B., 190

incineration, limitations of, 100
infant mortality rate, for Israeli Arabs and Jews, 45
injustice, environmental, 12–14, 43, 45, 46–47
inspectors general, xiii
Israel
   Arab activists, xxii, 42–47
   Arrabe, 43–45
   attitudes on environmental issues, xxi–xxii, 15, 18, 25–26, 37–39, 42, 78, 79, 120, 149–52
   conflict over Voice of America tower, 41
   early environmentalists, 17, 37–41
   environmental conditions, 16, 45–46, 114–24, 205n37
   Haifa, 66, 78–85
   interviews in, 188–90
   relationship of Arabs and Jews interested in the environment, 196n14
   requirements for grassroots environmental groups, 47

Sharon's plan to level areas of the West Bank, 39
See also Ministry of the Environment (Israel)
Italy, Seveso, 3

Jewish National Fund, 151
Jim, Russell, 34
jobs, arguments for preserving, 138–39, 147
Johnova, Ja'ra, 85–92, 169, 171, 180
Jurgi, Judith, 30, 174

Kana'aneh, Hatim, 43–47, 57, 176, 177, 181–82, 190
Kellog, Idaho, interviews in, 186
Kibbutz Mishmar HaEmek, 102, 114–15, 121, 132
Kirk, Susie Van, 145–49, 163, 209n17
Klaus, Vaclav, 156, 159–60

land, stewardship of, 105–6, 118–19
landfills, limitations of, 100
Laraña, Enrique, 94
leadership
   by women, xix, 60, 67–68, 84–85, 181, 204n11
   necessity of maintaining ties with grassroots, 130
   significance of, 57–60, 96, 178–79, 200n37
Life and Environment, 39
logging, controversy over, 142–43, 147
Love Canal, 3

Madres de Plaza de Mayo, 61, 92–93, 206n53
Marinov, Uri, 40–41, 120–24, 152
McCarthy, Eugene, 142
McKay, Tim, 141–45, 148
media
   coverage of environmental threats, 31, 59
   use of, 72–73, 81–82
Mehra, Sally, 70, 74–75
Melucci, Alberto, 94
Mendelssohn, Heyedrich, 17
Mendicino County activists, 209n11
methodology of studying social movements, 196n12

Meyer, Kathy, 7
Military Production Network, 9, 34
Ministry of the Environment (Czech Republic), 156, 161
Ministry of the Environment (Israel), xxi, 95, 114, 117, 119, 120, 123, 152, 154, 199n30, 210n33
Moldan, Bedrich, 156
Mothers Against Drunk Driving, 61
mothers' groups, 61–97
Muir, John, 139

Nagymoros dam, 50
Nalder, Eric, 31
National Audubon Society, xviii
National Commission on Superfund, 12
National Outline Scheme for Solid Waste Disposal, 114
National Planning Authority, 82
national security, and the environment, 18, 25–27, 36–39, 200n1
National Toxics Campaign, xviii, 128, 130
New Forestry, 141
Newman, Penny, 13–14, 63–64, 68–76, 83, 85, 169, 171, 175, 177, 178, 179, 180
Newsweek, quote from, 71
NIMBYs (not in my back yard), xxvi, 102, 110, 112, 121
Norit Americas, 10
North Coast Environmental Center, 143, 209n11
Nuclear Regulatory Commission, 4, 36

Office of Management and Budget, xiii
Ogden Martin, 100
Ojibwa Indians, 76
O'Leary, Hazel, 9, 35

Partnership for Eastern Europe, 162
Pensacola, Florida, 11
People Against Violence (VPN), 127, 130, 208n38
People of Color Environmental Leadership Summit, 13
personal transformation, of grassroots environmental leaders, 8, 15, 83, 85, 94–95, 101–2, 179
pollution
    air, 49, 78–85, 87–88
    water, xxi, 49

power, alternative networks of. See alternative networks of power
Prague, air pollution in, 87, 88, 92
Prague Mothers, 88–93, 180
preservation of nature, 138
"Principles of Environmental Justice," 13
privatization, and ecological concerns, xxiv, 126–27, 159–60
Putnam, Robert, 2, 148, 169

Rabanco, 110–11
Rabin, Yitzhak, 123
racism, environmental, 11–12
Rainforest Alliance, xviii
Reagan, Ronald, 30
Reagan administration, xix
Redwoods National Park, 142
redwood trees, 139–40, 208n3
right-to-know laws, xiii, 36
Robinson, Florence, 11–12
Rockwell Industries, 36
Rosenberg, Tina, 130
Ruddick, Sara, 62
Ruud, Casey, 31

Sagi, Yoav, 42, 154
Schwartz, Eilon, 149–50, 152–55
secrecy
    around Hanford Nuclear Reservation, 30–32
    in Czechoslovakia, xxiii, 48, 87
    and democracy, xiii–xiv
    and the environment, 25–27, 36, 59
sequoias. See redwoods
Seveso, Italy, 3
sewage disposal, as problem in Israeli-Arab community, 45–46
Shafran, Itsik, 118–19
Sharon, Ariel, 38–39
Shaul, Devorah Ben, 15–18, 84
Sierra Club, xviii
Sierra Club Legal Defense Fund, 146
Silmavy, Ivo, 20–22
Sinai, Sharon's plan to bulldoze, 38
Sinclair, Mary, 172
Slovakia
    environmental conditions, 125–31, 161–62
    waning of environmental movement, xxiv, 21–23, 56–57, 103, 129–30

Slovak Union of Landscape and Nature
  Protectors (SZOPK), xxv, 49–54, 127,
  157, 190
Smith, Michelle, 107
Smith, Tim, 107–8
Snitow, Ann, 62
social capital, 1–2, 3–6, 47, 70, 83, 167,
  168–71, 173
social movements, methodology of studying, 196n12
Society for Sustainable Living in Slovakia, 203n61
Society for the Protection of Nature
  (SPNI), xxii, 17, 38, 39, 41, 42, 80–81,
  154
solidarity
  of grassroots environmental activists,
    xv–xvi, 15, 32, 55, 108, 132, 159,
    177–80
  necessity of, 74
solid waste, xxi, 99–133
Šremer, Pavel, 50–51, 56, 57, 126, 156,
  157, 177
Steele, Karen Dorn, 31
Stembridge, Lynne, 34
Stringfellow, James, 68
Stringfellow Acid Pits, 68, 70, 73, 76
sustainable use of natural resources,
  155–56
Swerdlow, Amy, 71, 204n8

tactics, 8–10, 12, 14, 27, 33, 65, 81, 89–90,
  96, 101
Tal, Alon, 39–42, 47, 123, 189
Talias, Moti, 151
Thomas, Jim, 34
Thoreau, Henry David, xvii
toxic waste, 11–13, 28, 31–32, 35–36,
  69–70, 76, 99, 103–14
trust, breach of. See betrayal

Union for Environmental Defense, 26, 40,
  41, 123, 189, 210n33
U.S. Bureau of Indian Affairs, 113
U.S. Department of Energy, 7, 28, 34, 35,
  36, 95, 180

U.S. Geological Survey, 7
U.S. Office of Management and Budget,
  xiii
U.S. Forest Service, 140–42, 146, 147,
  209n8

Vavroušek, Josef, 155–56, 157, 160, 161
Voice of America
  publicization of Bratislava Nahlas, 54
  tower, 41–42, 202n33

Walton, Douglas N., 166–67, 171
Washburn, Cheryl, 166
Washington
  Benge, 103–4
  interviews in, 185–88
  southeastern, 103–14
  state of, 36
Washington State, Department of Ecol-
  ogy, 104, 109, 111
Washington Toxics Council, 108
Washpirg, 108 .
Waste Management Inc., 100, 101, 109,
  112
water pollution, xxi, 49
West Bank, Sharon's levelling of whole ar-
  eas, 39
Wheelabrator, 100, 101
whistleblowers, ix–x
Wilderness Society, xviii
Williams, Margaret, 11, 12
Woburn, Massachusetts, 3
women
  as environmental leaders, xix, 60,
    67–68, 84–85, 181, 204n11
  essentialist argument for participation
    in politics, 61–62
Women Strike for Peace, 71, 204n8
World Wildlife Fund, xviii, 59

Yakima Nation, and the Downwinders, 34
Yanai, Giora, 116, 122

Zamkovsky, Juraj, 127–31, 159, 172, 173,
  208n40
Zionist ideology, 38, 43, 66, 116, 150–51